SECOND-ORDER PRESERVATION

·

Second-Order Preservation

SOCIAL JUSTICE AND CLIMATE ACTION
THROUGH HERITAGE POLICY

Erica Avrami

University of Minnesota Press
Minneapolis
London

The University of Minnesota Press gratefully acknowledges the generous assistance provided for the publication of this book by the Graduate School of Architecture, Planning, and Preservation at Columbia University.

Portions of chapter 3 were published in a different form in Erica Avrami, Cherie-Nicole Leo, and Alberto Sanchez Sanchez, "Confronting Exclusion: Redefining the Intended Outcomes of Historic Preservation," *Change over Time* 8, no. 1 (Spring 2018): 102–20; copyright 2018 University of Pennsylvania Press. Portions of chapter 4 were published in a different form in Erica Avrami, Jennifer L. Most, Anna Gasha, and Shreya Ghoshal, "Energy and Historic Buildings: Toward Evidence-Based Policy Reform," *Journal of Cultural Heritage Management and Sustainable Development* 13, no. 2 (2023): 379–404; copyright 2021 Emerald Publishing Limited.

Published by the University of Minnesota Press
111 Third Avenue South, Suite 290
Minneapolis, MN 55401-2520
http://www.upress.umn.edu

ISBN 978-1-5179-1794-4 (hc)
ISBN 978-1-5179-1795-1 (pb)

A Cataloging-in-Publication record for this book is available from the Library of Congress.

Printed in the United States of America on acid-free paper

The University of Minnesota is an equal-opportunity educator and employer.

UMP BmB 2024

To my dad, for giving me a past

To my mom, for letting me root

To my son, for giving me a future

Contents

Preface

I begin from a place of privilege. As a White woman educated in predominantly White institutions of higher learning and working in the predominantly White field of heritage conservation in the United States, I am mindful of my identity and perspective.[1] Before I entered academia, much of my career was spent in international heritage organizations. The privilege of working in varied cultural and socioeconomic contexts and with diverse colleagues and publics has both educated and humbled me. I have had to grapple with how the field and its philanthropic intentions can perpetuate Whiteness, exclusion, and neocolonialism through what Laurajane Smith refers to as the "authorized heritage discourse."[2] At the same time, such cross-cultural cooperation can foster mutual learning, empower voices, provoke action, and support different knowledges and ways of knowing. That tension is, in part, why I embarked on writing this volume.

Friends and students sometimes ask me if I have a favorite heritage site. As a former director of the World Monuments Watch, one of the tremendous privileges I experienced was insight into the numerous heritage sites that vied for nomination every two years. Myriad places—famous, forgotten, remote, neglected, contested—passed across my desk and served as a poignant reminder of the seemingly universal human impulse to transfer place-based heritage across generations, to mark and remember our existence. My response is usually politic but sincere: how could I possibly choose when there are so many amazing places in the world?

Once a curious colleague pressed me further, "Well, what place have you visited the most, not counting for work?" The answer surprised me. I had traveled to the D-Day landing beaches in Normandy, France, half a dozen times in a thirty-year span, always with friends or family. I do not have a particular penchant for military heritage— quite the opposite. My father was a second-generation American who served in World War II, received an education through the GI Bill, and worked for the U.S. Department of Defense for more than three decades. His passion for U.S. military history meant that childhood family vacations were a seemingly endless string of car rides to battlefields, forts, and naval facilities. And I grew up in the town where the Continental army encamped in the winter of 1779–80, during the Revolutionary War, which meant countless class trips to the reconstructed soldier huts at Jockey Hollow and the stately home that served as General Washington's headquarters, both part of the Morristown National Historical Park. I'd had my fill of military heritage before reaching adulthood.

What rivets me each time I visit the D-Day beaches, and lures me back, is the sheer magnitude of collective action. I don't experience that simply by walking the coast and seeing the vestiges of the Atlantic Wall. The solemnity of the place as encountered today belies the brutal devastation and loss of life. It also masks the months of planning, cooperation, building, training, and coordination—across borders, languages, politics, and cultures—that culminated in that moment and locale. It is only because of the research, interpretive exhibits, oral histories, news stories, photographs, films, and more that I experience this meaning in this place. The landscape is complicit in hiding the past as much as it is in exposing it.

The hidden dimensions of human agency are what draw me to this particular place and to heritage in general, and specifically to policy. Public policy is, after all, an institutionalized form of collective action that pervades and shapes environments and lived experiences. Not always discernably so, policy scaffolds, constrains, and empowers human relations and governance. It legitimates and directs institutions and organizations. It shapes and is shaped by research, education, and practice.

I begin from a place of collective agency and accountability.

Heritage is messy and fraught. It is neither innocent nor neutral. It is political, powerful, and value laden. It is socially constructed. It grounds and dispossesses. It incurs consequences. I am careful in my use of words like *stewardship* and *guardianship*, as they connote protection of something that already is and can conceal the nonneutral agency involved in heritage-making.

Throughout this volume, I refer interchangeably to the *heritage enterprise* and the *preservation enterprise,* the former deriving from the global nomenclature of *heritage conservation* and the latter from the

FIGURE 1. The Allied landings on the beaches of Normandy, France, on June 6, 1944, initiated an extensive offensive to liberate northwestern Europe from Nazi occupation. More than 4,400 soldiers lost their lives on the beaches that day. By June 30, more than 850,000 troops, 148,000 vehicles, and 570,000 tons of equipment and supplies, from eight different countries, had arrived on this fifty-mile stretch of shore. Today, the serenity of the Normandy coast belies the physical and emotional magnitude of this history, reminding us how landscape can be complicit in both concealing and revealing the past. Upper photograph courtesy of the U.S. National Archives; lower photograph by Anton Bielousov under a Creative Commons Attribution-Share Alike 3.0 Unported license, via Wikimedia Commons.

term *historic preservation,* which is specific to the United States. Although *enterprise* has business connotations, I imply its more generic definition as "a project or activity that involves many people and that is often difficult."[3] Heritage policy, or preservation policy, is formed by and emerges from this enterprise and is repeated and fortified in institutions, tools of governance, and modes of practice. It is a vehicle of collective action that seeks to make sense of and order the messiness, in the interest of the public good.

Policy work carries great responsibility and accountability to each other, as individuals and collectives. It entails a mutual obligation that extends beyond justifying the importance of heritage to people; it compels consideration of what the heritage enterprise does for people, how policy benefits and burdens diverse publics and the environment. I begin from a place of hope.

Another definition of *enterprise* further expounds my position and use of the term: "the ability or desire to do dangerous or difficult things or to solve problems in new ways."[4] Problematic legacies of systemic exclusion and resource consumption pervade the built environment and the policy infrastructure that enables it, and this extends to and is complicated by the heritage enterprise. Premised on the principle that people are all equal, we all have equal responsibility to act, to be agents of change in response to the intractable and interlinked crises of injustice and climate change. The greatest challenge in contemporary heritage policy is mustering the desire for self-reflection and systemic reform. This involves pursuing new heritage information and perspectives, compromising and negotiating heritage values in the context of broader societal and environmental concerns, recognizing different knowledges and voices, and confronting the implications—positive and negative—of past and current practices. These are dangerous and difficult things not only because of their complexity but because they threaten the status quo.

As David Lowenthal noted in 1985, "only in this generation has saving the tangible past become a major global enterprise."[5] This volume acknowledges the maturation of the heritage enterprise into a pervasive form of public policy that has the power to profoundly impact human life and the planet. It seeks to challenge and to question, but also to tap the kind of future-oriented hope that first inspired preservation as a public endeavor.

Introduction

SECOND-ORDER PRESERVATION

After the bombardment and destruction of the House of Commons during World War II, Winston Churchill urged the House of Lords to reconstruct the building in its previous form rather than entertain a new architectural design. In his view, the old House had conditioned the style of parliamentary debates. Altering those spatial arrangements would change the character of those debates and thus the structure of English democratic governance. He famously noted, "We shape our buildings and afterwards our buildings shape us."[1]

The idea that historic places and objects, as tangible things, are created by humans and likewise condition the human experience echoes across heritage scholarship. In expounding the value and meaning of cultural resources, anthropologist William Lipe invoked the political philosopher Hannah Arendt: "the things that owe their existence exclusively to men nevertheless constantly condition their human makers."[2] Ian Hodder's concept of "entanglement" derives from the evolving codependent relationship of humans and things in the context of archaeological inquiry.[3] Jorge Otero-Pailos builds on Michel Serres's example of a soccer ball as a *quasi-object* to analogize heritage, noting that "the ball participates in and co-produces the human interaction we call soccer. . . . Without the ball there is no game."[4]

In teaching heritage policy, I build on this soccer analogy by likening policy to the rules of the game. I ask students to describe how they played soccer (or football, as it is known beyond the United States) in their youth. Many speak to how they improvised with friends to create a goal with garbage bins, or co-opted a backyard as a field, or made up their own rules. There are tales of joining leagues, playing for their school, qualifying for tournaments. As their participation became less localized and more formalized, the rules of the game became increasingly standardized to establish a platform for teams to play against each other at higher levels, like a state or national championship or the World Cup. Does everyone across the globe play soccer with the same set of rules all the time? Of course not. But the more we engage with others—across communities, institutions, and geopolitical boundaries—the more we need shared policies, so that we all understand the rules of the game.

I then ask students to turn this soccer analogy to heritage. Publics and societies across the world have diverse concepts of heritage; they preserve and transfer it differently across generations. But to engage governments and institutions in preservation, polities seek some form of agreement on how heritage might be protected, treated, and managed, so the rules of the game can be understood by all. The higher the level of governance, from local to national to international, the more functional it becomes to forgo nuances and establish shared norms through policy. Consider the degree of cultural difference among the 195 nation-states that are party to the United Nations Education, Science, and Culture Organization (UNESCO) World Heritage Convention.[5] Does everyone across the globe conserve heritage with the same set of rules all the time? Of course not. But participating in the World Heritage system and elevating heritage sites to that platform—in the same way a nation-state might bring its team to the World Cup—requires a shared commitment to and understanding of the rules of the game.

The soccer analogy compels an additional perspective beyond the dialectical relationship of people and object: the relationships among people, in which the object is instrumental. One might argue that the intention of the soccer game is for players to interact not simply with the ball but also with each other. The rules of the game govern both. Heritage policy also shapes our experience of and engagement with others and their stories. However, just because everyone is following the same set of rules does not mean that the playing field is even or that the game is fair. The impetus of policy to standardize can undermine difference, perpetuate dominant cultures and unjust power relationships, and reinforce systems of exclusion. The recursive nature of policy structures further fortifies standardization as well as consequent inequities, repeating and institutionally embedding potentially unjust processes across generations.[6]

Complicating the policy landscape further is the fact that heritage is not the only game in town. Especially because of its social-spatial dimensions, place-based heritage policy bumps up against and overlaps with policies for land use, economic and community development, affordable housing, climate mitigation and adaptation, and more. The extent to which heritage policy integrates with or distances from these competing or attendant policies varies, depending on the locale. For example, heritage management may be incorporated into tourism or resilience planning or may be addressed through discrete governance institutions and procedures. Returning to the soccer analogy, these varying policies with their distinct interests are vying for access to and influence on the same place, like different players seeking to play different games—soccer, rugby, baseball—on the same field. The soccer teams want to claim their space and prioritize their game, and prevent other teams from encroaching. Similarly, heritage policy fundamentally seeks to distinguish places as heritage, to claim those places, and to rationalize the importance, if not the primacy, of heritage interests and values in the policy landscape.

Circumstances change. Rules change too. Games akin to soccer date back millennia, but modern efforts to develop a common set of soccer rules began in England in the mid-nineteenth century. In 1882, a newly established international board formalized the rules; it continues to oversee their development. The rules of the game are standardized but have evolved and continue to adapt, for example, penalty kicks were introduced only in 1891, offside rules have changed multiple times, substitutions were not allowed until 1958, and red and yellow cards were added in 1970. The birth of television and other forms of social media influenced how the game was played and regulated. As medical data emerged about the brain health implications of heading a soccer ball, youth leagues began disallowing the practice, and some professional leagues limit the weekly number of headers per player during training.

This volume argues for revisiting and reimagining the rules of the game in the preservation enterprise. Social and environmental conditions have changed dramatically since heritage entered the mainstream of public policy. World population has doubled since the UNESCO World Heritage Convention entered into force in 1972; the U.S. population has increased by nearly 70 percent since the 1966 National Historic Preservation Act. Urban/rural population ratios also inverted across the globe, from less than 40 percent urban in 1972 to nearly 60 percent urban today; in the United States, more than 80 percent of the population now lives in urban areas, and those areas are increasingly plural in terms of racial and ethnic diversity. Climate change emerged as a global policy priority in the 1980s with the establishment of the Intergovernmental Panel on Climate Change in 1988. The built environment is now known to play a major role in climate change and is responsible for nearly 40 percent of global greenhouse gas emissions.[7] The long-term effects of racism, colonialism, and other forms of exclusion on publics and environments, and how they complicate the climate crisis, are increasingly recognized and researched.

These profound developments in how humans occupy, use, and protect places compel concerted examination of preservation policy so that it evolves with these transformative circumstances. As both a reflection and a provocation, this volume examines the social and environmental implications of laying claim to place as heritage through government action, with a lens toward contemporary urban geographies as places of plural identities, significant capital flows, and layered histories of occupation. It explores a heritage policy agenda that pursues and incorporates new knowledge, analyzes the implications of past practices and contemporary conditions, and advances more responsive and responsible policy reform.

The public policy infrastructure in support of preservation emerged in earnest in the twentieth century, with architects and architectural historians playing an outsized role. Its associated institutions, research, laws, and practices reflect and reinforce individual site-focused approaches that valorize the aesthetic and material care of the heritage *object*. This ubiquitous policy approach stems from the obvious first-order notion that no public benefit can ensue if the heritage is lost or irrevocably damaged.

Object-focused approaches are important; they navigate and acknowledge the critical formal and material dimensions of place, their meaning, and their experience as a spatial encounter. Object-focused preservation of places creates a multisensory medium through which narratives of the past are potently transmitted. That we can see, touch, hear, and smell place is profoundly evocative. That polities choose to recognize and protect heritage places, to maintain them across generations, amplifies the power of such experiences. That people rally for the protection of places and protest their potential loss underscores the community-building function of advocating for heritage places. Their survival is a collective act.

But object-focused approaches are not sufficient. As Daniel Bluestone notes, "the essential materialism of preserved places has led preservationists to steward these objects of preservation desire as if they are ends in themselves, often sapping preservation's vitality, relevance, and civic promise."[8] As a form of public policy, legal rationales for why government should take on the work of preservation undergird associated laws and ordinances and articulate that civic promise; they codify intentions well beyond the safeguarding of buildings and sites and their aesthetic and material qualities. These public policy rationales emphasize civic education, public health and welfare, economic stability, tourism, and more.[9] However, the practical work of government regulation centers overwhelmingly on the first-order logic of preventing loss, damage, and significant alteration through designation and procedural design review of proposed alterations to those designated places.

At site-specific scales, designation and design review processes do little to account for these public policy rationales. Local preservation commissions in the United States, for example, do not evaluate a proposed historic district based on projections for property value or affordability impacts, nor do they prioritize effects on community economies or greenhouse gas emissions when reviewing designs for an adaptive reuse project. Their purview centers on minimizing negative impacts to the historic and aesthetic qualities of place-based heritage. This narrow lens means that the social, economic, and environmental intentions of heritage policy are largely divorced from processes of decision-making about what to preserve and how.

At structural or systemic levels, this uncoupling of intentions and processes inhibits the ability to assess the outcomes of preservation in terms of its effects on publics, positive or negative. As Iris Marion Young observes, this is an endemic challenge for public policies and associated practices:

> many large-scale social processes in which masses of individuals believe they are following the rules, minding their own business, and trying to accomplish their legitimate goals can be seen to result in undesirable unintended consequences when looked at structurally.[10]

Although the conservation and interpretation of individual sites may effectively confront social exclusion and climate concerns, site-by-site approaches do not aggregate to systemic change, nor do they ensure equity across multiple places and publics and across time.

The soccer analogy is helpful as a simple illustration of the limitations of a heritage-as-object purview and its relationship to policy as a set of shared rules applied to the object. But it is insufficient for characterizing the wider political inquiry. Part of the work of policy is questioning and requestioning whom it serves and how. Public policy, as government action, by its nature compels accountability. That requires not only an aperture that frames heritage as both people and place but an obligation to interrogate policy histories, systems, and their implications.

Contemplating how to approach this sort of interrogation during the throes of a global pandemic, I found myself thinking about these policy challenges in relation to public health.[11] Whereas the medical professions focus on the care and treatment of individuals, the work of public health centers on populations. This duality recognizes that endemic issues cannot be addressed on a patient-by-patient basis. Public health policy and the methods it employs create an infrastructure of institutions, research, laws, and practices centered on confronting health disparities and promoting well-being at the community level and in systemic ways. In doing so, it interrogates standards of care, institutionalized norms that may contribute to bias and disparate treatment, and barriers to access, so as to advance equity and justice in policymaking and implementation.

Like medical practitioners, preservationists establish analytical criteria and standards for intervention, develop documentation and diagnostic technologies, research and implement physical treatments, and pioneer managed care approaches (e.g., cultural resource management) to guide the preservation of heritage places: buildings, archaeological sites, historic districts, and so on. The existing preservation policy infrastructure supports and reinforces this object-focused endeavor. Applying a public health–like lens to the preservation enterprise means looking beyond the first-order logic of saving buildings and sites as the sole intention of heritage policy; it requires second-order thinking.

Second-order thinking derives from discourses in multiple fields. In popular media and business-oriented literature, second-order thinking means looking beyond a particular objective to anticipate the longer-term implications of achieving that objective.[12] Actions have unintended consequences, and while they cannot always be predicted, the exercise of playing out a decision over time is a way of developing forethought and awareness about possible outcomes, positive and negative. By exploring multiple decision-making scenarios and looking several steps ahead, second-order thinking involves a more open-ended examination of alternatives, rather than a strategic pathway toward one particular end goal. Second-order thinking is thus future oriented, extending time horizons and incorporating the potential derivative effects of a decision. The intention is to improve decision-making so as to maximize benefits and reduce negative effects.

Emerging research around second-order science expands on the concept by advocating for reflexive analysis of systemic implications, as Karl H. Müller and Alexander Riegler observe:

> The science system becomes increasingly confronted with the effects of its own products, objects, technological designs, evaluations, interventions, etc. So science must be increasingly concerned about its own internal and external effects, and thereby become more aware of its own consequences and, at the same time, more self-reflexive in terms of its wider implications for societies and their environments.[13]

Michael Lissack argues that second-order science inherently involves revealing "hidden issues, problems and assumptions" that are often overlooked in the everyday practice of scientists. Such reflexive accounting of the supposed results of past decisions can lead to better tools and refinement of those already in use and can fundamentally reduce public doubt in science.[14] Second-order thinking in this construct thus adds a past-oriented dimension to understanding the effects of previous decisions, in order to improve outcomes.

The preservation enterprise faces similar challenges. The emergence of critical heritage studies launched a discourse characterized by second-order thinking.[15] In seeking to elucidate the implications of heritage practices, this discourse forged space in the academy for interrogating the histories and theories driving the preservation enterprise and its social consequences and is helping to shape different and more experimental modes of site-based practice. Instrumentalizing heritage is also a type of future-oriented, second-order thinking in that it looks beyond just saving a site to how different preservation scenarios might intentionally support broader social, economic, or environment aims.[16] However, such approaches still largely center heritage as a discrete place through which public purpose may be realized. Limited attention has been paid to the functioning of the preservation enterprise within a broader urban policy agenda concerned with equity, community development, built environment regulation, and climate mitigation and adaptation. And there is likewise less interrogation of how these policies function structurally, how they are embedded in institutions, how they aggregate and replicate people-contingent processes and outcomes, and how they scale beyond site-by-site heritage approaches. As government-sponsored action, it is incumbent on preservationists to interrogate the edges of harm in the heritage enterprise, to understand who is advantaged and disadvantaged and how the decisions it takes today may prevent recursive harm and spur alternative futures.

Applying second-order thinking to government-sponsored heritage policy means moving beyond the academy and individual sites to understand the preservation enterprise as an embedded, institutional *system*. Heritage is more than an aggregate of place-based resources and site-by-site approaches; policy has endemic effects on people at varying scales and across geographies. Like public health, first-order intentions of treating the object as patient are still essential to the enterprise. However, applying second-order thinking can help in understanding and unraveling the cumulative and repeated effects of those first-order actions and how institutionalized structures of governance inhibit or enable maximal benefits beyond the saved object.

Second-order preservation involves querying how the development and application of heritage policies and practices advantage and disadvantage certain publics and complicate collective claims, spatial and narrative, within our earthly environment. There are both past- and forward-facing dimensions to this, to understand how benefits and burdens are unevenly shared across spaces, populations, and time. Ultimately, such understanding can guide policy reform. It allows for the kind of reflexive analysis that can evolve preservation policy to more effectively meet contemporary challenges and better serve diverse publics. This volume tests this notion of second-order preservation by looking at how heritage policy began and evolved, and the implications of that structure today, to identify potential avenues of policy reform.

Much like the built environment itself, the structural dimensions of policy have a stratigraphy, with new constructions anchored by long-ago-laid foundations. There is injustice embedded deep within these footings, owing to what journalist Isabelle Wilkerson refers to as the "architecture of human hierarchy." Centuries of subjugation by race, gender, religion, and more are entrenched within the built environment. What survives today, and in what condition, is a consequence of those histories, as are the policies that guide their protection. Appropriate to the heritage enterprise, Wilkerson analogizes the need to structurally interrogate the underpinnings of injustice to a deteriorating plaster ceiling in her older home. Investigation of the attic and infrared imaging showed water infiltration that long predated her ownership of the house but that was presently threatening its structural integrity. Repairing the plaster was not sufficient to rectify the problem; it required digging far below surface conditions. Even those who did not produce these preexisting problems must contend with their consequences.[17]

Interrogating these antecedent foundations is not a matter of placing fault or anachronistically judging the past by the present. Young argues that accounting for the past is needed to understand how it contributes to contemporary injustice:

> Understanding how structural processes produce and reproduce injustice requires having an account of how they have come about and operated in the past coming up to the present. Having such a backward-looking account also helps those of us who participate in those processes understand our role in them. The purpose of such backward-looking accounts, however, is not to praise or to blame, but to help all of us see relationships between particular actions, practices, and policies, on the one hand, and structural outcomes, on the other.[18]

Second-order preservation involves revisiting these policy foundations as the rationales or intentions for government action, especially the conditions under which they were formed, by whom, and for whom. How multiple levels of governance (local, state, national, international) apply these policies, normalizing and embedding them within institutional structures, serves as an additional and interconnected avenue of inquiry. It questions how policy may reproduce power and vulnerability by repeatedly centering certain publics, places, and narratives over time and across geographies, thereby creating systemic and unintended consequences through site-by-site decisions and practices.

This second-order thinking also involves probing these policy intentions and their attendant processes in relation to evolving social and environmental conditions. Like the public health field and most other types of public policy, from education to clean air, this is not a one-and-done endeavor but rather an ongoing process of data collection, data analysis, and feedback loops to understand how policy intentions, processes, and outcomes are, or are not, effectively aligning. As a form of public policy, the heritage enterprise is accountable for the aggregate and disparate effects of its institutions and tools. Yet the first-order logic of "save the building, then other benefits will follow" suggests little accountability on the part of government to ascertain how, or even whether, its public purposes are actually being met consistently through preservation policy. Economic studies and some environmental ones seek to rationalize the accrued benefits of preservation at more systemic levels, but most of these are punctual and advocacy driven. They seek to protect the status quo of the preservation enterprise rather than to inform policy evolution, focusing on how intended consequences justify existing policy without interrogating how unintended consequences may necessitate revised policy. Second-order preservation thus entails both past- and forward-looking analyses to determine how public institutions may need to modify and restructure their remits, to both achieve and be accountable for their public policy actions.

Reform is an inescapable dimension of public policy. As the political scientist Charles E. Lindblom noted, "policy is not made once and for all; it is made and re-made endlessly. Policy-making is a process of successive approximation to some desired objectives in which what is desired itself continues to change under reconsideration."[19] There is an uncertainty to preservation consequences, an entropy that follows the collective claim to place as heritage due to intersecting public and private forces and changing social, economic, and environmental conditions. We cannot order and control the entropy of heritage, but we can be more cognizant of how policy influences it. Endeavoring to reflexively analyze and anticipate consequences will enable the preservation enterprise to evolve more responsibly and effectively in light of changing circumstances.

Preservationists are not simply protectors of heritage sites; we are caretakers of the enterprise as well. The preservation policy system is a complex structure. For it not only to survive but to perform effectively, to duly serve the public writ large, we must ensure its structural integrity. We cannot achieve that by simply expecting its foundations to last or assuming that cosmetic interventions will suffice. The dual climate and social justice crises are testing this structure like the combined forces of a perfect storm, exposing weaknesses and cracks, raising questions of incremental fixes versus reconstructing altogether. We must look backward and forward and beyond the immediate priority of preventing material loss of the object. Preservationists are acutely aware of the arc of history and the significance of time; we must expand that gaze to continually consider and reconsider the policy long view.

Through this volume, I am intentionally looking for cracks in the foundation. To address the challenges we face today and on the horizon, we must improve the policy infrastructure of the preservation enterprise. But first we must assess the foundations, as Young advises, "not to praise or to blame, but to help all of us see relationships between particular actions, practices, and policies, on the one hand, and structural outcomes, on the other." Some will take issue with this critical analysis, fearing that it may reflect poorly on the field and its many benefits and accomplishments. But when a property owner engages a conservation architect to undertake a condition assessment, the expectation is that they will identify problem areas in need of repair. This provides a basis from which both owner and consultant can prioritize and design effective interventions. This examination follows a similar logic. To enhance the policy infrastructure of preservation so that it more effectively serves people, and the causes of justice and climate especially, we must understand how disparate aims and inequities manifest through past and present decision-making.

This volume does not provide definitive answers to how policy should change but rather reframes what we ask of policy by questioning its implications. It embarks on a critical reflection by shifting the lens of inquiry from the object, how publics ascribe value to and preserve individual sites, to how the object-focused values of the field contribute to tensions and systemic biases in policy. It seeds the concept of second-order preservation by exploring and unraveling the consequences of policy and its first-order logic and by interrogating the broader social and environmental stakes of heritage policy and its recursive structures. In doing so, it joins a growing chorus of ever-hopeful practitioners, scholars, and policymakers confronting exclusion in the preservation enterprise and pursuing new horizons for collective agency.

1

Heritage as Place and Policy

When we talk about places, we are talking about life.

—Asa Briggs, "The Sense of Place," in *The Quality of Man's Environment*

Preservation policy seeks to protect people's freedom to collectively transfer heritage across generations. How that works in and through *place* provides important insights into how object-focused approaches to preservation—the ball as heritage—can obfuscate the implications of policy and reinforce first-order priorities. Defining heritage is not limited to how people view, characterize, or ascribe values to the object. Heritage that is place based or place associated functions as a social-spatial dynamic. Preservation policy intervenes in that dynamic, effectively seeking to manage change in ways that promote certain values over others, and thus certain publics over others. Understanding "place" in the preservation enterprise serves as a critical starting point for how concepts of place influence policy.

PLACE AS HERITAGE

Place is not simply an object or a thing; it is an inhabited space, an ever-evolving context for life, human and nonhuman. Claiming place as heritage is not simply about recognizing the history and importance of a particular site. People ascribe meaning, memory, and value to places deemed heritage to differentiate and privilege them. That is not to say that heritage exists only if designated or listed. There are places and practices of significance the world over that are not formally recognized as heritage, and the ways in which people form attachments to place are not necessarily contingent upon a heritage label. However, designation or listing is largely a precondition of collective action in the form of public policy; it enables polities to act on places, and their inhabitants, by institutionalizing and legitimizing these heritage claims.

Heritage places are often defined by scholars, policymakers, and professionals through descriptive typologies that may reflect production or use, disciplinary perspectives and remits, or physical and spatial characteristics. Terms like *monument, memorial, historic building, archaeological site, historic district, traditional settlement, historic corridor,* and more denote individual and collective human-made constructions because of their materiality, design, and function. *Immovable heritage* refers to these same sorts of land-connected resources and derives largely from legal discourse related to real property, differentiating it from movable heritage or property (such as artworks or museum objects). Heritage qualifiers, such as *industrial, urban, rural,* and *underwater,* further describe and categorize in terms of use and context, creating subgenres of research, practice, and advocacy that transcend individual sites or geographies. Umbrella terms like *built heritage,* the *historic built environment,* and the *heritage-scape*[1] generically frame the spatial and physical phenomena that are the primary foci of the preservation enterprise. The influential U.S. preservationist James Marston Fitch emphasized the object-focused lens of the field when he referred to historic preservation as "curatorial management of the built world," paralleling place to a collection of art or museum artifacts.[2]

From the spot on the steps of the Lincoln Memorial where Martin Luther King Jr. delivered his "I Have a Dream" speech to the Mississippi Delta National Heritage Area, which extends across eighteen counties, the varying geographic scales of historic places muddle notions of heritage as exclusively object or human-made construction. The Cliff of Bandiagara, a UNESCO World Heritage site in Mali, includes 289 villages and spans an area of more than fifteen hundred square miles, larger than the state of Rhode Island.[3] The heritage lexicon increasingly employs terminology like *cultural landscape,* which blurs the debated divides between humans and environments, and between cultural and natural resources, by acknowledging their inextricable linkages. *Historic urban landscape* connotes the complex and layered dimensions of heritage attributes and values in city contexts, as well as an approach that centers heritage in urban policy and decision-making.[4] Not unlike the soccer analogy of different sports teams seeking to claim space for and prioritize their game, these landscape terms and approaches are still tempered by object-focused

FIGURE 2. The diverse geographies, physical forms, spatial scales, and social dynamics of historic places complicate the notion of heritage as a typological *object.* A single paver at the Lincoln Memorial in Washington, D.C., marks the place where Martin Luther King Jr. delivered his "I Have a Dream" speech. The Cliff of Bandiagara, a UNESCO World Heritage site in Mali, includes 289 villages and spans an area of more than fifteen hundred square miles. Upper photograph courtesy of the National Park Service; lower photograph courtesy of Ferdinand Reus under a Creative Commons Attribution-Share Alike 2.0 Generic license, via Wikimedia Commons.

concepts of heritage as they endeavor to elevate preservation policy within broader urban and rural agendas.

Heritage places typically fall within the construct of tangible heritage, which has physical or material characteristics, as opposed to intangible heritage, which refers to cultural practices like oral traditions, performing arts, crafts, and more. Although heritage practitioners readily acknowledge that there are intangible dimensions to heritage places, institutional and disciplinary structures largely separate tangible and intangible heritage, and government policy related to the former is far more advanced.[5] The recognition of intangible heritage is an important policy frontier for many societies whose knowledge and practices are not as vested in material evidence and construction or do not comport with professionalized norms. It is also an important consideration for marginalized publics—Indigenous peoples, Black and Brown people, women, and others—whose ability to transfer heritage across generations is compromised due to oppression, dispossession, the lack of property rights, or the loss of physical vestiges. However, this tangible–intangible binary is, at times, a means of promulgating and reinforcing object-focused approaches to preservation that still elevate the material and the physical. By defining and centering what exists or survives in place as tangible heritage, the preservation enterprise runs the risk of discounting the potential placeness of heritage that is practiced or no longer survives and shifts the messy humanness of place to the more nebulous realm of intangible heritage. To suggest, for example, that the House of Commons is tangible heritage while parliamentary debates are intangible heritage belies the fundamental interconnectedness that Churchill sought to elucidate and reconstruct. It sidesteps the complexity of the social-spatial relationships that create and characterize place-based heritage by labeling everything that is not formal or material as intangible, establishing a false dichotomy.

In using terms like *place-based* or *place-associated heritage,* I seek to push the boundaries of object-focused approaches by disquieting the tangible–intangible binary and recognizing the social and political tensions and dimensions of place. In 2019, fieldwork with students and colleagues in Freetown, Sierra Leone, raised poignant questions about the many markets that characterize the city. Certain thoroughfares have served as corridors for informal street vendors for more than a century. The architecture along these arteries demonstrates significant change over time in construction materials, styles, heights, and massing. However, the social-spatial relationships and uses persist, with vendors continuing to occupy liminal spaces along the street wall and in front of buildings during market hours.[6] During similar fieldwork in Yangon, Myanmar, students identified street vending as a character-defining feature of the historic central business district, creating a distinct codependency between vending activities and building facades, especially how they were designed, accessed, and occupied.[7] To qualify these street markets as *intangible* heritage discounts the long-standing, place-based dimensions of these vending practices and their social-spatial implications. It likewise fails to more fully recognize the many people for whom this practice is a continuing form of livelihood, social interaction, and resource provision, in that particular place.

Disruptions of social-spatial relationships, which may not involve a direct intervention on the heritage object, further complicate tangible–intangible divides and what constitutes a heritage place. Fieldwork with students in 2015 and 2017 in Port-au-Prince, Haiti, investigated historic houses dating from the late nineteenth to the mid-twentieth century, known familiarly as gingerbread houses, to understand their evolution. Because of security and safety concerns in recent decades, tall, opaque walls have replaced low fencing around many of these structures, thereby eradicating the liminal spaces between houses and between house and street. Such spaces formerly allowed for neighborhood connections and views, porch-to-porch and yard-to-yard communication, and engagement with street-based cultural and economic activities. The spatial qualities of these properties and the social conditions of these aggregated spaces at neighborhood scales are interdependent. Protection of life and property is a valid priority, but one that has compromised community cohesion, in part, through the formal introduction of the walls.[8] Such alterations are distinct from the architecture of the gingerbread houses themselves but profoundly impact their use, meaning, and encounter.

Removal and loss further complicate object-related heritage distinctions. The mobility of place-associated heritage challenges strict adherence to movable versus immovable qualifiers. Can the Parthenon Marbles, relocated to the British Museum from Greece under contested terms, be considered *movable* heritage even though they were integral to the Parthenon building? Neither the capacity to be moved

FIGURE 3. The spatial and social conditions of heritage places are inextricably linked. The construction of increasingly higher and more opaque walls around historic gingerbread houses in Port-au-Prince, Haiti, has eradicated the liminal spaces between houses and between house and street. Such spaces formerly allowed for neighborhood connections and views and engagement with street-based cultural and economic activities. These physical alterations are distinct from the architecture of the gingerbread houses themselves, as heritage *objects,* but profoundly impact their use, meaning, and encounter. Photograph by the author.

nor the actual change in geography and environment negates their place-based origins and context. The importance of context and the complications of mobility are underscored by the fact that a building on the U.S. National Register of Historic Places may lose its listed status if moved. If a National Register home is relocated due to increased flooding, for example, does that decision to physically preserve the structure *ex situ* mean that historic significance is compromised or simply recontextualized?

Heritage as place incurs connections to environments, geographies, and publics that exist beyond the aperture of an object-focused lens. The preservation enterprise acknowledges and reflects this, to some extent, as a question of context, often expressed through expanding geographic boundaries of districts and landscapes, by delineating buffer zones around heritage sites, or by analyzing social and economic contexts as part of management planning processes. The idea of an object in context nevertheless still centers, and thus valorizes, the object. I purposefully use the term *valorize* to connote the way in which the preservation enterprise adds value to places through such actions, rather than simply discovering or assessing their existing value. A priori identifying something as heritage invokes the rules of the preservation game and claims the field, as in the soccer analogy. Heritage cannot be everything all at once, so some degree of object centering may be valid. But place incurs people, and people are not just context. The social-spatial relationships of place are contingent upon people; they affect and are affected by them. Heritage policy runs the risk of othering associated publics as secondary when it does not adequately account for the social and environmental dimensions of place or the social and environmental implications of policy structures.

Deconstructing the concept of place is an important starting point for balancing and expanding the object-focused heritage lens. Theories of place vary across disciplines and worldviews, and wide-ranging literatures explore and debate its definition and examination.[9] The following key dimensions, from sociologist Thomas R. Gieryn, provide a basis for understanding place in the context of heritage policy:

Geographic location. Place is sited somewhere, though its boundaries may not be fixed and may vary in scale.

Material form. Whether the result of direct human intervention or not, there is a physicality to place. "Places are worked by people" in that they are created, used, managed, altered, destroyed, and/or challenged. "Social processes (difference, power, inequality, collective action) happen *through* the material forms."

Investment with meaning and value. Places are further constructed and reimagined by publics who identify, name, narrate, interpret, and valorize them. "In spite of its relatively enduring and imposing materiality, the meaning or value of the same place is labile—flexible in the hands of different people or cultures, malleable over time, and inevitably contested."[10]

That people and communities ascribe meaning and develop attachments to places is broadly acknowledged, though the conditions and factors influencing such attachments are diverse, relating to specific geographies, cultures, and knowledges. Place attachment and sense of place serve as overarching concepts for characterizing the complex social-spatial dynamics and processes that intertwine humans, their environs, and their material dimensions.[11] Exploration of these attachments can be employed to support public engagement in community preservation and planning processes by acknowledging identities, stories, and values.[12] They likewise are associated with social resilience, particularly postdisaster. Such attachments can also encumber individual and collective decisions about which places should be protected, for example, in the face of climate change and when habitability becomes too much of a risk.[13]

Attachment to places may manifest as a sense of collective identity and a claimed right to place as heritage, but ownership in the legal sense further complicates what is preserved and by whom. The geography of place is inextricably linked to issues of land access, acquisition, and dispossession; it is a medium of conflict. More than cultural object or property, place-based heritage is geopolitical territory. It is acreage and floor area. For example, buildings designated by the New York City Landmarks Preservation Commission occupy more than 30 percent of the tax lots in Manhattan.[14] People depend on these spaces to live, work, learn, create, build wealth, and more. Place-based heritage is a form of spatial production, and space has power.

Debates about place and space, their distinctions and intersections, shed light on how the production and use of space, and claims to place as heritage, constitute a political act with social, economic, and environmental consequences. Social science scholars assert the spatial and geographic dimensions of social theory[15] and expose the ways in which power, difference, and injustice are produced and reproduced through place and time.[16] As Edward Soja cautions, "we must be insistently aware of how space can be made to hide consequences from us, how relations of power and discipline are inscribed into the apparently innocent spatiality of social life, how human geographies become filled with politics and ideology."[17] The discourse of cultural geography shares common threads with that of heritage scholarship regarding the dialectical relationship of humans and that which they create. However, the perspective of space (as opposed to object) and social organization as interdependent more directly acknowledges the histories and dynamics of human conditions and processes as inextricably bound up in place, thereby centering questions of politics and social justice.[18] Claiming place as *heritage* means, to some extent, recognizing geography, materiality, and value, per Gieryn's attributes, at a particular moment in time. But the attributes of place can both reveal and conceal, obscuring what alternatively might have been, what may have existed or happened before, and the forces that shaped what is.[19] They may likewise be reflective of inequities and power dynamics within communities, valorizing particular places over others because of the agency and influence of some, but not all. The bequest of place is not simply the object we see today. It is the complicated conditions, and often injustices, that enabled that place to become and to persist. In prioritizing the object, claims of heritage skew toward commemorating what survives and the narratives and publics associated with it. This physical and symbolic form of placemaking centers those narratives and privileges those publics through material, spatial, and representational reinforcement that influences people's lived experience of an environment over time and their identity.[20] Claiming place as heritage affects people, not just objects, in potentially positive and negative ways.

The preservation enterprise has tremendous power and responsibility in claiming place. When recognized through government policy, heritage places in effect become the most "fixed" and formally valued elements of landscapes and built environments; their continued survival is codified as a public priority. While affording the intergenerational transfer of particular spatial experiences, forms, knowledge, and associated narratives, such political acts nonetheless can discount both the past and the future. In safeguarding the physical vestiges of a particular period in time, the preservation enterprise may be complicit in devaluing who and what previously occupied a space or may preclude alternative futures for that space and its associated publics. The climate crisis compounds these justice implications. Climate mitigation and adaptation raise complex challenges for existing built environments and communities, which are further complicated by historical inequities in claims to space and contemporary place attachments. More frequent and severe climate events, such as flooding and fire, disrupt much more than the material dimensions of place and are compounded by the valorization of heritage and the object-centric priorities it connotes.[21]

Claims to place as heritage also afford important opportunities for squaring or righting history and understanding the social-spatial dynamics of place. More than a form of stewardship or protection, the deeply historical function of preservation may help reveal what landscapes and the built environment may conceal and reinvent power and agency through new stories of the past.[22] As Keith Basso observed in his experience with the Western Apache, such interrogations are an alternate "way of constructing history itself, of inventing it . . . a means of reviving former times but also of *revising* them, a means of exploring not merely how things might have been but also how, just possibly, they might have been different from what others have supposed."[23]

HERITAGE AS POLICY

Societies throughout time have established practices of transferring heritage across generations. This is not simply an act of inheritance or the stewardship of objects; it is a form of self-determination within our environments and communities. As Elizabeth Kamarck Minnich observes:

> we are not just products or objects, nor are we self-contained subjects existing in a void. We are unique, related subjects whose freedom is conditioned—not determined—by worlds not of our making but in our care, open to the effects of our actions.[24]

Through public policy, place-based heritage and its collective conservation are sanctioned by and become the purview of government. Throughout this volume, I refer to the heritage or preservation *enterprise* in part due to the inextricable interaction among the public, private, and third (including not-for-profits and academia) sectors in forging and operationalizing contemporary policy. But government is a foundational framer of that interrelationship through public policy, one that has accountability to its populace, particularly under democratic ideals. Understanding the general arc of policy history provides further insight into its recurring focus on first-order priorities, as well as important efforts to recognize publics through policy.

Early government forays into heritage policy in Europe were often rooted in questions of property ownership. Heritage inventories cataloged assets—buildings, lands, and objects—to which the state laid claim, often to distinguish between church and state control and possession. A long history of monarchs appropriating ecclesiastic properties dates to at least the fourteenth century and was systematized in England under Henry VIII and Cromwell through the 1535 *Valor Ecclesiasticus*, which inventoried and assessed Church property.[25]

The idea that heritage was more than simply an asset of the state but rather a progressive, nation-building enterprise in which the state should engage emerged most notably through the writings of the Abbé Grégoire in the 1790s. Responding to the desecration and destruction of cultural property caused by the French Revolution, he advocated for the republic's role in preserving heritage as *public* objects, not simply through ownership by the state but as places of cultural significance in which the people writ large had a vested stake. His vision for state-sponsored heritage stewardship was somewhat realized through the establishment of the Commission nationale des monuments historiques some four decades later, though under the reign of Louis-Philippe rather than as a project of Grégoire's republican rationale.[26] In the nineteenth century, national governments in Europe increasingly took on the work of identifying and protecting heritage within their territories.[27]

Geopolitical conflict and efforts to codify the rules of war provided early platforms for advancing heritage protection transnationally and internationally. The Lieber Code (1863) commissioned by President Abraham Lincoln during the U.S. Civil War, the Brussels Declaration (1874) initiated by Czar Alexander II of Russia, and the Oxford Manual (1880) prepared by the International Institute of Law all included sections that advocated for cultural property to be spared from bombardment and other forms of damage. The Hague Conventions of 1899 and 1907 established agreed-upon terms for international conflict through a treaty of states parties. Its articles on the protection of historic monuments and similar properties derived from the earlier codes. But the process of ratification by multiple governments through a signed treaty was a critical step in formalizing policy and advancing its adoption. The Roerich Pact, initiated during World War I, was the first multistate treaty dedicated specifically to protecting heritage in times of war and was ratified in 1935 by more than twenty countries across the Americas, including the United States. The 1954 Hague Convention for the Protection of Cultural Property, advanced by UNESCO, likewise focused explicitly on heritage and has been ratified by more than 131 countries. Even though states' self-interests may conflict with collective interests, these multilateral agreements establish common grounds for cooperation. Like the soccer analogy, these signed treaties constitute a government-endorsed commitment to standardizing the rules of the game for all players.

These treaty regimes and their policies regarding the wartime treatment of heritage, along with early heritage inventories and protective legislation within discrete countries, set important precedents for advancing and standardizing preservation policy beyond the nation-state. The Athens Charter for the Restoration of Historic Monuments was a seminal statement adopted at the First International Congress of Architects and Technicians of Historic Monuments in Athens in 1931 and published in 1932. Earlier national and transnational doctrines were dedicated to preserving heritage places, such as William Morris's manifesto for the Society for the Protection of Ancient Buildings (1877) in Great Britain and the Recommendations of the Sixth International Congress of Architects held in Madrid (1904), but the Athens conference marked an important orientation toward multilateral policy development. It was organized under the auspices of the International Museums Office, established by the International Commission for Intellectual Cooperation of the League of Nations. The charter expressly advocated for national-level heritage policies and served as a call for international cooperation, though representation at the conference was largely European. However, the Athens Charter was a text drafted by a group of professionals; it was not an intergovernmental treaty formally ratified by nation-states.

After World War II, the establishment of UNESCO in 1945 and, through UNESCO, the creation of the International Center for the Study of Preservation and Restoration of Cultural Property (ICCROM) in 1956 brought renewed attention to heritage protection as multilateral policy. In 1964, the Second International Congress of Architects and Technicians of Historical Monuments convened in Venice. Some thirty years after the first congress, conference participants mostly from Europe produced a more elaborate doctrine of international standards for preserving built cultural heritage, known as the Venice Charter. Representatives of both UNESCO and ICCROM, which are intergovernmental organizations whose members are nation-states, were involved in the conference. However, the Venice Charter itself was not formalized through an international convention or treaty.

Despite the lack of multilateral nation-state ratification, the Venice Charter was a highly influential document that set precedent in national and international preservation policy. It sparked the establishment of the International Council on Monuments and Sites (ICOMOS) in 1965, which officially adopted the charter the same year. Though ICOMOS has national committees, it is a nongovernmental organization whose membership is made up of individuals, largely heritage professionals. But this professionally endorsed charter informed the operational guidelines and criteria of the UNESCO World Heritage Convention, an intergovernmental treaty established in 1972, for which both ICCROM and ICOMOS serve as official advisory bodies.

The Venice Charter likewise served as a critical reference in the development of U.S. preservation policy. In 1965, building on the momentum of the Venice Charter, a blue ribbon committee of congressional delegates, mayors, and preservation advocates traveled to Europe. The fact-finding mission led to the publication of *With Heritage So Rich* in January 1966, which advocated for establishing new federal legislation and policy infrastructure in support of heritage.[28] Later that same year, the U.S. National Historic Preservation Act was signed into law. The Venice Charter also served as a critical reference in the drafting of the U.S. Secretary of the Interior's Standards for the Treatment of Historic Properties in the 1970s, which endure as a seminal government policy document through multiple revisions.

Charters, standards, and similar guidance documents continue to emerge from the professional heritage community, especially through the many scientific and national committees of ICOMOS.[29] Notable among these is the Australia ICOMOS Burra Charter, which the national government adopted and incorporated into policy. Its values-based approach highlights the incorporation of diverse stakeholders in heritage decision-making and has consequently helped to reframe heritage discourse internationally. The 2005 Council of Europe Framework Convention on the Value of Cultural Heritage for Society, known as the Faro Convention, echoes similar democratic perspectives on heritage participation. Ratified by twenty-three member states of the Council of Europe (as of 2022), it functions as a "framework convention" that suggests action, rather than obligating its signatories.[30]

Whether through formal or informal channels, these declaratory tools influence and underpin government-endorsed policy. A global infrastructure of organizations and agencies, legislation, and programs developed in tandem, creating iterative dynamics of policy development and reinforcement. They collectively bear witness to the maturation of heritage conservation as a realm of public policy implemented across varying levels of governance. Global governance manifests movements toward regularization owing to the aforementioned professional charters and intergovernmental agreements. At the same time, the international heritage arena, though reinforcing and self-replicating, manifests diversity across the laws, policies, and institutions of discrete nations and is derivative of those national heritage policies and attendant institutions. Similarly, national heritage policies themselves can be aggregates of local policies and in turn can influence and standardize local policies.

Although ownership, recognition through listing, and the development of intervention standards serve as core government functions in the heritage enterprise, a broader range of policy tools developed in the twentieth century. Emerging from a 1995 Salzburg Seminar, "Preserving the National Heritage: Policies, Partnership, and Actions," John de Monchaux and J. Mark Schuster characterized five fundamental actions of government:

Ownership and operation. The state might choose to implement policy through direct provision, in this case by owning and operating heritage resources.

Regulation. Alternatively, the state might choose to regulate the actions of other actors, particularly those private individuals or institutional entities that own and occupy heritage resources.

Incentives (and disincentives). The state might provide incentives or disincentives designed to bring the actions of other actors with respect to heritage resources into line with a desired policy.

Establishment, allocation, and enforcement of property rights. The state can establish, allocate, and enforce the property rights of individual parties as these affect the preservation and use of heritage resources.

Information. Finally, the state can collect and distribute information intended to influence the actions of others who might be engaged in the preservation or use of the built heritage.[31]

Not all tools function or are applied at all levels of governance, and many tools do not fit squarely within a specific category. Listing may be primarily an informational tool, but it can trigger or incur regulation and influence property rights, depending on the locale. The United States has federal-level historic tax credits and some state-level tax credits; these function as incentives but likewise incur some degree of regulation, as project designs must be reviewed and approved by state historic preservation offices and by the National Park Service in the case of federal credits.

Similar to the soccer analogy, local governance demonstrates a range of diversity with regard to both policy tools and institutional infrastructure. As the primary administrator of property taxes and land use, local governments in the United States have significant authority to regulate place. Distinct municipal agencies may be dedicated to preservation, for example, the New York City Landmarks Preservation Commission. Alternatively, preservation functions may be embedded within a city's planning department. Some incorporate preservation within zoning or through zoning overlays, whereas others define preservation as a separate land use policy distinct from zoning. Many centralize review of changes to designated sites, whereas others defer to neighborhood-level boards like those established for the historic preservation overlay zones (HPOZs) in Los Angeles, California. Municipal preservation entities may identify, regulate, or administer heritage in different ways and beyond traditional buildings, sites, and districts. For example, cities like Madison, Wisconsin, and Washington, D.C., protect view sheds of their historic capitol buildings by regulating building heights; Denver, Colorado, regulates views of the surrounding mountain landscape. Programs in San Antonio, Texas, and San Francisco, California, seek to protect legacy businesses.

These local policies and governance infrastructures can be diverse but are nonetheless influenced by higher levels of government, thereby reinforcing standardization to varying degrees. For example, more than 85 percent of recently surveyed U.S. municipal ordinances cite

FIGURE 4. Many U.S. cities centralize preservation design review processes under a single commission that oversees the entire municipality, such as New York City. Others, such as Seattle, Washington, and Los Angeles, California, have established neighborhood-based boards for their historic districts, affording more localized participation. Changes in design and use within the now designated Pike Place Market Historical District in Seattle (seen here circa 1922) are reviewed by the Pike Place Market Historical Commission, comprising citizen volunteers appointed by the mayor. The Angelino Heights neighborhood in Los Angeles similarly has a district-specific HPOZ board that reviews design changes and advances preservation plans. Upper photograph courtesy of the Seattle Municipal Archives; lower photograph courtesy of Konrad Summers under a Creative Commons Attribution-Share Alike 2.0 Generic license, via Wikimedia Commons.

or use designation criteria similar to those of the National Register, and many refer to the Secretary of the Interior's Standards as guiding policy in the review of alterations to designated properties.[32] State enabling legislation and state-level model preservation ordinances reinforce consistency across local laws.[33] The U.S. National Park Service's Certified Local Governments (CLG) program works to build linkages across federal, state, and local levels of governance. Local governments are incentivized to comport with CLG policy criteria, as the program affords access to technical assistance, funding, and planning resources.

The international, national, and local levels of heritage governance do not necessarily reflect a hierarchy of authority or power. In the United States, the most robust regulatory powers, namely, designation that protects against demolition and requires approval of proposed alterations to a property, whether publicly or privately owned, tend to be at the municipal level. And in some localities, for example, in New York City, such designation does not require owner consent. Inclusion on the National Register of Historic Places, which may be distinct from or in addition to local designation, allows owners to object to listing and provides no protection from demolition, though the use of federal monies triggers review and mitigation of a project's adverse effects on National Register properties, familiarly known as Section 106 review.

Whereas UNESCO World Heritage status involves a reporting and monitoring system for properties included on the list, nation-states maintain their sovereignty in establishing and implementing policies respective to their heritage sites. The World Heritage Committee, composed of rotating representatives of the nation-states participating in the convention, does not have authority to intervene in national or local heritage policy or site management. As a multistate treaty and system, World Heritage functions primarily as an informational policy tool through listing and monitoring sites, establishing guidelines, and conducting collaborative research about managing heritage sites. When proposed or implemented actions adversely affect World Heritage sites, the committee has little recourse beyond requesting monitoring missions and state of conservation reports, communicating concern to the nation-state, advocating for consideration of improved management or alternative approaches, suggesting alterations to site boundaries, and delisting sites when negotiations and warnings fail.[34]

To date, the committee has delisted only three properties in the history of the convention, from among more than eleven hundred on the World Heritage list as of 2023.

These varying levels of governance, degrees of authority, and diverse tools demonstrate a complex and broad-ranging heritage policy landscape. Nonetheless, the bulk of government action remains focused on heritage-as-object approaches. Protecting the materiality and meaning of place-based heritage is paramount in most charters, guidelines, and standards and in the well-established and pervasive regulatory processes governing the review and approval of property alterations, eligibility for incentives, and the exercise of property rights. Many U.S. municipalities and government agencies appoint citizen-led commissions and use public hearings as a means of engagement when taking decisions about designation or design changes. Participation-oriented and rights-based tools, like the aforementioned Burra Charter and Faro Convention, center the role of stakeholders in heritage decision-making. However, such tools still focus largely on how discrete places as objects are valued, preserved, and managed. People are integral constituents of *place,* and thus of *place-based heritage,* and the intended addressees of public policy. How publics are advantaged or disadvantaged by policies like designation or regulatory design review, as well as how they bear the burden of and/or benefit from the preservation enterprise over time and at systemic levels, remain largely underexamined in the development, implementation, and revision of heritage policy.

2

Victimizing and Valorizing

> The immensity of man's power to destroy imposes a
> responsibility to preserve.
> —Representative John F. Lacey, 1901

Second-order preservation involves interrogating the fundamentals of policy—how certain ideas about the role of government in the heritage enterprise were seeded and grew. Governments instituted a system of exceptionalism, a way of differentiating "heritage" from other places to focus their actions and achieve their public purpose. Changing historical contexts and interests motivated those public purposes; thus the shared impulses that underpin the differentiation of heritage involve a range of environmental, economic, social, political, and aesthetic intentions.

At its core, the intention of protecting heritage for future generations is righteous and good. The value of places as spatial encounters with the past, as spiritual embodiments, and as physical reminders of people and stories cannot be overstated. In acknowledging that collective value through policy, governments promote heritage-making as a vibrant medium of civic memory, codifying the legacy of humankind through the built environment. At the same time, in serving as a necessary protector of shared resources, governments recognize and reify the vulnerability of heritage places. This duality of valorizing and victimizing is embedded in and repeatedly reinforced by heritage policy, creating inherent tensions in how government actions affect not only places but people.

Even when intentions seem righteous and good, associated processes and outcomes may engender inequities, especially over time. The legacies of some may be privileged over those of others, the right to claim place may be disproportionately afforded to some and not to others, and the power and agency of some may marginalize others. Victimizing and valorizing places consequently victimizes and valorizes people, which is not effectively addressed in preservation policy. This victimology is complex and often contradictory based on people's identities and perspectives. In the context of public policy, collective intentions and outcomes transcend a traditional victim–perpetrator construct. It isn't simply that one property owner or community may victimize another through heritage decision-making; publics can be both advantaged and disadvantaged by preservation or the lack of preservation. Time and geography can further complicate how we define who benefited or was burdened by heritage decision-making.

Applying a second-order preservation lens involves exposing historical foundations and recursive patterns of decision-making to understand how government-endorsed policies structurally enable or inhibit justice-oriented reform. Acknowledging positionalities beyond the object-focused traditions of preservation is imperative to this interrogation in order to understand the diverse perspectives of those positively and negatively affected by the heritage enterprise. The purpose is not to make preservation policy vulnerable but rather to identify where it might be reinforced or repaired. The following past-facing explorations shed light on the early and embedded intentions of policy and on how these often obscured foundations complicate the repeated origin stories of preservation policy and the pathways toward reform.

HOPE AND FEAR

As a child, one of my favorite books told the story of a little house in a bucolic country setting. The humanized and gendered house had expressive windows as eyes and a front stoop that curved in the semblance of a smile. With the passage of time, a city grew around the little house, and she became a victim of encroaching development. Though left sad and derelict in the shadow of tall buildings and elevated train tracks, "she was just as good a house as ever underneath."[1] Then one day, the great-great-granddaughter of the man who built the little house saved her. The little house was relocated to a country field and restored, and she was happy again.

The idea that buildings and sites are *victims* in need of saving speaks to the way in which the preservation enterprise grafts a fear of discontinuity onto places-as-objects, seeking to intervene in the life cycle of a

FIGURE 5. The cover of Virginia Lee Burton's *The Little House* (Boston: Houghton Mifflin, 1942) depicts a humanized and gendered house; over time, she becomes neglected and endangered by encroaching development. Such depictions reflect how heritage is both victimized and anthropomorphized through characterizations of threat and rescue. Courtesy of Houghton Mifflin.

structure or landscape by preventing material decay or thwarting loss. This victimization likewise anthropomorphizes heritage. In ascribing values to physical forms and materials, we give voice and feeling to places. We use them as conduits for the hopes and fears about ourselves and the world around us.[2] Their ill treatment serves as a critical rallying cry for preservation action, for confronting threats to both our understanding of the past and our vision for the future. Heritage conservation is thus framed as an act of rescue, as aid to places that are vulnerable, in danger, or neglected.

Risk and loss aversion are threaded throughout the heritage enterprise and in many ways are engrained in policy structures.[3] Endangered lists are a primary means of advocacy in the field, used to draw public and media attention, financial resources, and government awareness toward place-based heritage. Documentation and condition surveys are undertaken with the assumption that heritage is vulnerable to change, degradation, or destruction. Perceptions of loss predicate public policy, and threats to heritage serve as a critical means of policy agenda setting.

The 1966 U.S. National Historic Preservation Act (NHPA) cites the threat of "ever-increasing extensions of urban centers, highways, and residential, commercial, and industrial developments" as part of the public purpose of the law. The 1980 amendments to the NHPA expanded the public policy rationale, and its dependence on risk, by adding that "historic properties significant to the Nation's heritage are being lost or substantially altered, often inadvertently, with increasing frequency."[4] The 1972 UNESCO World Heritage Convention opens by noting that heritage is "increasingly threatened with destruction not only by the traditional causes of decay, but also by changing social and economic conditions which aggravate the situation with even more formidable phenomena of damage or destruction" and goes on to underscore "the magnitude and gravity of the new dangers threatening" heritage.[5]

In 2008, the World Heritage Committee codified these dangers by adopting a list of fourteen primary threats, plus associated subthreats, to World Heritage sites.[6] The expansiveness and exactitude of this list suggest that much of human action imperils heritage. Such threat regimes not only create a dichotomy between heritage-as-object and people; they also fuel an oppositional relationship. Heritage is cast as a victim of human agency, from conflict to climate change, when in many respects, threats to heritage are fundamentally a clash between different people's claims to place and their respective values regarding its use.[7]

Heritage is, at the same time, an embodiment and commemoration of human agency, albeit selective. These are not just places but exceptional places; they are "irreplaceable," per both the UNESCO World Heritage Convention and the NHPA. Placed-based heritage serves as a conduit of collective memory and shared values, endorsed by government. Heritage places, above all other places, have histories and meanings deemed significant to communities at potentially local, national, and international levels. They have symbolic and emotional value. As Caitlin DeSilvey observes:

we live in a world dense with things left behind by those who came before us, but we only single out some of these things for our attention and care. We ask certain buildings, objects, and landscapes to function as mnemonic devices, to remember the pasts that produced them, and to make these pasts available for our contemplation and concern.[8]

Being worthy of rescue is a means of valorizing. The act of preserving, of marshaling government policy tools to protect places, produces value.[9] That is not to say that all heritage places served by policy are in immediate danger, but the mere act of designating or listing place-based heritage at once denotes significance and connotes potential risk. Designation itself is both a platform for communicating significance and a form of triage in that it determines what places deserve added care. Public policy rationales for preservation demonstrate the evolving fears and ideals that drive government action toward care and the first-order aims of saving the heritage object. Characterizations of heritage as victimized and valorized reflect contradictory tensions in those fears and ideals and how they are grafted onto places and the publics who inhabit them.

---

1. Buildings and Development

Housing
Commercial development
Industrial areas

Major visitor accommo-
dation and associated
infrastructure
Interpretative and visitation
facilities

2. Transportation Infrastructure

Ground transport infrastructure
Air transport infrastructure
Marine transport infrastructure

Effects arising from use of
transportation infrastructure
Underground transport
infrastructure

continued on next page

FIGURE 6. UNESCO has defined the primary threats to World Heritage. Abridged by the author from https://whc.unesco.org/en/factors/.

Figure 6 continued

3. Utilities or Service Infrastructure

Developments in relation to infrastructure for energy utilities (i.e., gas, electricity, and water) and other service requirements

Water infrastructure
Renewable energy facilities
Nonrenewable energy facilities

Localized utilities
Major linear utilities

4. Pollution

All types of pollution (residential or commercial) as well as garbage, solid waste

Pollution of marine waters
Groundwater pollution
Surface water pollution

Air pollution
Solid waste
Input of excess energy

5. Biological resource use/modification

Collection or harvest of wild plants and animals (forestry, fishing, hunting, and gathering) and harvest of domesticated species (silviculture, agriculture, and aquaculture)

Fishing/collecting aquatic
  resources
Aquaculture
Land conversion
Livestock farming/grazing of
  domesticated animals
Crop production

Commercial wild plant
  collection
Subsistence wild plant
  collection
Commercial hunting
Subsistence hunting
Forestry/wood production

6. Physical resource extraction

Mining
Quarrying

Oil and gas
Water extraction

7. Local conditions affecting physical fabric

Environmental or biological factors that promote or contribute to deterioration processes of the fabric of heritage sites

Wind
Relative humidity
Temperature
Radiation/light

Dust
Water (rain/water table)
Pests
Micro-organisms

8. Social/cultural uses of heritage

Social factors that contribute to deterioration processes of the fabric of heritage sites; some uses might have a positive impact as they enhance certain values (e.g., ritual, religious), whereas others might compromise ascribed values and could lead to the deterioration of the heritage site

Ritual/spiritual/religious and associative uses
Society's valuing of heritage
Indigenous hunting, gathering, and collecting
Changes in traditional ways of life and knowledge systems

Identity, social cohesion, changes in local population and community
Impacts of tourism/visitors/recreation

9. Other human activities

Illegal activities
Deliberate destruction of heritage
Military training

War
Terrorism
Civil unrest

10. Climate change and severe weather events

Storms
Flooding
Drought
Desertification

Changes to oceanic waters
Temperature change
Other climate change impacts

11. Sudden ecological or geological events

Volcanic eruption
Earthquake
Tsunami/tidal wave

Avalanche/landslide
Erosion and siltation/deposition
Fire (wildfires)

12. Invasive/alien species or hyperabundant species

Translocated species
Invasive/alien terrestrial species
Invasive/alien freshwater species

Invasive/alien marine species
Hyperabundant species
Modified genetic material

13. Management and institutional factors

Management system/management plan
Legal framework
Low-impact research/monitoring activities
Governance

High-impact research/monitoring activities
Management activities
Financial resources
Human resources

14. Other factor(s)

Any factor not already covered

THE LIST

At the core of government action is the process of designating or creating lists, differentiating that which is officially recognized as "heritage" from that which is not. The list reinforces a dialectical tension between victimizing and valorizing yet, at the same time, seeks to reconcile it by compelling just cause for protection. Listing likewise establishes an essential binary between what is worthy of saving and what is not worthy of saving as an object of government policy. The list serves as a fundamental gatekeeper to most other policy tools, such as design regulation, grants and loans, tax incentives, and code exemptions; those on the list have access to these tools.[10] Yet designation involves policy implications and compliance, playing by the rules of the game. The binary of listed–not listed, with its victimizing and valorizing, incurs a sort of brinkmanship: if not listed or designated, a heritage place-as-object can be lost. Not listing may suggest a dereliction of duty on the part of property owners and government and sets up heritage policymaking and implementation as an arena of conflict politics, rather than as a negotiated process of community building.

The guidelines and standards associated with the physical treatment of heritage places can further fuel these binaries and brinkmanship by valorizing interventions that minimize change and maximize original materials. The Secretary of the Interior's Standards, for example, use a "recommended–not recommended" taxonomy to guide decision makers toward responsible practice.[11] This binary taxonomy reduces the burden of decision-making but, in effect, undermines how "standards" and "rules" are meant to function differently. As legal scholars Cass R. Sunstein and Edna Ullmann-Margalit explain:

> the central difference between a rule and a standard is that a rule settles far more in advance and allows on-the-spot judgments to be quite mechanical. . . . In law, the contrast between rules and standards identifies the fact that with some legal provisions, interpreters have to do a great deal of work in order to give law real content. The meaning of a standard depends on what happens when it is applied. Of course the nature of the provision cannot be read off its text, and everything will depend on interpretive practices.[12]

In seeking to provide more directed guidance, these object-centric and binary-framed policy documents may not adequately allow for diverse interpretations of how listed heritage may be treated. Applying standards too much like rules pushes policy toward strategic decision-making that centers the first-order aim of saving the heritage place-as-object. In theory, standards should enable scenario-driven planning, which could envision a more robust spectrum of alternatives that consider potential second-order outcomes. Such alternatives might allow for more creative approaches to preserving the social-spatial dynamics of place-based heritage and recognizing more diverse publics and values in decision-making.[13]

By focusing on place-as-object and failing to internalize heritage as people contingent, the list in many ways inhibits the ability to build a civil society around heritage that can effectively engage with other social and environmental concerns. For example, other United Nations (UN) divisions, such as UN-HABITAT and the UN Environment Programme (UNEP), forge critical networks of government agencies, nongovernmental organizations, and not-for-profits and empower these actors as collaborators with shared missions. When UN meetings and conferences regarding housing or the environment occur, masses of network representatives participate as a result. Because the place-based heritage arm of UNESCO centers on the World Heritage Convention and its attendant list, its agency focuses primarily on the states parties to the convention and the properties on the list. The list is the nucleus and organizing precondition of civic engagement. The on the list–not on the list binary and gatekeeping extend from places to people; publics are included and excluded as a function of the list.

The list complicates efforts on the part of the heritage enterprise to engage with pressing social and environmental causes like climate displacement and affordable housing. Heritage places are the primary target of project support and philanthropic funding, as well as policy, thereby defining the remit of preservation agencies and third-sector organizations. The issues affecting people in place-based heritage contexts are points of potential intersection and areas of common ground between the preservation enterprise and those in allied fields of social justice, community development, sustainability planning, and other policy agendas. Lists and their inherent place-as-object definitions can inhibit more robust cooperation and alliance building with policy arenas more directly focused on public welfare.

Because of its first-order logic of saving places, the concept of the list also makes interrogation of the systemic aspects of the heritage enterprise, a key aspect of second-order preservation, especially challenging. It hinders the ability to understand the implications of policy in structural and distributive ways because government data and decision-making center on places, not on the broader social and environmental intentions and implications of preservation policy.

Listing is not simply an inventory, nor is it neutral; it is a decision to valorize and invest in some places more than others.[14] This inherently means investing in some publics more than others. Any place can have heritage value to some; government cannot recognize or protect all places of value. Valorizing through a list is dependent on centering and othering narratives, and those connected to them. Listing may thus advantage or disadvantage those associated with or inhabiting place-based heritage.

Because listing serves a gatekeeper function, social inequities related to it can be repeated through and reinforced by consequent policy tools. Being more cognizant of this power to privilege or disprivilege, and the way in which it has shaped policy to date, is critical to second-order preservation. Unraveling structural circumstances means interrogating the evolving public policy rationales that undergird listing and other tools and how their contradictions forged systemic conditions that continue to complicate preservation policy's benefits and burdens.

EXPLOITATION AND STEWARDSHIP

An object-oriented heritage lens means that buildings and sites cannot save themselves. Akin to how one might paternalistically characterize an innocent child or a person without means, this perspective evokes a protective response. Preservationists are caretakers, custodians, and keepers; preservation policy elevates this stewardship to an obligation of government.

Early forays into historic preservation in the United States were generally object-focused ventures led by civil society organizations and philanthropists, and at times, local and state legislatures laid a foundation for government stewardship. The rescue of Independence Hall, Mount Vernon, and many more historic edifices in the nineteenth century, by concerned citizens, set in motion the communication, if not the realization, of a shared desire to preserve heritage places.[15] This planted the preservation enterprise in the public consciousness and eventually helped to legitimize it as an activity within the sphere of democratic institutions. It likewise relied on a victimizing and valorizing discourse, as Charles Hosmer noted in his seminal account of early preservation in the United States: "once a group of people saw a notable building in danger, every argument imaginable supporting the idea of preservation came sharply into focus."[16]

As a fledgling republic established through settler colonialism and the dispossession of Native American peoples, what constituted *heritage* in the early decades of the U.S. government was not, however, historic buildings. Wilderness functioned as a unifying heritage ideal to a nation prospecting and parceling a vast frontier of land.[17] Distinct from the heritage of the "Old World," America's bountiful natural resources and landscapes catalyzed a unique perspective on patriotism and human inspiration, reinforced by mid-nineteenth-century paintings, treatises, and expeditions. Protecting these resources for the public benefit thus entered the bailiwick of government. This wilderness stewardship stood in stark contrast to the Homestead Act of 1862, which turned over millions of acres in the public domain to settlers willing to cultivate the plots. The federal government was at once incentivizing the large-scale consumption of land and pioneering large-scale protection.

Commercialization and local landowner claims at Niagara Falls, one of the great scenic destinations in the early nineteenth century, prompted government concerns over the exploitation of America's natural wonders and the need for stewardship. When the Yosemite Valley in California experienced similar land claims and tourism speculation in the 1850s, Congress withdrew the land from alienation, meaning it could not be disposed from the public domain and acquired by settlers. Congress then ceded Yosemite Valley and the Mariposa Grove of Giant Sequoias to the state of California for the creation of a public preserve in 1864.[18] A report to the governor of California by landscape architect Frederick Law Olmsted codified the preservation of Yosemite as both an obligation to and inspiration for the American public.[19] Beginning in 1890, Congress passed several acts to protect additional lands near Yosemite, and in 1906, the valley and Mariposa Grove reverted back to the federal government as part of a larger national park.

Driven in large part by the early state-level success of Yosemite, in

1872, Congress established the very first national park, Yellowstone, which occupies nearly thirty-five hundred square miles of land in what is now the U.S. states of Wyoming, Montana, and Idaho. Historian Mark David Spence provides a stark account of Yellowstone's origins and the intertwined histories of developing the national park system and forcing Native Americans from their ancestral lands. With the Yellowstone Act came increased management of Indigenous people's lives and their claims to the land. The creation of the national park disregarded previous treaties recognizing the rights of multiple Native American Tribal communities (including Crow, Shoshone, Bannock, and Tukudeka) to the Yellowstone lands. These Tribal communities used it for hunting, gathering food, and trading and relied on its natural resources; the Tukudeka lived in the higher elevations of Yellowstone. The mountains and geysers of Yellowstone likewise held spiritual value for these peoples.[20]

Tukudeka remained on the Yellowstone lands until 1879, at which time they and other Indigenous communities found their access to Yellowstone increasingly curtailed by park officials. Park administrators and wilderness advocates regarded Native Americans' use of Yellowstone—what had been their traditional lands—as a threat to the park and the protection of its natural resources. In 1886, the U.S. Army took over the management of the park to prevent access by Native Americans. The creation of the state of Wyoming in 1890 and the U.S. Supreme Court case *Ward v. Race Horse* of 1896, which came just weeks after *Plessy v. Ferguson,* rationalized the government's right to keep Native Americans off public lands, even if previous treaties had afforded them access. The court cited the creation of Yellowstone National Park in 1872 and the Lacey Act of 1894, which restricted hunting within the park, as clear demonstrations of the government's intentions for the preservation of the land and natural resources, which Native American use threatened.[21]

By 1890, managers at Yosemite likewise raised concerns about the continuing presence of the Yosemite Tribal community in the park. Unlike Yellowstone, they advanced a more gradual program of "Indian removal" through military administration, curtailed rights, forced relocation, and eviction that stretched over decades. Naturalists like John Muir advocated for the protection of wilderness heritage but saw no place for Native Americans in the landscape.

Wilderness was a sublime environment, restorative to humankind

FIGURE 7. This 1905 stereograph of the Great Falls in Yellowstone highlights the natural grandeur of the national park and illustrates early tourism, both of which were integral to preservation policies that displaced Native Americans. Courtesy of the Library of Congress.

and inspirational to the American project. It was also, as Spence notes, the "depraved conditions from which savages needed uplifting."[22] Removal was rationalized as an act of benevolence, to civilize Indigenous peoples and to preserve the landscape as heritage object. In casting the wilderness as victim, the preservation narratives of both Yellowstone and Yosemite center and valorize the innovative stewardship role that government forged in creating national parks for the benefit of the people, or certain people. A century later, after the UNESCO World Heritage Convention was established in 1972, Yellowstone was among the first sites listed, and Yosemite followed in 1984.

FIGURE 8. This 1866 Currier & Ives lithograph depicts Native Americans camping in the Yosemite Valley, with Bridalveil Fall in the background. Published just two years after the creation of the California public preserve, it suggests that the early romanticism of Yosemite was integrally linked to its Native American inhabitants, even though the government ultimately sought their removal from the national park. By Fanny Palmer for Currier & Ives. Courtesy of the Library of Congress.

The cruel oppression and disenfranchisement of Indigenous peoples is not simply a dark era of history; it is a foundation on which preservation policy builds. The segregation of place and publics, the effective dehumanizing of the heritage object, repeats and reverberates. Ongoing debates over the use of national parks and federal lands, from grazing to rock climbing, underscore how "public benefit" can exacerbate privilege and exclusion in the complicated social-spatial relationships involved with claiming place as heritage. As evidenced by the myriad threats to cultural heritage cataloged by UNESCO, humans victimize heritage. But they are likewise victims of the policy structures that seek to preserve it.

Displacement and dispossession, in many cases, are not simply a consequence of preservation; they are tools that continue to be wielded in the name of heritage. As early as the 1960s, preservationists noted the deleterious effects of nearby human settlements on the churches of Lalibela, Ethiopia, a complex of rock-hewn religious structures that are approximately eight hundred years old. Lalibela was among the first properties designated as UNESCO World Heritage in 1978, prompting national and international efforts to preserve the site and to promote its tourism potential. By 2000, the World Bank was involved, sponsoring a tourism development plan that included the resettlement of those living in traditional and self-built housing around the perimeter of the site. The World Bank and Ethiopian officials viewed relocation as a means of protecting the heritage values of the churches-as-object; they did not fully consider the social-spatial dimensions of this sacred place or how displacement might rupture the social fabric of the community. The resettlement project relocated nearly three thousand residents, pushing them far away from the churches and market, which were places of daily spiritual, economic, and social interactions.[23] A 2018 UNESCO mission report noted, "The resettlement programme has taken place, but it has left a denuded and abandoned open space around the churches as well as a displaced community around Lalibela."[24]

A UNESCO-supported project at New Gourna, in Egypt, similarly

FIGURE 9. The resettlement program at the Rock-Hewn Churches of Lalibela, Ethiopia, involved the relocation of more than three thousand residents who lived in the immediate environs of the churches and frequented them regularly, to advance conservation of and tourism at the site. Their predominantly self-built homes were demolished, with the exception of a selection of *gojos,* a vernacular form of residential construction. These *gojos* were considered important elements in the integrity of the landscape and were noted in the site's inclusion on the UNESCO World Heritage list. Many of the *gojos* now sit largely vacant. Photograph by the author.

considered displacement of residents as a potential tool in restoring the village, which was designed and constructed by renowned architect Hassan Fathy in the 1940s. The Egyptian government contracted Fathy for a project intended to relocate the residents of Gourna, a village close to the pharaonic tombs in Luxor, an increasingly popular tourist destination. Fathy championed the participation of residents in the design and construction process, which employed traditional earthen materials and forms. But many residents resisted the relocation, and the success of the project is heavily debated.[25] Nonetheless, the village evolved over time into a thriving and close-knit community.

Decades of village occupation resulted in changes to the earthen buildings of New Gourna; families modified homes and, in a number of instances, replaced houses with concrete structures, owing to a combination of social, economic, and environmental factors. In response, the international community, valorizing Fathy's original design and earthen materials, joined forces to promote conservation of the village. New Gourna falls within the boundaries of the UNESCO World Heritage site of Ancient Thebes, with its Necropolis, inscribed in 1979. The inscription did not identify New Gourna as a contributing heritage element at the time, but its geographic inclusion within the World Heritage site afforded agency to international actors. Owing to the touristic value of New Gourna, Egyptian authorities began incentivizing relocation to residents, and a preliminary 2011 UNESCO proposal included the possible resettlement of 120 households from the core conservation area.[26] UNESCO efforts subsequently shifted away from displacement as a conservation strategy, in part because of community-engaged research by World Monuments Fund, and the restoration of public buildings has been the focus of UNESCO work completed since 2017.[27]

The valorization of heritage at national or international levels, and the responsibilities to larger collectives that it entails, influences the agency of local populations. Claims to place multiply and diversify, and geographic proximity may no longer be a primary determinant of the publics who have a stake in a heritage place. Preservation of the object takes increasing precedence because of these multiplying interests. As power dynamics become more complex, the object serves as a common denominator, a first-order priority upon which all interests depend. The social-spatial relationships characterizing heritage may be discounted,

FIGURE 10. Social, economic, and environmental conditions have led residents of New Gourna Village, Luxor, Egypt, to significantly alter the original earthen architecture buildings, designed by Hassan Fathy. Part of the UNESCO World Heritage site of Ancient Thebes, local and international actors raised concerns about the loss of historic significance and material integrity in the village, and the national government saw opportunities to advance tourism development and relocate residents in the name of heritage conservation. Photograph by the author.

thereby making local populations more vulnerable and more easily exploited in the interest of international or national stewardship.[28]

PROGRESS AND GREED

Indigenous peoples were not the only threats to U.S. wilderness heritage in the late nineteenth century. The richness of resources in the American West was a draw for industrialists and speculators. Railroads, in particular, posed a double-edged sword. Connecting the vast territories, dispersed resources, and scattered inhabitants of the United States was important to national and social progress. Even the parks themselves were dependent on development to enable visitors to experience them.

Backlash against the Industrial Revolution and exploitative robber barons fueled public support for exercising government legislative power over the nation's natural resources. Concern over the depletion of resources, raised by conservationists like George Perkins Marsh, likewise drew attention to the role of the state in managing the country's natural assets for future generations.[29] This philosophy undergirded the 1891 Forest Reserve Act as well as the creation of the U.S. Forest Service in 1905 and the National Park Service (NPS) in 1916. President Theodore Roosevelt championed this vision, chastising the "short-sighted men who in their greed and selfishness will, if permitted, rob our country of half its charm by their reckless extermination of all useful and beautiful wild things" and claiming:

> Our duty to the whole, including the unborn generations, bids us restrain an unprincipled present-day minority from wasting the heritage of these unborn generations. The movement for the conservation of wild life and the larger movement for the conservation of all our natural resources are essentially democratic in spirit, purpose, and method.[30]

It was under Roosevelt's administration that Congress passed the Act for the Preservation of American Antiquities in 1906, which broadly extended the federal government's concern toward the economic exploitation of cultural resources as well. Until this point, individual sites were the object of the federal government's actions. For example, in 1889, Congress allocated funds to conserve the Native American ruins of Casa Grande in what is now the state of Arizona, and in 1892, President Benjamin Harrison signed an executive order establishing the 480-acre Casa Grande Reservation, making it the first federal cultural and archaeological preserve.[31] The Antiquities Act afforded broad powers to the executive branch to protect cultural and natural resources, driven largely by concerns about indiscriminate archaeological excavations on public lands and the commercialization of ancient Native American artifacts. That the exploitation of Native American objects was cause for government protection while the exploitation of Native American peoples was regularly endorsed and instrumentalized by that same government suggests yet another contradiction in the victimizing and valorizing intentions of early preservation policy.[32]

The economic utilization of heritage was cast as an act of greed on the part of morally corrupt individuals and businesses. In parallel, the symbiotic relationship between tourism and heritage was acknowledged and valorized, as *encounter* with heritage was largely understood to be the means through which the public could most directly benefit. However, the inherent economic dimensions of heritage tourism were largely absent from early policy doctrines. This changed dramatically in the second half of the twentieth century, when the economic benefits of preservation served to rationalize evolving government action in the Americas.

In the wake of conflicts in the Americas over land and borders, such as the Mexican–American War (1840s) and the War of the Pacific (1879–84), the United States held the first International Conference of American States in 1890 to fundamentally promote peace and prosperity. This led to the creation of a regional coalition for multilateral cooperation within the Americas, the Pan American Union, now known as the Organization of American States (OAS). It was through this platform that the Roerich Pact, protecting cultural heritage in times of war, was signed by twenty-one nation-states in the Americas (though it was ultimately ratified by only ten).

After the establishment of UNESCO post–World War II and the development of the Venice Charter in 1964, the OAS took on heritage conservation as a multilateral concern in the context of Latin America, convening a group of experts from the region in 1967 in Quito, Ecuador. This meeting was just a few months after a major OAS summit of heads of states in the region, which focused on the industrialization and economic development of Latin America. The Quito meeting produced a region-specific adaptation of the Venice Charter, referred to as the Norms of Quito. Whereas the Venice Charter focused on the treatment of the heritage object, the Norms of Quito asserted, "Cultural heritage resources are an economic asset and can be made into instruments of progress." The norms explicitly sought to promote the reconciliation of urban growth and industrialization with the protection of environmental and historic values and to recognize the economic and specifically touristic value of heritage.[33]

The notion that heritage conservation has a decidedly economic value also emerged in U.S. policy in the mid-twentieth century and intertwined with questions of urbanization—specifically urban renewal and federal highway construction—as a cause of heritage destruction and reuse of heritage as a means of urban regeneration. The Housing Act of 1949 was a major legislative foundation for federally supported urban renewal in cities across the country; the 1949 law and other legislation helped to create what Francesca Russello Ammon refers to as a "culture of clearance" to address urban decay and renewal.[34] Amendments, through the Housing Act of 1954, introduced rehabilitation as a feasible approach to renewal, thus forging common ground between preservation and urban renewal, though often in problematic ways.[35] It underscored, through federal policy, the mutually beneficial relationship between the reuse of older, existing building stock and economic revitalization.

The synergetic relationship of preservation and economic development echoed throughout municipal preservation legislation enacted in the second half of the twentieth century. The 1965 New York City Landmarks Law, as part of its public policy rationale, called out the role of heritage in tourism, property value stabilization, and the overall economic vitality of the city.[36] A review of municipal ordinances across the United States reveals that more than half include the justification to strengthen the economy and/or stimulate economic growth, and an equal percentage notes the stabilization and improvement of property values.[37]

The 1970s oil crisis, which underscored energy as a national security and economic issue, further forged codependencies between preservation and economics through revitalization and rehabilitation policies. Research on the energy needed to produce new construction materials quantified the embodied energy required for a replacement building; this valorized the reuse of older buildings by demonstrating the energy, and thus money, that could be saved. This energy research also supported the revitalization of existing city centers and neighborhoods, as a means to conserve energy at an urban scale. The Housing and Community Development Act of 1974 built on this economic rationale of reinvesting in existing urban areas to conserve resources, renew communities, and curb "the growth and persistence of urban slums and blight." Reinvestment in older neighborhoods fundamentally cast displacement as a positive objective, not merely a consequence, of revitalization efforts, as codified in the 1974 law:

> an increase in the diversity and vitality of neighborhoods through the spatial deconcentration of housing opportunities for persons of lower income and the revitalization of deteriorating or deteriorated neighborhoods to attract persons of higher income; and . . .

the restoration and preservation of properties of special value for historic, architectural, or esthetic reasons.[38]

The Tax Reform Act of 1976 further supported revitalization through rehabilitation by eliminating financial inducements to construct new buildings and demolish old ones. The new law provided for amortization and accelerated depreciation options to incentivize building rehabilitation and allowed taxpayers to amortize over five years the costs associated with rehabilitating a property on the National Register of Historic Places.[39] In 1980, Congress amended the NHPA to include the *energy* and *economic* benefits within its public policy rationale, codifying intentions of the heritage enterprise well beyond inspiration and stewardship.

Acknowledging and asserting the economic value of heritage as a driving force for government action triggered a host of new policy tools at national, state, and local levels in the United States, such as state- and local-level tax incentives and abatements, the transfer of development rights, easements, tax increment financing, and public–private partnerships.[40] This complicated and continues to complicate policy intentions around the issues of economics and the commodification of heritage. The policy of listing or designation essentially seeks to protect heritage places, whether publicly or privately owned, from the financial pressures of market forces because of their perceived public benefit. Government-sponsored, market-driven incentives essentially provide taxpayer resources, or reduce taxpayer coffers, in service to private property and owners, with the expectation that the public expenditure will result in a return on investment through preservation.

Touting preservation as a means of regeneration and a competitive advantage in market-driven contexts has implications. Sharon Zukin asserts that neoliberal economies contribute to the commodification of heritage, which is part of a symbolic economy with two parallel production systems: "the *production of space,* with its synergy of capital investment and cultural meanings, and the *production of symbols,* which constructs both a currency of commercial exchange and a language of social identity."[41] In highly competitive real estate markets, preservation can become an increasingly fraught form of public policy as it seeks to intervene in these spatial and symbolic economies. This is in large part due to the engrained paradigm of listing more and more heritage places, which are in turn privileged by government and play by a different set of land use rules.

Consumerism, especially tourism, further complicates this dialectical tension. Harking back to the early problems of wilderness tourism, public policy rationalizes preservation as having positive benefits for people, but people are at the same time perceived as threats:

> "The dark side, of course, is consumption," said Francesco Bandarin, assistant director-general of Unesco and head of its World Heritage Center, speaking of the consumerism that so often surrounds heritage sites. "And consumption and preservation do not go together." If a site is "within an hour of a harbor," he added, "it becomes inundated by a flood of tourism and geysers of money."[42]

Economics, for better or for worse, is one of the primary ways in which the heritage object and people are most directly linked. With money serving as a common denominator and policy language, there are by far more economic studies regarding heritage policy than environmental or social. Across urban and rural environments, and across time, as Young noted, the self-determination marginalized peoples seek more often than not concerns "access to land and resources in order to enhance their economic well-being," which inherently involves heritage places.[43] Who can access these economic incentives and how various publics financially benefit from or are burdened by preservation policy remain largely underresearched.

NATURE AND CULTURE

The concept of a truly *natural* landscape is questionable. One might argue that there are no natural landscapes; the direct and indirect effects of human activities influence every corner of the globe through climate change. In addition, the anthropocentric notion that humanity, as culture, is somehow distinct from nature is likewise debatable.[44] Nevertheless, the preservation enterprise has both distanced and associated nature and culture in policy, in increasingly problematic ways.

Addressing nature and culture through common policy approaches emerged in the United States through the Antiquities Act of 1906 and was codified through the establishment of the NPS in 1916. Whereas wilderness-as-heritage drove the development of early parks, in the

1920s and 1930s, administrators at the NPS advanced a robust program of developing historical parks, reinforced by the Historic Sites Act of 1935.[45] A series of NPS reports in the late 1950s and early 1960s on the state of national parks provoked a major overhaul of management approaches and valorized ecosystem preservation.[46] That, coupled with growing environmental awareness in the 1960s and 1970s, underpinned a host of environmental laws at the federal level protecting, among other things, air, water, and wilderness. Among these, the 1970 National Environmental Policy Act forged a critical link between nature and culture by requiring procedural review of any federal actions significantly affecting the quality of the human environment. This includes review of impacts on cultural resources, those locally recognized as well as properties listed on or eligible for the National Register of Historic Places, which came to fruition through the 1966 NHPA. The 1990s saw the amplification of environmental justice and concerns over the disparate pollution and environmental burdens borne by communities of color, leading to the integration of environmental justice in federal decision-making through Executive Order 12898.

This emphasis on environmental policy created both opportunities and challenges for preservation policy. Energy policy specifically helped open the door to new rationales for preservation policy and new tools but did not significantly alter object-focused approaches. Concerns about ceding ground (think soccer field and competing interests for the same policy space) may have also inhibited more robust investment in policy reform, as noted preservationist Robert E. Stipe expressed in his 2003 compendium *A Richer Heritage*:

> The preservation community needs to recognize that direct, active involvement with issues related to environmental protection, growth management, and land-use planning, though achieving societal ends, also has the potential to seriously jeopardize the identity and effectiveness of the historic preservation movement itself. . . .
> . . . There is nothing wrong with joining the many planner-environmentalists opposed to sprawl, big-box retailing, or promoting environmental sustainability. Some of the outcomes advanced by this recent movement will be socially, economically, and aesthetically beneficent for preservation. However, the more closely identified we become with these and related trends, the

closer [preservationists] come to losing our identity as the keepers of cultural tradition.[47]

In the United States, the making and remaking of policy is more engrained in the institutions and structural processes dealing with nature and the environment. Civil society, researchers, practitioners, and government actors moved beyond nature as an object to be preserved and site-by-site approaches. Without abandoning protected places as a legitimate dimension of policy, environmentalists actively sought to probe the systemic issues affecting the human environment. New knowledge is valorized as feedback to refine environmental policy intentions, processes, and outcomes. Research into the systemic effects of air and water pollution buttressed new legislative action on the environmental front. The introduction of energy performance codes and now greenhouse gas laws is the result of evolving knowledge around the role of buildings in energy consumption and carbon-based emissions. Even U.S. federal laws like the Clean Air Act involve periodic cost–benefit analyses to evaluate the burdens and benefits of the legislation to the public.

This stands in stark contrast to the cultural heritage policy regime. The Secretary of the Interior's Standards and other information policy tools are periodically updated and expanded, for example, to provide sustainability and flood guidance. Congress has also amended the tax credit law a few times, most recently to eliminate the 10 percent credit. In total, and compared to the environmental field, the legislative infrastructure and policy tools of the preservation enterprise, especially at the federal level, have seen comparatively limited change.

At the international level, environmental and cultural interests likewise intersect through early policy developments and continue to seek common ground, despite nature–culture divides. The International Union for the Conservation of Nature (IUCN) was founded in 1948 as the first international body devoted to environmental conservation. It forged efforts with the UN to advance a list of protected international parks in 1958, and a preliminary list was presented in 1962 at the First World Congress on National Parks. The same year, UNESCO issued its "Recommendation Concerning the Safeguarding of Beauty and Character of Landscapes and Sites," which urged members to develop national policies for protecting natural and cultural heritage places. Three years later, upon the twentieth anniversary of the UN, the White House convened a conference on international cooperation in which it introduced the concept of a Trust for the World Heritage, echoing the UNESCO merger of cultural and natural heritage concerns. By 1970, IUCN and UNESCO were working in concert and solidified the concept of World Heritage at the UN Conference on the Environment in Stockholm in 1972. UNESCO took on the development of the convention and published the first list of cultural and natural sites in 1978.

In addition to catalyzing World Heritage, the 1972 Stockholm conference was a watershed moment for environmental policy, forging pathways beyond the protection of discrete natural preserves. There was growing awareness of the toll humankind was taking on natural resources through urbanization and development. It is important to note that at this time, the concept of development (itself disparate and debatable) was largely based on a premise of economic growth: that increasing productivity and thus income was a fundamental vehicle through which to achieve improved quality of life. The economic boom of the post–World War II era created a postmaterial society (in the Global North) that could afford to acknowledge and prioritize the impact industry and growth have on land, resources, water, and air—and thus on the human condition.[48]

In 1983, the UN established the World Commission on Environment and Development, known as the Bruntland Commission, to examine this intersection of environment and development. The commission's seminal 1987 text, *Our Common Future,* merged these arenas under the term *sustainable development,* defined as "development that meets the needs of the present without compromising the ability of future generations to meet their own needs."[49] The next year, amid growing concerns and mounting evidence of climate change due to greenhouse gas emissions, and its potentially catastrophic effects, the UN established the Intergovernmental Panel on Climate Change (IPCC).

In 1992, the UN Conference on the Environment and Development—more familiarly known as the Rio Earth Summit—took place in Rio de Janeiro, Brazil. The result was a dense action plan, entitled Agenda 21, that outlined goals and strategies for sustainable development that integrated environmental, economic, and social concerns at the international, national, and local levels. An important element of the plan was acknowledgment of the disparity between lesser and more industrialized countries (or the North–South divide) and the need for global cooperation to effectively address equitable progress and responsible management of resources.

This linking of human and natural systems, and its justice implications, also helped to mark shifts in thinking from an environmental paradigm that was anthropocentrically focused to an ecological paradigm that placed humankind within a more complex system of biodynamics. The priority was no longer protecting natural and cultural sites, as objects, with defined borders. It established the environment as part of the "global commons," transcending geopolitical boundaries.[50] In effect, Agenda 21 proffered that "think globally, act locally" was not enough: the nations of the world needed also to "act globally." Growing scientific research was demonstrating that local activities like emissions and deforestation had profound global effects. Multilateral cooperation was imperative.

To effectively address sustainability issues and translate Agenda 21 principles to the building and construction sector, the International Council for Research and Innovation in Building and Construction initiated the development of *Agenda 21 on Sustainable Construction.* Published in 1999, it provided a framework for conceptualizing the link between sustainability and the built environment so as to utilize natural resources efficiently, minimize waste and energy consumption, manage land use effectively, and improve quality of life—in ways that are both globally and locally responsive. But a more sustainable built environment cannot be achieved through solely technical means, as *Agenda 21 on Sustainable Construction* indicates:

> A decade ago, the emphasis was placed on the more technical issues in construction . . . and on energy related design concepts. Today, an appreciation of the non-technical issues is growing and these so-called "soft" issues are at least as crucial for a sustainable development in construction. Economic and social sustainability must be accorded explicit treatment in any definition. More recently also the cultural issues and the cultural heritage implications of the built environment have come to be regarded as pre-eminent aspects in sustainable construction.[51]

The built environment is not, physically, the same the world over, nor are its inhabitants. *Agenda 21 on Sustainable Construction* was strongly dominated by thinking about what could or should be accomplished in industrialized countries, as the most egregious greenhouse gas emitters. Though lesser industrialized countries face some similar challenges, challenges vary or may be more intense (such as housing security, a lack of infrastructure, rapid urbanization, and limited institutional capacity). This resulted in the subsequent *Agenda 21 for Sustainable Construction in Developing Countries* in 2002.[52]

These Agenda 21 efforts, as well as prior and subsequent UN-supported policy milestones (such as the current sustainable development goals, or SDGs, which reframe the objectives of Agenda 21 as the basis for sustainable development), continue to create opportunities to reimagine heritage policy, to think beyond site-by-site, put-it-on-the-list approaches and beyond nature–culture divides. Efforts by UNESCO, ICOMOS, and the IPCC are afoot to engage and align heritage policy in the context of the climate crisis, though they are in large part reflective of a "heritage as victim of climate change" positionality. Due consideration is afforded vulnerable publics, especially Indigenous communities, at the front lines of sea level rise, and the inextricable link between people and place forges new ground beyond the traditional object-centric focus of preservation policy. Climate justice rightly serves as an explicit aim of policy action. However, how place-based heritage policies structurally influence climate change and the publics impacted by it, and the injustices that may produce, is an avenue of policy inquiry that warrants further interrogation.[53]

COHESION AND PLURALISM

The establishment of Yellowstone and the expansion and elevation to national status of Yosemite in the late nineteenth century marked more than a valorization of nature and wilderness heritage. During the post–Civil War period of Reconstruction, in the words of Peri Arnold, "it was an impulse to locate in the state of nature, and protect, a source of energy for the American republican project."[54] Parallel to these government actions was the establishment of military parks marking critical Civil War battlefields and honoring the dead. The year 1890 saw the establishment of the Chickamauga and Chattanooga National Military Park, followed by Shiloh (1894) and Gettysburg (1895). Establishing the Gettysburg park involved a legal battle over lands owned by the Gettysburg Electric Railway Company that the federal government sought to acquire through eminent domain. The case set legal precedent for government stewardship of heritage for public benefit, stating in its judgment:

> Upon the question whether the proposed use of this land is [a] public one, we think there can be no well-founded doubt. . . . The battle of Gettysburg was one of the great battles of the world. . . . The importance of the issue involved in the contest of which this great battle was a part cannot be overestimated. The existence of the government itself, and the perpetuity of our institutions, depended upon the result. . . . Can it be that the government is without power to preserve the land, and properly mark out the various sites upon which this struggle took place? Can it not erect the monuments provided for by these acts of congress, or even take possession of the field of battle, in the name and for the benefit of all the citizens of the country, for the present and for the future? Such a use seems necessarily not only a public use, but one so closely connected with the welfare of the republic itself as to be within the powers granted congress by the constitution for the purpose of protecting and preserving the whole country.[55]

The government, and the court, regarded the protection of these battlefields as a conduit for valorizing the ideals of a unified nation and the struggles it endured to achieve that unity. Part of the nation-building project was a civic education that roused sentiments of patriotism and a shared past and future. Places became an important trope for centering and conveying these narratives. Stemming from the notion, as legal scholar Carol M. Rose characterized, that "visual surroundings work a political effect on our consciousness,"[56] buildings and sites with historical associations could inspire the observer with a sense of nationalism and instill the duty of stewardship, much like natural sites.

Underpinning these principles is the role of government in promoting social cohesion through not simply public ownership but a *collective* claim to place-based heritage. Public policy frames a common responsibility for ensuring the intergenerational transfer of these heritage places and their associated narratives, a responsibility shared by all publics and realized through government action. The people are at once the stewards and the benefactors; government is merely a conduit.

The driving concerns of the Antiquities Act of 1906, namely, the exploitation of Native American sites and artifacts, underscored this idyllic notion of communal responsibility. That a government so vested in policies of violence, dispossession, and radical cultural assimilation regarding Native Americans would concomitantly valorize Native American heritage seems like a profound contradiction. But it speaks to the colonizing power of claiming place as heritage. Requiring excavation permits and restricting the trade of artifacts established government as the proxy for decision-making and management; it acts in the interests of the collective good. By promoting this shared responsibility, government effectively removed decision-making power from Native American communities about the treatment of their heritage and thus fractured their ability to self-determine how to transfer that heritage across generations, or not.[57] Subsequent legislation sought to redress these injustices, such as the Native American Graves Protection and Repatriation Act of 1990, and the Antiquities Act has since helped to protect many acres of land significant to America's Indigenous peoples.[58] However, the underlying principles of collective action and responsibility are embedded in the foundations of preservation policy in problematic ways. And by centering heritage-as-object, valorized by a collective claim, policy can obfuscate how vested publics may be marginalized through decision-making.

The UNESCO World Heritage Convention contends that "cultural and natural property demonstrate the importance, for all the peoples of the world, of safeguarding this unique and irreplaceable property, to whatever people it may belong."[59] As a multilateral agreement, the convention duly respects national sovereignty, and nation-states maintain authority over the ownership and management of sites within their respective territories. But it nonetheless echoes long-standing heritage debates, rooted in property rights, regarding cultural nationalism versus internationalism.[60] The notions of "world" heritage and outstanding universal value suggest not only a shared claim but a shared geography, challenging notions of proximity and how local and distant publics equitably participate in and share the burdens and benefits of World Heritage and its attendant polices.[61] Claims to place-based heritage are not necessarily singular, further complicating shared constructs. Multiple groups, cultures, religions, or societies may have previously occupied or constructed a place, or may presently value it, making such claims cumulative and complex.

The shared rules of the game, the standardized principles that guide what sites should be listed and how a site should or should not be preserved, may not equally respect the very diverse values and vested interests of the multiple publics associated with those heritage places. Criteria and guidelines themselves can be exclusionary and colonizing in that they may inherently valorize some knowledges and ways of knowing and the publics associated with them. The largely European influence over the Venice Charter and World Heritage raises troubling questions about international preservation policy that are equally applicable to the United States. The post–World War II multilateral landscape promoted through World Heritage affords new political spaces for nation-states, old and new, in a postcolonial era.[62] But how respective states parties influence and exercise the rules of the game may not always be equitable.[63] Designation is a means of privileging certain places over others. If Whiteness underpins the systems of valorizing heritage places, in what ways do the recursive structures of policy continue to privilege Whiteness in place-based heritage and the built environment writ large?

At the local level in the United States, these recursive tools, like designation and regulatory design review of changes to heritage places, may valorize certain ways of knowing and thus certain publics. Freer from the issues of sovereignty characterizing the international arena, local governments apply policy tools across publicly and privately owned properties by operationalizing self-determination as a collective, community-based act. Much of U.S. preservation law is undergirded by the 1954 *Berman v. Parker* case, in which the Supreme Court rationalized a community's collective right to regulate private property on the basis of community aesthetics and appearance. Ironically, the case established the right to demolish a building that was blighting a neighborhood and helped rationalize urban renewal projects as well as preservation.

In this sense, the right to preserve and the right to destroy are co-constitutive; there is a co-logic.[64] The role of government is not simply to promote social cohesion through preservation policy but to protect the right for publics, as discrete collectives, to self-determine their preservation desires. As legal scholar Carol M. Rose contends, "a major public purpose underlying modern preservation law is the fostering of community cohesion, and ultimately, the encouragement of pluralism. . . . The most important substantive contribution of preservation law has been recognition of the political aspect of our physical surroundings . . . and the consideration of which kinds of physical environment are appropriate to a nation of democratic communities."[65]

Contemporary discourse is pressing on the question of pluralism, examining the ways in which claims to place as heritage constitute a human right.[66] Much of this emerges from concerns over how political actors use the performative destruction and seizure of cultural heritage to oppress vulnerable populations. Applying a lens of human rights puts the protection of places on par with the protection of people and highlights how territorial sovereignty limits international action to support the rights of local publics in cases of noninternational conflict and injustice.[67]

The aforementioned Faro Convention recognizes "that every person has a right to engage with the cultural heritage of their choice, while respecting the rights and freedoms of others, as an aspect of the right freely to participate in cultural life." It likewise underscores "the need to involve everyone in society in the ongoing process of defining and managing cultural heritage."[68] The tensions of collective duty and individual right complicate how government can hold these interlinked yet at times contradictory concepts in view and create policies that ensure just processes and just outcomes.

The debates over Confederate monuments in the United States serve as an illustrative point. Many argue for the right to display these statues as part of their Southern heritage; others argue that they symbolize a racist ideology that fractured the country and constitute a form of continuing oppression. Where the heritage rights of some infringe upon the rights and freedoms of others is a fraught milieu, made even more fraught when claims to place—to land and public space—are at the core. Removing a problematic statue from a park may reclaim a more equitable space. Does that extend to plantations and townhomes where generations of Black people were enslaved? Or to the many public and private buildings across the country constructed with slave labor? These have more problematic conditions of occupation and ownership, complicating collective claims to both space and narrative.

3

Social Consequences

An interviewer recently asked me if I expect preservation organizations to become social justice organizations.[1] I argue that they inherently are, whether or not they embrace the role. At its core, preservation policy is about protecting people's freedom to collectively transfer heritage across generations. Doing so in *place*—where space may be occupied, owned, and layered with histories—is a complex process of evaluating those freedoms against others. A government-endorsed claim to heritage creates privileges and burdens. These may include expenditures of taxpayer money, access to grants, additional layers of or exemptions from regulation, or changes to property rights; even lists that simply recognize heritage without providing physical protection require resources for reviewing and maintaining information. Whenever policy actions may be privileging or burdening some publics over others, questions of justice are manifest.

With a never-ending mandate to keep saving places, and accumulative lists of heritage places, the preservation enterprise is perpetually growing. Organizations, especially government agencies, often face these ballooning responsibilities with limited funds and staff. A lack of resources may curtail efforts to address social justice and climate robustly. However, concerns over "mission creep" and claims of limited mandates likewise predominate. By focusing on the first-order logic of saving the object, the preservation enterprise seeks to direct its resources toward concerns clearly within its purview, but in doing so, it defines a scope that effectively skirts social consequences as a nucleus of its work. Of the dozens of charters and declarations issued by heritage institutions like ICOMOS and UNESCO, very few substantially focus on or even mention people, how to cooperate with communities, and how preservation may impact various publics. Although both scholarship and evolving modes of practice are increasingly recognizing the social dimensions of the preservation enterprise, most standards and professional ethics center on how to treat the heritage object, defined in chiefly material terms.[2] How to be accountable for and to people in the preservation enterprise remains a largely impromptu dimension of policy and practice.

Second-order preservation compels an interrogation of the social consequences of heritage policy as a primary intention. Putting people on par with the object and internalizing the social-spatial dimensions of heritage require considered reflection about not only the historical motivations that underpin policy (as discussed in chapter 2) but also the ongoing conditions of decision-making that may reinforce or challenge the marginalization of people, or some publics, in the preservation enterprise.

Borrowing from and adapting legal definitions of justice, I explore these consequences through four lenses: representational justice, procedural justice, distributive justice, and restorative justice. Each brings a distinct perspective to the preservation enterprise, but they intersect significantly and are not mutually exclusive. This orientation compels a centering of people to understand how the heritage enterprise is representing diverse stories and voices, promoting fair processes of decision-making, ensuring equity in outcomes, and redressing past wrongs.

REPRESENTATIONAL JUSTICE

Because preservation focuses on the past and the places-as-objects that symbolize it, representational justice is not simply a matter of who currently has access to or is part of the heritage enterprise. It involves issues of space and time. Who heritage represents engenders questions of how the stories of different publics can or cannot be encountered in geographies and through the built environment. As an interrogation of public policy, it incurs questions of how claims to place as heritage may contribute to or counter disparities in who is represented through the listing or designation of heritage places, which valorizes certain histories. It further raises questions of who presided over and participated in the foundational formation of policy and how their identities and positionalities may bias recurrent decision-making.

The built environment is an uneven groundwork of representation. There are long histories of spatially marginalizing populations—especially Black and Brown people, Indigenous peoples, the foreign born, the poor, and women—thereby limiting their power to claim land and material property. Such legacies of racism, subjugation, and exclusion are entrenched within the built environment and landscapes, through omission and design. This is complicated by the way in which place can itself conceal, rather than reveal, history, burying layers of memory and use over time.[3] The following provide a brief—and incomplete—illustration of how publics may be unevenly represented in the built environment and landscapes encountered today:

The built environment reflects who had and has the right to freedom. Millions of enslaved Africans were forcibly transported to the Americas and deprived of the right to self-determination through centuries of subjugation and violence. Their ability to construct place-based heritage or to transfer heritage practices across generations was fundamentally undermined.

The built environment reflects who had and has the right to occupy land and how. The forced relocation of Indigenous peoples is an atrocity committed across time and across the globe. For example, as a consequence of the 1830 Indian Removal Act, more than sixty thousand Native Americans were forcibly relocated from their ancestral homelands in the southeastern United States to areas west, as part of what is familiarly referred to as the Trail of Tears. Beyond land dispossession, the Dawes Act of 1887 authorized the U.S. government to break up commonly held tribal lands into allotments, fundamentally fracturing how communities used and occupied lands.

The built environment reflects who had and has the right own property. Even after emancipation, Black Americans faced significant challenges to purchasing and maintaining ownership of land and property owing to legal restrictions, discrimination, and racial terror. In the United States, married women were not allowed to own property until 1848, and unmarried women gained that right only with the 1862 Homestead Act.

The built environment reflects who could and can live in certain places. Cities were shaped and defined by who had a right to live in certain neighborhoods. Many municipalities in the United States enforced racial and other forms of restrictive covenants, controlling where people who were Black, Jewish, or Asian could rent or own a home. These restrictions were reinforced through Federal Housing Administration manuals.

These populations were often relegated to areas with environmental vulnerabilities, such as flood risks or nearby polluting industries. And even after courts ruled on the illegality of such restrictive covenants, practices persisted through social enforcement.

The built environment reflects who had and has access to capital. The government-sponsored Home Owners' Loan Corp, in collaboration with the banking industry, produced maps in the 1930s for most major municipalities in the United States indicating risk ratings for mortgage lending in various neighborhoods. These became known as redlining maps, as the areas in red—for highest risk—often demarcated communities of color, immigrants, and the poor, thereby undercutting their access to capital and their ability to build wealth through property ownership and maintenance.

The built environment reflects who had and has political power. The mid-twentieth century in the United States saw major federal programs that contributed to significant changes in the urban landscapes of its cities through the construction of highways and urban renewal. These developments often had the most severe impacts on impoverished communities and communities of color.[4]

Black and Brown communities, enslaved and Indigenous peoples, non-Christians, immigrants, the economically disadvantaged, people with disabilities, women, and those identifying as LGBTQ+ could not historically occupy space freely or equally. Spaces representing their narratives have been underinvested in and undervalued and were often made invisible or systematically destroyed. They are at a profound disadvantage when it comes to claiming *place* as heritage.

Places are not words in a book or images on a screen. Spatial encounters in the built environment bear repeated witness to particular ideas of self and community that are profoundly experiential. Like Churchill's observation of the House of Commons, these formal conditions shape social-spatial dynamics. Names on buildings and streets (toponymy), statues and monuments in public spaces, and architectural forms all mediate social-spatial dynamics and contribute to representations that, in the context of the United States, often skew toward those who are White, male, wealthy, and powerful. When the stories of some are disproportionately represented in place, it defines and conditions those experiences and relationships by centering particular narratives and publics, creating potential exclusion.

The preservation enterprise is, at times, complicit in perpetuating and exacerbating this unevenness of representation in the built environment. Early projects influenced public views and thus framed foundational perspectives on preservation policy. Cameron Logan's work on preservation in Washington, D.C., and Dennis Gale's work on gentrification and urban renewal independently draw on the case of Georgetown to illustrate the complicated ways in which the preservation enterprise historically engaged with broader land use issues and real estate speculation. In the 1920s, residents of means stoked interest in the "rebirth" of historic Georgetown, which by the early twentieth century was in decline. They successfully petitioned to amend zoning in the neighborhood, limiting building heights to forty feet, thereby preventing the area from becoming vulnerable to larger-scale development. The marketing and desire for historic properties brought new middle- and upper-class homebuyers and renters, displacing lower-income Black residents, who, in 1930, represented over 40 percent of Georgetown's population. The District government further abetted this displacement through the demolition of alley dwellings, which were deemed unsanitary, though in some cases the government allowed White families to purchase the alley dwellings instead, thus making them the object of gentrified restoration.[5] Long before these historical accounts of Georgetown's past examined this problematic preservation legacy, more than half a century ago, legal scholar Michael deHaven Newsom noted:

> The true history of Georgetown—until the preservationists' interests in it—was an integrated history. The black elements in that history have now been destroyed, resulting in a perversion and distortion of history.... What preservationists have done to black history is not unique.... Blacks have attempted to correct the distortions in the teaching of history, and they are attempting to do the same thing with history as seen and as acted upon by the preservationists.[6]

Narratives and associations more proximate to Whiteness and power may predominate in the built environment because they are what disproportionately survive or prevail over other claims. The unfairness and inconsistency of capital investment may repeat historic patterns of devaluation (like redlining), making properties more vulnerable to disinvestment. This can in turn create conditions and rationales for reinvestment framed as slum clearance, renewal, rehabilitation, and revitalization. Often cast as progressive programs to benefit communities, they may nonetheless engender displacement of marginalized publics and erasure of their stories.

Even preservation-oriented efforts to recognize multiple narratives in urban landscapes may not justly represent a diversity of publics. As part of a studio in Montgomery, Alabama, which brands itself as the first capital of the Confederacy and the cradle of the civil rights movement, students experimented with questions of narrative representation in the landscape through an alternate survey. They walked the historic downtown recording and mapping the narratives they encountered—what stories they experienced or witnessed as an average pedestrian—through sites, buildings, monuments, and signage. Although both Confederate and civil rights narratives were prevalent, several stories and publics were largely absent from the landscape. For instance, little could be found of Montgomery's role as a critical transfer point of Indigenous peoples on the Trail of Tears or of the city's role as a hub of the domestic trade of enslaved peoples before emancipation.[7] And in comparing Confederacy and civil rights narratives, students found that a significantly higher proportion of Confederacy-related sites were physically preserved, whereas many civil rights narratives relied more heavily on signage to mark places that no longer survived.

Heritage lists and designation rosters can echo and reinforce these patterns of exclusion, disproportionately recognizing the places that dominate in the built environment and the publics and stories they represent. A number of scholars, including Dolores Hayden, Gail Dubrow, and Ned Kaufman, pioneered early research about the underrepresentation of women, people of color, and other marginalized populations in the preservation sphere, largely through case-focused research.[8] But data about the systemic effects of these disparities suggest that there is still much work to do. For example, by one estimate, only 2 percent of the properties listed on the National Register relate to African American history.[9]

The preservation enterprise has been aware of these disparities for decades and continues to seek to address them. An early government effort to address representational inequities is *Five Views: An Ethnic Historic Site Survey for California,* a 1988 report and survey that focuses on the histories of Native Americans, Black Americans, Chinese Americans, Japanese Americans, and Mexican Americans in the state and sites associated with those stories.[10] It served as a form of community engagement that sought to give voice to publics underserved by the heritage enterprise and policy. Municipalities in California continue to employ similar historic-context approaches in their efforts to identify heritage places and engage underrepresented publics, for example, Los Angeles's "African American Historic Contexts" and San Francisco's "Development of Sexual Identity Based Subcultures Historic Context."[11] Los Angeles supported its efforts through a comprehensive survey of the built environment, SurveyLA, and an ancillary platform, MyHistoricLA, to facilitate community participation.

National Historic Landmarks theme studies, undertaken by the NPS, likewise seek to build place-associated histories and identify sites related to various publics, such as "Japanese Americans in World War II" and "Civil Rights in America: Racial Discrimination in Housing."[12] Alternate platforms of recognition, like the New York City LGBT Sites Project, seek to make invisible histories more visible by telling stories about significant places that survive, even if they are not designated or listed. Funding through both government and nonprofit sources, such as the National Trust's African American Cultural Heritage Action Fund, further incentivizes research, designation, interpretation, and conservation efforts.[13]

All of these examples demonstrate the concerted efforts on the part of preservation practitioners and policymakers to address disparities and, in doing so, promote representational justice. These are essentially additive approaches; they seek to expand heritage rosters, and thus to increase representation, by adding or recognizing more and more sites. This is an important way of confronting the publics and places excluded from heritage rosters and preservation action. But is quantity, or quantity alone, a measure of justice? Simply growing the number of heritage sites does not get at the structural issues in heritage policy that led to these representational disparities, nor do site-by-site approaches to funding.[14] The intractability of systemic biases compels deeper policy interrogation. Even in Los Angeles, where historic contexts for many disadvantaged publics increasingly inform preservation decision-making, the diversity and intersectionality of an urban population characterized by more than 140 nationalities are difficult to wholly represent, let alone spatialize through discrete places.[15]

Concerns over representational inequalities are particularly salient in the international arena, where equity and agreed-upon rules underpin cooperation. From its inception, the World Heritage system afforded new representational opportunities and discursive possibilities for nations in an increasingly decolonizing world.[16] Of the more than five hundred UN multilateral treaties, the World Heritage Convention, with 195 states parties as of 2023, is among the most ratified, which underscores the power of heritage as a shared global concern. UNESCO had a prior history of investment in heritage conservation, which early on was recognized as a conduit for international cooperation and a form of diplomatic currency, for example, through the oft-cited Nubian campaign.[17] But the 1972 convention sought to standardize the rules of the game and level the political playing field of heritage policy through a multilateral system, one that relies on the process of listing to recognize heritage and thus define the places within UNESCO's remit. The "one nation, one vote" concept theoretically sought to allow equal representation, but the political realities of shared decision-making in a multilateral system do not always bear that out.[18]

Concerns about uneven and unfair representation emerged in the early 1990s, reflected largely through the high concentration of World Heritage sites in Europe and the overwhelming prevalence of cultural, as opposed to natural, sites. These imbalances prompted several actions. After ratifying the World Heritage Convention in 1992, Japan spearheaded a joint UNESCO, ICOMOS, and ICCROM initiative to broaden understanding of diverse approaches to cultural heritage conservation, to better recognize non-Eurocentric worldviews and inform how heritage places were assessed for inclusion on the list. The initiative sought to clarify criteria and reduce the barriers to nomination that many countries faced owing to differing cultural interpretations of the concept of "authenticity." This produced the Nara Document on Authenticity in 1994 and a series of regional conferences that expanded the discourse.[19]

That same year, UNESCO launched the World Heritage Global Strategy in an effort to increase "representativity, balance and credibility" of the World Heritage list. As a multilateral platform and list, there was concerted interest in ensuring greater equity and parity among its sites and geographic regions (Europe and North America, Africa, Asia Pacific, Latin America, and the Arab States). The strategy involved some structural changes that continue to be adjusted, for example, shorter terms for states parties on the committee to enhance diversity in decision-making, a cap on the number of nominations that may be brought forth by a states party in a given year, and a cap on the overall number of nominations that the committee will consider in a given year. But this has not effectively resolved the structural unevenness, and a 2021 study of the program found mixed results, further complicated by the overwhelming increase in the number of sites as the list expanded from 410 to 1,121 properties over the twenty-six-year span. At the onset of the Global Strategy in 1994, 47 percent of properties were located in Europe and North America; by 2020, that proportion remained at 47 percent.[20]

Echoing the UN umbrella system, representation in the World Heritage system is defined geopolitically; the heritage site (as object) is seen to represent the nation-state and thus its people. Using place, specifically political geography, as a proxy for people is a simple shorthand for questions of representation but nonetheless problematic when viewed through a justice lens, because identities—and thus associated heritage—are not only geopolitical; they are racial, cultural, religious, and more. For example, using the UNESCO website, a general search of the term "church" produces a list of 310 World Heritage properties (27 percent of all properties); a search for the term "mosque" produces a list of 88 (8 percent of all properties). From a world population perspective, approximately 32 percent are Christian and 24 percent are Muslim.[21]

Looking at the World Heritage list in terms of sheer population numbers, disparities are likewise rife and call into question whether the number of World Heritage sites within countries equitably reflects the representation of people as global citizens. For example, China had fifty-six properties on the list as of 2022, among the highest number for any nation; from the perspective of population, that is one site per 25.4 million people. Italy has fifty-eight properties on this list, which translates to 1.02 million people per site. Sweden and South Korea each has fifteen sites on the list, with a population ratio of 691,000 and 3.46 million people per site, respectively. A number of states parties have nine sites on the list, including Israel (973,000 people per site), Colombia (5.7 million), Ethiopia (12. 8 million), and Indonesia

(30.2 million). Nigeria has the poorest representational ratio at more than 104 million people per listed site, with Bangladesh following at 55.8 million. More than twenty-five states parties to the convention have no representation on the list, meaning no sites within their borders have been successfully nominated. Their populations constitute approximately 82 million, or 1 percent of people worldwide. And when calculated by the regions to which nation-states are assigned for the purposes of the World Heritage system, the disparities are equally striking (Figure 11).

These are rudimentary and incomplete analyses of populations vis-à-vis sites, but they trigger complex questions about how people are being represented or not *by* heritage listing. While the aforementioned theme studies in the United States seek to advance greater recognition of underrepresented publics and the sites associated with their histories, they fundamentally look to promote the recognition of more heritage places. Second-order analysis of representational justice and the multifaceted ways it manifests in heritage designation and listing have yet to be internalized as part of policy review and reform, which relies so heavily on the first-order logic of prioritizing heritage-as-object.

The use of the list further complicates an object-focused versus a people-focused lens by emphasizing heritage typologies, such as those discussed in chapter 1, as a metric for representation and balance. By categorizing sites as vernacular, urban, archaeological, industrial, and so on, analyses suggest some connections to social contexts, but without squarely addressing the publics associated with and thus represented by the sites. Who is being represented through heritage is far more complicated when place-based heritage is approached as a social-spatial dynamic, especially in a postcolonial world in which many societies are becoming increasingly plural. For example, Taos Pueblo is a Native American sovereign nation within the United States; from the perspective of World Heritage listing, it is a U.S. site. The Bamiyan Valley in Afghanistan is a World Heritage site largely associated with Buddhism, even though it has not been practiced there since the fourteenth century. This global platform both reveals and conceals how claims to heritage transcend geographic proximity of place and publics, as discussed in chapter 2, and may effectively disempower local communities and/or empower those whose claims to place are complicated by histories of dispossession or migration. Parsing whose stories or histories are represented or not is highly complicated, but

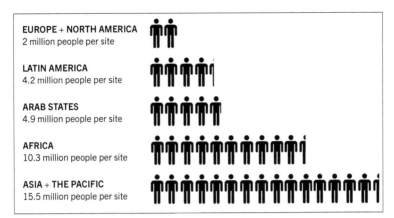

EUROPE + NORTH AMERICA
2 million people per site

LATIN AMERICA
4.2 million people per site

ARAB STATES
4.9 million people per site

AFRICA
10.3 million people per site

ASIA + THE PACIFIC
15.5 million people per site

FIGURE 11. The distribution of World Heritage sites is shown by population, per regional groupings of UNESCO. Data sources: World Heritage 2020 statistics; U.S. Energy Information Agency population data set 2020. Figure by the author.

preparing an extensive nomination dossier for World Heritage consideration is already a complex, costly, and time-consuming endeavor. More just representation cannot be achieved until the system intentionally and directly accounts for people.

Justice questions also implicate who is represented in the archive; Andrea Roberts's work is particularly salient on this point.[22] So much of the object-centric work of preservation hinges on the evidence available to understand historical conditions about the physical attributes of a place or space, as well as who designed, constructed, occupied, or used it, and how. Many of the same publics underrepresented in the built environment are also underrepresented in the traditional sources of data that are used for preservation, because they did not or could not document these places and associated experiences or were compelled to keep both places and information hidden. Heritage knowledge and ways of knowing may be informal or nonmaterial, shared over generations or through furtive networks, and thus are accumulated, practiced, and recorded in different ways. Preservation policy systems undervalue some publics and their histories, and their ways of knowing, "othering" those whose heritage practices are more divergent or for whom the normative rules are not accessible.[23]

Those historically marginalized by government and academia may be reticent to share their materials, knowledge, and stories with institutions that have been complicit in their exclusion. They may likewise mistrust and resist compliance with a system of knowledge and conservation that does not comport with their worldview. This may extend to concerns over listing or designating properties as well, which compels a potentially ongoing relationship with government and conformity with its standards.

Native American experiences illustrate how policy may adapt to augment representation, but enhanced representation does not itself rectify structural injustice. The 1966 NHPA did not originally recognize Tribal communities, but amendments in 1992 gave federally recognized Tribes a role in the preservation of historic properties on Tribal lands. A Tribal community may choose to participate through the creation of a tribal historic preservation office (THPO), which functions much like a state historic preservation office (SHPO), and as of 2020, there were more than two hundred THPOs. While representation is enhanced, procedural justice issues persist, as Tribal communities must still comply with federal regulations that do not adequately recognize their values, their perceptions of heritage, and their relationships to the land.[24]

At the core of representational justice, and inextricably tied to procedural justice, is the question of who has authority to narrate and represent. Who was at the table when heritage policies were forged—whether through declarative documents, multilateral treaties, or legislation—matters. Of the twenty-three people who served on the committee that drafted the Venice Charter, twenty-two were men, nineteen of whom were from Europe.[25] The eleven members and ex officio members of the U.S. Special Committee on Historic Preservation, which advanced the 1966 NHPA, were all White men.[26] Representational realities in the heritage enterprise today extend from these foundations.

Maturation of the preservation profession included the establishment of a multidisciplinary field of study and realm of expertise, mutually reinforced by institutions of higher learning that offer degrees in historic preservation or heritage conservation, and by NGOs/IGOs, like ICOMOS and ICCROM, that provide professional training. This globalizing enterprise gave rise to a community of experts and institutions who inform governments and the policies they produce. Both the identities and the positionalities of these experts matter. Advocacy organizations like Latinos in Heritage Conservation and Asian and Pacific Islanders in Historic Preservation demonstrate how publics are mobilizing to ensure representation in the heritage enterprise. How-ever, in the United States as of 2020, fewer than 1 percent of profes-sional preservationists were African American, and 80 percent of NPS staff are White.[27]

Effective representation is not simply a matter of increasing diver-sity in the ranks of the heritage enterprise. The theories and practices forged through the professionalization of the heritage field are still largely object focused and reinforced by preservation policies founded on first-order logic. Heritage professionals are not necessarily versed in or trained to analyze or represent a diversity of public values and inter-ests. There are potential conflicts between how professionals uphold standards and reinforce policy systems and how they effectively serve publics with diverse heritage claims, as legal scholar Lucas Lixinski argues:

> Experts and expert organizations, after all, are meant to translate communities' desires . . . and a system that sees heritage as an end in itself is less likely to be able to accurately convey community aspirations that largely see heritage as an instrument in the pursuit of broader goals. . . . Communities are brought in under someone else's umbrella, playing under someone else's "stage management" rules, and never in full.[28]

Professional focus on the first-order logic of saving the object may set up fundamental impediments to understanding, and more justly rep-resenting, the second-order concerns of those who claim heritage places. Contemporary policy reinforces a conditional relationship: preserve the object so that benefits can ensue. Communities may en-vision and experience a much more dynamic interplay between pres-ervation and the burdens and benefits it may beget. Professionals are thus mediating between how to apply and leverage policy and how to represent a community's interests—strategies that are not always aligned. New kinds of preservation praxis and practitioners, not nec-essarily educated in the academy, are challenging representation issues on the ground, generally through site-based action. But the extent to which this activism engages with and influences policy is yet to be seen, as much of this advocacy work pursues additive approaches of listing more sites.

PROCEDURAL JUSTICE

Parallel to the professionalization of the field is an evolution of policy that privileges expert knowledge. Early NPS directives acknowledged the very complicated nature of preservation decision-making and also underscored the role of experts, as in this excerpt from a memorandum on "General Restoration Policy" from 1937:

> The demands of scholarship for the preservation of every vestige of architectural and archeological evidence—desirable in itself— might, if rigidly satisfied, leave the monument in conditions which give the public little idea of its major historical aspect or importance. In aesthetic regards, the claims of unity or original form or intention, of variety of style in successive periods of building and remodelling, and of present beauty of texture and weathering may not always be wholly compatible. In attempting to reconcile these claims and motives, the ultimate guide must be the tact and judgment of the men in charge.[29]

From today's vantage point, and particularly as part of a justice-oriented second-order analysis, we may question the degree to which experts are vested with decision-making power. As Cameron Logan observes,

> despite the fact that expert control of the process of identifying historic significance in the built environment is the norm, the idea that an expert can adjudicate such claims according to objective criteria is difficult to sustain. As critical, historical research on the development of historic preservation has advanced in recent years, it has become ever clearer that in practice a designation of historic significance is never purely the result of careful inspection of the place itself. Rather, such designations are also the products of the various regimes of assessment and evaluation that affect the cultural perception of place in the broadest sense. Such perceptions are inextricably tied to social codes and patterns of judgment that cannot be addressed by reference to given criteria of significance and the immanent qualities of a building or district.[30]

By setting criteria and standards, and producing declarations and charters, the heritage enterprise influences and directs processes of preservation decision-making from site to systemic levels. The gatekeeper of policy processes is listing or designation. Those places on the list can access the protections and benefits and may also be subject to additional regulation. How places make it onto the list or get designated is thus a foundation of policy and the starting point for questions of procedural justice. Beyond that, how decisions are made regarding interventions and management further incurs procedural processes that may advantage and disadvantage certain publics and worldviews regarding heritage. The intentions of these processes, the transparency and equity of rules and decision-making, and how fair access and participation are facilitated all contribute to understanding the procedural justice implications of preservation policy.

Survivorship Bias

The identification of heritage places for policy action is predicated, in large part, on survival in the landscape. When I was first studying historic preservation more than thirty years ago, we learned how to identify heritage through observational surveys of the existing built environment. We practiced how to "read" architecture, assessing potential significance based on period style, formal aesthetics, design and structural features, and material quality and integrity. While consideration for listing or designation involves additional research, such observational practices imply that what we physically see in the present can evince the important stories of a place and its peoples. Relying on first-order logic, preservationists look for what survives in the built environment because we seek to bring policy to bear upon the *object*.

Decisions about what to list or designate rely on far more than material endurance, but this precondition is fundamentally a form of *survivorship bias* that complicates procedural justice. What survives in the built environment is not necessarily a reliable or inclusive narrator of history, as discussed from the perspective of representational justice. By focusing on that which successfully persisted physically and spatially, that is, what stands today, preservationists make the significance of a place and its stories contingent on what exists in the present, which bends toward wealth, power, and privilege.[31] Whiteness dominates in the U.S. built environment, in part because of who had the resources and agency to invest in it. Many publics are at a profound disadvantage when it comes to physical evidence, endurance in place, and the capacity to claim and maintain property. Preservationists may exercise and repeat survivorship bias through surveys, designation criteria, and intervention standards.[32]

The Covid-19 pandemic presented a unique opportunity to interrogate the issue of survivorship bias and its consequences. In a semester-long studio taught remotely, with students spread from California to China, we focused on Harlem, specifically the period of the Harlem Renaissance in the early twentieth century, when the neighborhood became a Black mecca.[33] Students researched various historic context themes relevant to the place and time, some of which were commonly associated with the Harlem Renaissance, such as literature and political activism, and others of which were more tangential, like Black-owned businesses and education. As part of their research, we asked them to identify place-based historic assets related to their respective themes: places that were significant to the people and story of the Harlem Renaissance, regardless of whether those places still existed. Students used historic imagery and maps, literary accounts, tax photos, period newspapers and journals, interviews with community-based organizations, and more to identify and map these assets, which included buildings and enterprises, such as beauty parlors and nightclubs, schools and medical facilities serving the Black community, and art studios and homes where literary salons occurred. They also mapped open-space assets, such as streetscapes where political parades marched and sidewalks where soapbox orators regularly preached and numbers runners plied their trade.

Then students determined which assets survived and which did not. They used Google Earth and Street View, and a few New York City–based students got out into the neighborhood with a camera to ground-truth their findings. They found that only 35 percent of the buildings they identified as historic assets significant to the Harlem Renaissance were still standing. And when they analyzed how survival correlated to their historic context themes, they found that assets related to more popularized narratives—like literature, religion, and politics—had higher rates of survival.

Most of the surviving assets were not recognized through designation or listing, but some were. Students analyzed those that were designated as New York City landmarks or part of historic districts to understand whether their significance tied to the Harlem Renaissance. Fewer than half of the designation reports referenced Black histories, and less than 10 percent mentioned any association with the Renaissance period. Students also found that the surviving buildings in Harlem, as well as National Register listing and local designation, underrepresented certain publics and narratives, including women, who played critical roles in journalism, business, performing arts, politics, and more; LGBTQ+ communities, who had a very rich and significant history during the Renaissance through the performing and literary arts, drag balls, and more; and economically disenfranchised publics whose spatial claims were often open spaces like streets and sidewalks. This exercise enabled students to excavate histories that they could not have understood if they had looked only at what survived in the built environment. And it compelled students and faculty alike to deeply consider how traditional surveys, as a foundational preservation procedure, may disprivilege or exclude publics and their narratives.

Beyond revealing concealed histories of a public, geography, or era, such research is a litmus test in the interrogation of systemic processes in preservation policy and how bias may be embedded and repeated. Even in locales where context research and statements guide heritage surveys, such as Los Angeles, the intention is to identify what survives, what the built environment *reveals* at the time of the research or survey. While promoting inclusion of publics and the places associated with their stories, context statements may likewise rely heavily on survivorship and do not interrogate how the structural dimensions of preservation policy may be complicit in perpetuating concealment and exclusion.

Survivorship bias echoes through designation and listing criteria, as well as standards of intervention, particularly through notions of *integrity* and *authenticity*. The first-order logic of these concepts privileges the persistence of historic form and material as a precondition for claiming place as heritage. As Herb Stovel recounted, the concept of integrity first emerged in the 1950s through the NPS as "a composite quality connoting original workmanship, original location, and intangible elements of feeling and association."[34] It became an essential listing criterion for the National Register, and current guidance now includes seven aspects of integrity: location, design, setting, materials, workmanship, feeling, and association. Though not strictly a heritage-as-object characterization, integrity nonetheless has a strong physical contingency and binary function as part of National Register criteria:

Integrity is the ability of a property to convey its significance. To be listed in the National Register of Historic Places, a property must not only be shown to be significant under the National Register criteria, but it also must have integrity. The evaluation of integrity is sometimes a subjective judgment, but it must always be grounded in an understanding of a property's physical features and how they relate to its significance. Historic properties either retain integrity (this is, convey their significance) or they do not.[35]

As discussed from the perspective of representational justice, many publics are at a severe disadvantage when compelled to comply with the integrity criterion, because their ability to maintain original features and materials has been historically compromised through exclusionary policies regarding land use, property ownership, lending, and more. The listing process is further biased toward survivorship by the added National Register criterion of a period of significance, which per NPS guidelines is "the length of time when a property was associated with important events, activities, or persons, or attained the characteristics which qualify it for National Register listing." This temporal framing is critically tied to integrity in that "the property must possess historic integrity for all periods of significance" that are identified.[36] Despite the very long histories of a place and those associated with it, National Register listing requires a discrete time frame that signifies when and, accordingly, who were most important. This period of significance, codified as a matter of public record, may then guide decision-making about a site, its conservation, and, in some cases, its interpretation by focusing interventions and centering narratives on that period. This structural element of policy fundamentally discounts what and who came before and after and fails to account for how change may have been an unavoidable consequence of exclusion.

Although municipalities need not necessarily comply with National Register guidance in defining their own designation criteria, the reinforcing nature of policy across varying levels of governance, particularly through the Certified Local Government program, means that most do.[37] A vivid example of the procedural injustice that these criteria can perpetuate is the case of 857 Riverside Drive in New York City.[38] The nineteenth-century home in Upper Manhattan was owned by known abolitionists, and research suggests that it may have been a stop along the Underground Railroad, a furtive network of safe houses to abet freedom-seeking enslaved persons. Precisely because of the clandestine nature of the Underground Railroad, documentation of such safe houses is scarce, and only seventeen designated landmarks in New York City are associated with abolitionist history. However, despite avid community and political support, the New York City Landmarks Preservation Commission did not consider 857 Riverside Drive for designation because of integrity issues, as recounted in the *New York Times*:

> "As a result of the extensive modifications that have been made to the house and its architectural details, it does not appear to retain the integrity necessary for consideration as an individual landmark. . . . The alterations include the removal of the octagonal cupola and wraparound porch along with their decorative trim, replacement of windows and doors and removal of their enframements, and the addition of the permastone veneer." . . . The house . . . therefore "retains neither the historic appearance nor adequate historic fabric from the 19th-century abolitionist era."[39]

FIGURE 12. Shown is 857 Riverside Drive, New York, New York, circa 1937 and 2023. The lack of design features associated with its nineteenth-century period of significance, when it is purported to have been used as part of the Underground Railroad, disqualified the site for landmark designation. Such sites, which were intentionally furtive because of the clandestine nature of the abolitionist enterprise, are often underdocumented and disadvantaged by standards of material integrity. Left photograph by Berenice Abbott, courtesy of the New York Public Library; right photograph by the author.

The physical changes to and deterioration of the house do not negate the important and underserved social histories associated with this particular space. But an aesthetic regime dominates in preservation such that guidance is predicated on the notion that places must retain certain visual and material features to perform as heritage.[40] The object-focused nature of designation criteria, which prioritize historic fabric and form as critical conduits of value, exemplifies how first-order logic creates procedural barriers to claiming place, particularly by historically marginalized publics.

Integrity criteria also disfavor relocated properties, which can further compound bias and perpetuate procedural injustice. As Janet Hansen and Sara Delgadillo Cruz have recounted, the Kinney–Tabor house in Venice, California, was denied heritage status in 1968 because

FIGURE 13. The Kinney–Tabor House was inherited by Irving Tabor, an African American, in 1925. Racial covenants at the time prevented him from taking up residence in the home, so he relocated the house to Oakwood, a Black neighborhood in Venice, California. The relocation disqualified the house from historic status in 1968. In 2008, half a century later, the decision was reconsidered and the property was designated a Los Angeles historic-cultural monument. Courtesy of Downtowngal under a Creative Commons Attribution-Share Alike 4.0 International license, via Wikimedia Commons.

it had been relocated and altered. Abbot Kinney was the founder of Venice, and he bequeathed the house to his longtime employee and confidant Irving Tabor, who was Black. In 1925, racial covenants and opposition from neighbors thwarted Tabor's attempt to occupy the home, so he moved the house to Oakwood, an African American enclave of Venice. In an example of restorative justice, the house was reconsidered and formally designated in 2008.[41]

The biases of these designation criteria are reinforced by guidelines for intervention as well, such as the Secretary of the Interior's Standards. Publics whose heritage places were devalued, neglected, or purposefully destroyed may have properties with compromised or nonmaterial integrity. But reconstruction as a means of reclaiming that heritage is expressly discouraged by the Standards: "because of the potential for historical error in the absence of sound physical evidence, this treatment can be justified only rarely."[42] And owing to bias regarding "evidence" and the lack of traditional archival materials relating to many marginalized publics and their heritage, some degree of conjecture may be unavoidable when reconstructing such heritage. Debates over whether reconstruction is or is not appropriate are also directly linked to processes of designation, as reconstructed properties generally are not considered eligible for the National Register unless they are "accurately executed in a suitable environment and presented in a dignified manner as part of a restoration master plan, and when no other building or structure with the same association has survived."[43] Such circular reasoning contributes to a self-reinforcing pattern of exclusion by constraining options and creating hurdles for those whose ability to transfer heritage across generations has already been historically impeded.

There are, for example, a number of reconstructed soldier huts at national parks associated with the Revolutionary and Civil Wars: Valley Forge in Pennsylvania, Manassas in Virginia, and Fort Donelson in Tennessee, to name a few. Because the original huts did not survive, these projects relied on archaeological evidence, military records referencing the general construction and layout, and in some cases visual documentation, such as a sketch or plan. Among the earliest reconstructions are those at Jockey Hollow in New Jersey, where the Continental army encamped during the winter of 1779–80. They are part of the Morristown National Historical Park, the very first national historical park established by the NPS in the 1930s. Rebuilt multiple times since, archaeological and historical research confirms that neither the location nor the fabrication of the huts is historically accurate (for example, they have concrete foundations).[44] As a counterpoint to the oft-preserved "George Washington slept here" homes where commanders commonly quartered, these replicas demonstrate the severe and crowded conditions under which soldiers labored to survive the harsh winters of war. The desire to portray a more thorough history seems to outweigh the "potential for historical error" raised by the Standards.

More considered debate surrounds the reconstruction of non-surviving dwellings of enslaved peoples. At Monticello, the home of Thomas Jefferson, a similar mix of archival evidence and archaeological research informed the Mountaintop Project, which investigated the Mulberry Row area of the site and the lives of enslaved people on Jefferson's plantation.[45] Staff at Monticello note that the re-creation of a slave dwelling and storehouse, though informed by historical evidence and extensive consultation with preservation professionals, did not meet the standards for reconstruction because of potential inaccuracies. But because the site is owned by a not-for-profit and the project received private funding, strict adherence to the Standards was not necessary.[46]

Though these reconstructed spaces afford a spatial encounter with important and underrepresented narratives of Black history, the interpretation of the lives of enslaved peoples at Monticello and other historic sites is often criticized by visitors who want or expect stories reflecting more centered, and White, histories.[47] Those held in bondage sacrificed and toiled under severe and inhumane conditions yet contributed significantly to the building of the United States. That the reconstruction and interpretation of soldier huts in government-owned national parks is less scrutinized, by preservation professionals and visitors alike, than the reconstruction and interpretation of the dwellings of enslaved peoples on privately owned historic sites gives pause. As Laurajane Smith contends, such bias is reflective of how heritage-making through site interpretation can facilitate or impede representational and distributive justice.[48] The object-centered rules and procedures established by the preservation enterprise about what is or is not acceptable, and the uneven application of those standards, hamper the ability for underrepresented publics and their stories to claim place, contributing to procedural justice disparities.

FIGURE 14. The replica soldier huts at the Morristown National Historical Park, which serve to commemorate the suffering of soldiers in the Continental army during the Revolutionary War, are inaccurate reconstructions, as are a number of such huts across battlefields within the National Park Service system. Whereas these replicas have posed little to no controversy, the recreated dwellings of enslaved people at Monticello, Thomas Jefferson's plantation in Virgina, have been the subject of debate by preservationists owing to concerns over their authenticity. Left photograph by the author; right photograph courtesy of the Thomas Jefferson Foundation, copyright Thomas Jefferson Foundation at Monticello.

Efforts to counter the social consequences of survivorship bias and object-focused criteria as a matter of procedural policy are evident at the international, national, and municipal levels. The American concept of integrity entered the development of World Heritage in the 1970s as *authenticity*, defined by tests related to four physical attributes: design, material, setting, and workmanship.[49] Two decades later, as part of efforts to redress inequities and misunderstandings within the multilateral system, the 1994 Nara Document on Authenticity emerged from "the World Heritage Committee's desire to apply the test of authenticity in ways which accord full respect to the social and cultural values of all societies."[50]

Similar to how significance is contingent on integrity in the U.S. context, Nara affirmed that "authenticity . . . appears as the essential qualifying factor concerning values." At the same time, the declaration acknowledged, "All judgements about values attributed to heritage as well as the credibility of related information sources may differ from culture to culture, and even within the same culture. It is thus not possible to base judgements of value and authenticity on fixed criteria."[51] As Dawson Munjeri argues in relation to Africa, the concept of authenticity is culturally relative, and many societies do not base their concepts of heritage or its authenticity on "the cult of physical objects, the tangible, and certainly not on condition and aesthetic values."[52] Subsequent revisions to the *Operational Guidelines for the Implementation of the World Heritage Convention* incorporated language from the Nara Document to better acknowledge different forms of evidence and ways of knowing and expanded the attributes related to authenticity to include "form and design; materials and substance; use and function; traditions, techniques and management systems; location and setting; language, and other forms of intangible heritage; spirit and feeling; and other internal and external factors."[53]

Some efforts in the United States to recognize cultural differences as a matter of preservation policy centered on Native Americans and their heritage. In 1989, the Senate mandated the NPS to collaborate with the Bureau of Indian Affairs and report on historic preservation funding needs on Tribal lands. The resulting publication, *Keepers of the Treasures: Protecting Historic Properties and Cultural Traditions on Indian Lands,* elevated a much broader dialogue around fundamental differences in how heritage is understood, experienced, and communicated within Tribal communities.[54] As noted, the establishment of THPOs followed, along with a new typology of heritage: traditional cultural property (TCP).

The criteria for National Register eligibility pointedly address properties defined as buildings, structures, sites, objects, and districts. Per the NPS, TCPs also could include natural areas and features but, more importantly, acknowledged "association with cultural practices or beliefs of a living community. TCPs are rooted in that community's history and are important in maintaining the continuing cultural identity of the community."[55] This acknowledgment of heritage as an ongoing, place-based social dynamic and practice, and not just as an object, represented important, though limited, progress toward justice. But a new heritage typology did not necessarily address structural biases in the system. For example, as NPS staffer and key author of the National Register guidance on TCPs acknowledged, the moniker "traditional cultural property" is offensive to some Tribal communities, and for many, their sacred sites and traditions cannot be geographically bounded as a property. Although the intention, in theory, was to create more just processes for those with other worldviews, knowledges, and ways of heritage-making, National Register staff sought "to make traditional cultural properties fit within the existing structure as much as possible without rendering the concept meaningless."[56] Tribal communities are still compelled to follow existing federal policy processes and criteria.

At the municipal level, more liberal views of heritage as a social-spatial dynamic are evinced by the emergence of legacy business programs in a number of U.S. cities in the last decade, including San Francisco, California; San Antonio, Texas; Seattle, Washington; Cambridge, Massachusetts; Birmingham, Alabama; and Miami Beach, Florida. Following on precedents in Barcelona, Paris, London, and elsewhere, these policies recognize the cultural contributions of local businesses as well as the integral links between preservation interests and economic development. More than just a new heritage typology compelled to follow existing preservation norms, the programs seek to support the survival of locally owned businesses through object- and people-focused policy tools, including registries and awards that enhance promotion, funding for operations or capital improvements, and capacity building for business operators.[57]

The introduction of cultural districts in San Francisco in 2018 likewise acknowledges the integral relationship of people and places. This district typology pushes beyond heritage-as-object to identify "legacy businesses, nonprofits, community arts, and traditions" and to "support specific cultural communities or ethnic groups that historically have been discriminated against, displaced, and oppressed."[58] Districts recognize diverse publics and their claims to urban life and geography, such as Japantown, the American Indian Cultural District, SoMa Pilipinas, Compton's Transgender Cultural District, and the Leather and LGBTQ Cultural District. They emerged through growing recognition that preservation policies focused on the physical survival of buildings and sites did not prevent displacement of vulnerable publics.[59] The recognition of impeded claims to property by and social-spatial codependence in marginalized communities undergirded the

FIGURE 15. Although the typology of traditional cultural property (TCP) has largely been used to recognize Native American heritage, Bohemian Hall and Park, in Astoria, Queens, was included on the National Register of Historic Places in 2000 as a TCP because of its significance to the Czech American community as a still vibrant place of community gathering, particularly through its beer garden. Upper photograph courtesy of Jim.henderson, in the public domain via Wikimedia Commons; lower photograph from the Bohemian Hall and Park National Register nomination, courtesy of the National Park Service.

typology of cultural districts. And district-specific activities are determined by neighborhood-based organizations, meaning that participation is a critical dimension of policy.

Participation

Who determines what is heritage and how it is preserved is at the core of procedural justice questions. Intersecting with issues of representational justice, heritage policies detail the role of some publics in decision-making processes, affording them agency and influence. Heritage professionals, for example, have clearly defined positions and responsibilities in designation and design review procedures, across municipal to international levels of governance. Conversely, the engagement of others—nonprofessionals or community members—is more uneven and ad hoc across policy structures. Calls for human rights–based approaches to preservation and enhanced community engagement proliferate in the field, but discourse has yet to robustly shift policy toward accommodating and systematizing more inclusive participation.

Before the preservation enterprise matured through legislation and professionalization, heritage interests were often disadvantaged in U.S. urban planning and policy. Mid-twentieth-century federally funded urban renewal and highway construction projects wreaked havoc on many U.S. cities, causing the destruction and division of neighborhoods, largely in marginalized communities. The power and resource disparities between local residents and the federal government afforded little recourse to affected publics.

Two important avenues of legal action bolstered the development of preservation policy with the intention of empowering local communities. In 1954, the U.S. Supreme Court *Berman v. Parker* decision established the foundations of aesthetic regulation. Although the case was about the government's right to claim a property for demolition and redevelopment to improve neighborhood quality, as discussed in chapter 2, the premise also underpinned the government's right to preserve for similar purposes. This paved the way for the New York State Bard Law of 1956, which enabled municipalities to enact preservation ordinances on similar grounds.[60] The 1965 New York City Preservation Law resulted, serving as a critical court-tested gold standard for municipal-level preservation legislation and fortifying the regulation of aesthetics within the bailiwick of local governments.

The passage of the NHPA in 1966 enacted important procedural protections that further empowered localities in safeguarding heritage places. Any federal undertaking, including projects that receive federal funding, is subject to Section 106 review to determine if historic properties, meaning those on or eligible for the National Register, are affected and to mitigate adverse effects. The Advisory Council on Historic Preservation oversees these processes. The National Environmental Act provides similar procedural protections by requiring an assessment of the impact of federal agency actions on historic resources, as does section 4(f) of the Department of Transportation Act. Similar state-level legislation requires assessment when state-funded projects may impact properties on the National or State Register. The policies and institutions established by this cadre of legislation marked an important shift in government accountability and procedural justice vis-à-vis preservation.

These growing government functions required review processes and professional evaluations, such as environmental impact assessments, to legitimize community-based concerns about the potential loss of or negative outcomes related to place-based heritage. Preservation professionals emerged as both experts and facilitators, bringing specialized knowledge to bear and representing the heritage interests of diverse collectives. However, many saw the work of the preservationists less as a profession and more as a pioneering and socially progressive movement, as characterized by Adele Chatfield-Taylor, Antoinette Lee, and Ned Kaufman, respectively:

And far from being a form of nostalgia, as an interest in old buildings is frequently seen to be, it was—even in its beginnings, even in its most primitive, inarticulate form—a pioneering, heroically revolutionary, and completely avant-garde activity.[61]

In . . . the 1970s and 1980s, many preservationists regarded their work as pioneering. They approached historic properties surveys with an almost missionary-zeal.[62]

Once upon a time, historic preservation was a passionate protest. Now it's a prudent profession.[63]

That early activism was critical in raising awareness about the loss of neighborhoods and historic places and in propelling preservation toward the purview of public policy and democratic institutions. But with the expansion of government-sponsored policy tools came the professionalization of the enterprise. Historic preservation in the United States emerged as an academic field of study in the 1960s, when James Marston Fitch introduced it at the Graduate School of Architecture and Planning at Columbia University. Today, more than sixty U.S. institutions offer programs in historic preservation, including certificates and degrees at the bachelor's and master's levels.[64] The symbiosis of policy development and professionalization, as introduced in chapter 1, regularized education as well as criteria, standards, and decision-making (like the soccer analogy's rules of the game), thereby reinforcing an object-focused mission in the heritage enterprise.

In the United States, the NHPA compels each state to maintain a "primarily professional" board to review National Register nominations and provide advice for statewide preservation plans and grants as well as to the SHPO. Per the NPS manual for state boards, "the law requires that a majority of the members . . . be professionals qualified in the following and related disciplines: history, prehistoric and historical archeology, architectural history, and architecture."[65]

Ordinances in most counties and municipalities function similarly, generally outlining the chiefly professional membership of commissions or review boards, which take decisions about the designation of properties and evaluate proposed design changes to properties already designated. In New York City, for example, the Landmarks Law requires the eleven-person commission, appointed by the mayor, to include a minimum of six professionals (three architects, a historian, a city planner or landscape architect, and a realtor), as well as one resident from each of the city's five boroughs. The same commission designates properties, with final approval by the City Council, and reviews design changes that are not minor enough to be handled at a staff level. San Francisco has a similar seven-person commission of city residents, "qualified by reason of interest, competence, knowledge, training and experience in the historic, architectural, aesthetic, and cultural traditions of the City," which proposes designations to the Board of Supervisors and regulates historic resources after designation.[66] To ensure professional representation, smaller municipalities sometimes allow nonresidents to serve on preservation commissions. For example, Morristown, New Jersey, has a seven-person historic preservation commission of which three members must have expertise, including two knowledgeable in building design and construction or architectural history and one in local history. These three experts need not live in the town, but the remaining four commissioners must be residents.[67]

At the international level, the UNESCO World Heritage system further codifies the essential role of professionals in the conceptualization of heritage authority. Each states party identifies representatives of its choosing to participate in World Heritage meetings and processes; such individuals may or may not be heritage professionals. As a political, multilateral platform of diplomatic relations, sovereignty dictates each nation's right to self-determine its representation. However, to ensure that heritage expertise informs decision-making, the convention identifies three advisory bodies—ICCROM, ICOMOS, and IUCN—to prepare documentation, monitor the state of conservation of World Heritage sites, assist in implementing World Heritage Committee decisions, and, in the case of IUCN and ICOMOS, evaluate nominations to the World Heritage list. The convention and the work of the committee are further supported by a secretariat, the World Heritage Centre, which is staffed primarily with heritage professionals.[68] In monitoring missions and evaluations, the advisory bodies purposefully send experts who are not from the nation in which a heritage site under assessment is located. This serves the practical purpose of avoiding conflicts of interest, in that a nonlocal professional might be more objective and apolitical. Nonetheless, this underscores a sort of universalization of professional heritage expertise such that it transcends cultural and geopolitical contexts.[69] In doing so, it suggests that the professionalization of heritage somehow counterbalances the politics of heritage.

Professionals have significant authority in designation and design review processes, from local to international levels. That the profession is not biased, or that its presumed objectivity somehow compensates for the bias of others, reinforces a professional–nonprofessional binary that influences power and participation. Professional knowledge, and its object focus, is valorized in decision-making structures and processes, and the recursive nature of policy in turn reinforces that knowledge in the public realm.[70]

A comparative review of legislation across the United States interrogated the public policy rationales of municipal-level preservation ordinances, meaning how public investment in preservation is justified. While aesthetic regulation was an important basis for the development of municipal legislation, these public policy rationales clearly outline second-order intentions for the heritage enterprise. More than 60 percent cite the social benefits of preservation, including education and public health and welfare. Economics also prevail in more than half of the ordinances sampled, noting the intention of preservation to stimulate economic growth, stabilize or improve property values, and drive tourism. More than a quarter note preservation's regenerative role in rehabilitation and redevelopment as well as in managing urban growth. Despite its legal history, regulating aesthetics and design compatibility serves as a public policy rationale in approximately 20 percent of sampled preservation ordinances.[71]

Despite these legally established second-order intentions, designation and design review constitute most of the regulatory processes of municipal-level preservation agencies. The first-order logic of the profession—save the building, then other benefits will follow—dominates. Most of the social, economic, and environmental intentions of public policy are all but absent from designation criteria and standards for design intervention, which prioritize the aesthetics and material integrity of the object and largely follow the National Register criteria and the Secretary of the Interior's Standards, respectively.[72] And despite the second-order rationales that underpin their legal foundations, most municipal agencies have no mandate or few resources to undertake research regarding the socioeconomic or environmental effects of their work and the justice implications of their procedures.

This first-order priority of government procedures echoes professional knowledge that centers the object; in tandem, they influence the missions of civil society organizations that advocate for heritage as well as the aims of individuals who support preservation. As part of the aforementioned study of municipal ordinances, colleagues and I tested this notion in 2016 through an online survey of public interest in preserving historic districts in New York City. More than sixteen hundred respondents rated the importance of various public policy rationales for preservation. At the top was protecting historic architecture and features, and maintaining the aesthetic character of neighborhoods ranked third. At second was preserving walkability and street life, which suggests an interest in the social-spatial dynamics of urban streetscapes, though regulated through form and design. Other socially oriented rationales, such as promoting civic engagement, maintaining cultural diversity, preventing displacement, and protecting affordability, ranked in the middle third. Economic rationales were in the bottom third of the rankings.[73]

The demographic profile of the respondents raised troubling questions about who participates in preservation and why questions of diversity, equity, and inclusion warrant further interrogation beyond the demographics of preservation professionals themselves. The survey was offered in English and Spanish, disseminated through community boards and other neighborhood-based organizations (preservation related and not), and advertised through local and social media. Ninety-five percent supported the designation of historic districts, suggesting that respondents had a strong affinity toward preservation. Demographically, the respondent pool was overwhelmingly Whiter, better educated, older, and wealthier than the city average.

Procedural justice is about who participates in and has agency in decision-making and the transparency and fairness of that decision-making. Confronting the lack of diversity in publics supporting or with an affinity toward preservation is a challenge, as the role of non-professionals and community members in policy procedures varies across localities and levels of governance. Policy structures expressly call for professional knowledge and establish distinct responsibilities for preservation experts. Those community groups whose interests align with the professional values mirrored in policy procedures may be at a significant advantage in the preservation enterprise. Different publics with different knowledges or ways of knowing may be discounted as a consequence, thereby limiting their power and influence.

In an effort to recognize nonexpert knowledge, U.S. policy shifts intended to afford more just representation and standards to Native Americans, as previously discussed, through THPOs and traditional cultural properties. NPS officials likewise sought to empower Tribal communities by recognizing their authority vis-à-vis heritage professionals:

> One fundamental difference between traditional cultural properties and other kinds of historic properties is that their signifi-

Table 1. Demographic comparison of New York City preservation-minded community

ATTRIBUTE	NEW YORK CITY PRESERVATION-MINDED COMMUNITY (SURVEY RESPONDENTS) (%)	NEW YORK CITY POPULATION (%)
Race: White	86	33
Education: college degree	91	36
Age: 55 years and older	>50	<25
Income: $100,000 or more per year	>50	<25

2016 survey respondent pool compared to 2010 U.S. census data for New York City. From Erica Avrami, Cherie-Nicole Leo, and Alberto Sanchez Sanchez, "Confronting Exclusion: Redefining the Intended Outcomes of Historic Preservation," *Change over Time* 8, no. 1 (2018).

cance cannot be determined solely by historians, ethnographers, ethnohistorians, ethnobotanists, and other professionals. The significance of traditional cultural properties must be determined by the community that values them.[74]

This distinction recognizes that Native American communities ascribe values to heritage in ways that do not necessarily comport with the expertise of preservation professionals. Elevating their authority seeks greater procedural justice, though arguably, there is more work to be done given histories of racism and dispossession. Through a wider lens, this distinction intimates that determining the significance of non–Native American heritage places can be done "solely" by professionals and does not necessarily require input from "the community that values them." Does this presuppose that heritage experts can effectively represent everyone *but* Native Americans in heritage decision-making? Or that all non-Indigenous peoples ascribe value to heritage in the same ways?

In the highly plural society of the United States, this raises troubling concerns. In New York City, as of 2020, 60 percent of the population were immigrants and the children of immigrants (nearly 40 percent and over 20 percent, respectively).[75] This stands in stark contrast to 1965, when both the New York City Landmarks Law and the federal Immigration and Nationality Act were enacted. The latter overhauled U.S. immigration policy, which previously enforced quotas based on country of origin, highly privileging those emigrating from Europe. In 1965, foreign-born residents composed only 20 percent of the New York City population. Nationally, the foreign-born population grew from 9.6 million in 1965 to 45 million in 2015 and became significantly more diverse. During that same fifty-year span, the White, non-Hispanic share of the overall population declined from 84 percent to 62 percent.[76]

Eurocentric views toward preservation predominated at the time significant heritage legislation, namely, the New York City law of 1965 and the federal law of 1966, came into being. Taken together, the recognition of that foundation, the change in demography since these foundations were laid, and the contemporary racial and socioeconomic characteristics of preservation advocates (as suggested by the aforementioned survey) compel scrutiny. The assumptions made then did not anticipate how multiple publics participate in the preservation enterprise and how policy procedures may reflect a bias toward Whiteness in its privileging of first-order priorities and professional knowledge.

The concept of consent echoes across various levels of preservation governance and constitutes a foundational form of nonexpert participation in the listing or designation of heritage. At the international level, only the nation-state in which a heritage place is geographically located can include a property on its tentative list and nominate it to the World Heritage list.[77] The *Operational Guidelines for the Implementation of the World Heritage Convention* encourage states parties to

> adopt a human-rights based [*sic*] approach, and ensure gender-balanced participation of a wide variety of stakeholders and rights-holders, including site managers, local and regional governments, local communities, indigenous peoples, non-governmental organizations (NGOs) and other interested parties and partners in the identification, nomination, management and protection processes of World Heritage properties.[78]

Consent is called out expressly in relation to Indigenous populations, and state parties are asked to demonstrate that "the free, prior and informed consent of indigenous peoples has been obtained, through, inter alia, making the nominations publicly available in appropriate languages and public consultations and hearings."[79] However, each states party maintains its sovereign right to self-determine the nature of participation within its borders. UNESCO has limited agency in ensuring in-country participation beyond requesting that a nomination dossier include documentation about the participatory process.

In the United States, for a heritage site to be considered for potential World Heritage listing, it must have full written consent of the property owner. This owner consent provision in U.S. law creates substantial obstacles for nominating historic districts, urban centers, and other multiowner landscapes for World Heritage consideration. The onus of securing universal consent from vast numbers of private property owners contributed to the failed nominations of both Newport, Rhode Island, and Savannah, Georgia, as potential World Heritage sites.[80]

The NHPA takes a different view toward consent when listing on the National Register in that an owner may formally *object* to the inclusion of their property, thereby preventing listing. In proposed National Register historic districts, if more than 50 percent of property owners formally object, the district will not be listed. Although the objection provision was not originally included in the 1966 NHPA, the 1980 amendments added the provision in response to concerns regarding property rights and potential burdens on owners.[81] However, even if an owner objects, government review may still determine the property as "eligible" for inclusion, which means that it is still subject to the procedural implications of Section 106 review, described earlier, even if it is not formally listed.[82]

Preservationists claim that the stakes of consent are low for many owners, as National Register listing does not necessarily infringe on property rights. A property owner could list their property on the National Register and then significantly renovate it or tear it down without ramifications (presuming municipal regulations, such as demolition/construction permitting and added local landmark designation, do not restrict such action). Only when federal funding or licensing/permitting is involved in a project do procedural reviews take effect, such as Section 106 or the use of federal historic tax credits, which may regulate impacts on or changes to a property. However, in many municipalities, inclusion on the National Register automatically triggers local designation and thus regulation. The benefits afforded by National Register listing can be significant to owners, including access to tax credits, energy performance waivers, and more, and will be discussed in subsequent sections. The 1976 Tax Act created disincentives for demolition and accelerated depreciation on replacement structures, thereby creating potential financial encumbrances for owners seeking to replace an older or historic building.[83] And some of the most significant burdens placed on owners is in the process of preparing the documentation for potential National Register listing, which generally requires professional assistance to undertake research and prepare nomination forms and thus may be a barrier for some publics.

At the local level, much like the soccer analogy's rules of the game, consent or veto power is more nuanced and may be guided by state-level enabling legislation. It likewise has higher stakes, as such designation has significant implications for owners' control of their property. Most municipal designations prevent demolition and regulate formal exterior modifications to buildings, and interior modification if designated as an interior landmark. Owners must submit proposed changes to local commissions for design review and approval, which can potentially add time and costs when undertaking alterations. Municipal planning and preservation agencies generally afford opportunities for members of the public to propose a potential landmark or historic district, but the interplay between and respective responsibilities of publics and government officials vary across localities.

In Connecticut, state law calls for municipalities to prepare studies for proposed landmarks or districts and outlines procedures for owner consent or objection similar to the National Register. However, in the case of historic districts, a Connecticut municipality can designate the district only if more than two-thirds of property owners consent.[84] New Hampshire state law empowers local communities, specifically residents, to designate historic districts according to municipal governance arrangements.[85] Neighborhood representatives voluntarily put forward the proposal for a district, often with assistance from local government agencies, and work to develop a district-specific plan and ordinance. Per the municipal handbook prepared on behalf of the New Hampshire Division of Historical Resources,

> the ordinance is treated just like any other amendment to the zoning ordinance. In cities and towns operating under a council form of government, the local legislative body determines the details of

how the district ordinance is adopted. In towns operating under a town meeting form of government, or within a village district that has been specifically authorized by law to enact a zoning ordinance, the neighborhood heritage district ordinance is adopted by a ballot vote of the municipality.[86]

New Hampshire state law also provides for a clear option to abolish historic districts, affording residents significant procedural agency, which may make designation more acceptable to property owners. If a petition to abolish a historic district is signed by at least twenty-five voting residents of the municipality, the local commission is obliged to hold two public hearings and to call a vote at a town meeting. If two-thirds of the local legislative body vote in favor of the petition, the historic district must be abolished.[87]

Warren, Rhode Island, makes inclusion in a historic district voluntary. Owners whose properties are more than one hundred years old may choose to participate in the district and abide with regulations and receive associated preservation benefits. This makes for uneven aesthetic control at the neighborhood scale but provides more protection than no district and balances concerns over property rights.[88] Many other municipalities do not have citizen voting or owner consent provisions, including New York City, meaning that the local government can effectively designate an individual property or district against owners' wishes, although in some municipalities, like Jersey City, New Jersey, an objection from the owner triggers a super majority vote by the commission.[89] In Chicago, the designation of religious properties requires the consent of owners, but the designation of nonreligious properties does not require consent.[90] Generally, nonconsent/nonobjection municipalities seek some sort of demonstrated community interest before moving forward, and there are detailed legal provisions for informing property owners and residents and for engaging them in designation procedures, including mailed notices, periods of public commentary, and public hearings. Multiple political bodies may also be involved in the review and approval process.

The advantages and disadvantages of owner consent (or objection) are debatable with regard to procedural justice. While owner consent may engender a binary yes–no vote, such procedures are commonly preceded by public meetings and other forms of owner engagement. However, residents, business operators, and civic organizations who may lease or rent in a district, or are located outside of it, have little to no agency in policy contexts requiring owner consent. This may significantly disadvantage places with high residential rentership, which often correlates to publics with lower income levels. While nonowners may advocate and engage in public meetings, ultimately, the capacity to claim place as heritage hinges on individual rights of property ownership when owner consent is compelled by policy.

In localities without owner consent, designation processes rely considerably on deliberation and may include publics well beyond owners. In these policy contexts, heritage "ownership" is not a matter of individual property rights but a collective claim by the community. Drawing on Grégoire's notion of heritage as *public* objects in which the people have a shared stake, as discussed previously, municipalities vest power in political bodies to take decisions in the interest of the common good[91]—though as previously delineated, these political bodies comprise largely heritage professionals. In such deliberative processes, much depends on how government institutions engage multiple publics beyond professionals but also on how easily diverse publics can gain access to and fluency with these policy procedures. In many cases, public hearings are simply open platforms often dominated by those who can speak and present in ways that comport with the norms and language of the heritage profession.

The work of claiming a historic place begins long before such deliberative processes, and questions of public participation extend far beyond the decision to list or not. But the spectrum of nonexpert engagement before and after designation is less defined in laws and policy structures. Per the aforementioned review of U.S. municipal ordinances, only 10 percent of public policy rationales call out preservation as a vehicle for civic engagement.[92] And especially in localities without consent provisions, who participates beyond those appointed to a commission is a matter of self-selection. In New York City, there is a hardy and resolute network of professionally staffed or assisted civil society organizations and not-for-profits advocating for preservation, many focused on particular neighborhoods, such as the Upper East Side, the Upper West Side, and Greenwich Village. Who supports and engages with these groups influences preservation dynamics within the city writ large, as they serve as critical advocacy voices in public hearings, community board meetings, and the media. The demographic profile of the NYC survey respondents noted previously suggests that this community of preservation-minded activists, while exercising their participatory agency, may not be effectively representing diverse publics. Nor are pathways for broader engagement—beyond advocating for designation or protesting a proposed demolition or alteration—clearly charted. The role of nonexpert publics in identifying and producing knowledge about place-based heritage tends to be limited and ad hoc, organized or defined by a particular project dedicated to community-engaged documentation, cultural mapping, inventorying, or crowdsourced data collection.

As discussed previously, the histories of many publics are underrepresented in archives and traditional forms of physical documentation. More robust participation in identifying heritage may be compromised by a lack of historical evidence and by differing perspectives on what constitutes historical evidence. Typical processes of heritage identification and mapping prioritize the object and rely on particular ways of ordering land and geography, using cadasters, geopolitical boundaries, and property ownership to structure knowledge about place and thus people. Many societies do not adhere to these normative standards of geographic information and do not equate the right to use land with ownership. Heritage documentation and research in communities that have suffered exclusion and repeated trauma may itself be viewed as yet another form of dispossession and extraction, whereby experts collect data and record conditions according to their professional principles, with limited local input.

Even documentation technologies like laser scanning and remote sensing can be exclusionary. They may rely heavily on proprietary software and high-capacity hardware, reliable internet and point cloud access, trained professionals to undertake recording and process data, and particular biases in what is recorded and how data are prioritized. This may disadvantage communities who do not have or do not valorize these technical capacities, as they may be obliged to cede control of their knowledge to others. Who defines evidence and data standards, and who can access or own information about a public's heritage, raises profound procedural justice questions often overlooked within technical discourse.

These justice questions are compounded by the disproportional emphasis on professional standards to document and conserve the heritage object, versus ethics that may inform interactions with publics integral to the ongoing social-spatial dynamics of heritage places and how they are revealed or concealed. The growing discourse of critical heritage studies plumbs this disparity through the lens of social sciences like anthropology, archaeology, and ethnography, exposing the many problematic ways in which standardized practices and policies in the heritage enterprise do not sufficiently account for social difference and human rights.[93] Scholars like Jeremy Wells and Barry Steifel advocate for greater interdisciplinary engagement with the social sciences to advance human-centered preservation education and practice.[94] But the translation and development of these critiques from discourse into systemic policy reform is at best protracted, especially in urban contexts, where the preservation enterprise unavoidably intersects with land use planning and economic and community development.

Policy frameworks like the Faro Convention of the Council of Europe seek to "put people and human values at the centre of an enlarged and cross-disciplinary concept of cultural heritage." Faro defines a *heritage community* as "people who value specific aspects of cultural heritage which they wish, within the framework of public action, to sustain and transmit to future generations." But it offers limited concrete guidance with regard to how governments can ensure more just and participatory decision-making:

encourage everyone to participate in:

– the process of identification, study, interpretation, protection, conservation and presentation of the cultural heritage;

– public reflection and debate on the opportunities and challenges which the cultural heritage represents;

take into consideration the value attached by each heritage community to the cultural heritage with which it identifies.[95]

And although Faro advocates for "democratic participation," it implies differences in knowledge and agency among people:

take steps to improve access to the heritage, especially among young people and the disadvantaged, in order to raise awareness about its value, the need to maintain and preserve it, and the benefits which may be derived from it.[96]

The need to raise public awareness about and care for heritage is rife in preservation literature, advocacy, practice, and policy. While seemingly benign, its undertones suggest concerns worthy of interrogation with regard to procedural justice. The first is the premise that people universally benefit from heritage, but not enough people realize it. The preservation enterprise draws public attention to heritage in part because of this presumption, often framing heritage as a victim in danger and need of stewardship, as discussed in chapter 2. Such activism and rhetoric serve as critical means of mobilizing communities and leveraging government and private-sector action, and some argue that historic preservation is one of the last remaining community-driven tools in a U.S. land use planning toolbox that is largely bureaucratized.[97] But in recursively emphasizing the need to raise awareness about the value and benefits of heritage among broader populations, preservationists may also be seeking to educate the masses and get others to appreciate, and thus define, heritage *like they do.* This raises concerns about whether heritage advocates and practitioners seek to convince others to share/ascribe to their values or to enable a pluralistic process by which diverse publics can use or instrumentalize what they view as heritage to work out and realize their own values.

This attitude of needing to educate and convince others evokes a degree of paternalism, which can hinder the development of more robust participatory policies. It suggests that publics cannot fully engage in heritage decision-making because they do not (yet) understand how important heritage is or why it warrants investment. Per Sherry Arnstein's seminal ladder of citizen participation, such attitudes can engender "manipulation" and "therapy" rather than genuine participation. "Their real objective is not to enable people to participate in planning or conducting programs, but to enable powerholders to 'educate' or 'cure' the participants."[98]

More robust citizen power can be seen in some U.S. municipalities where historic or conservation districts have neighborhood-based committees that undertake design review for modifications within their respective districts. For example, Seattle, Washington, Columbus, Ohio, and Los Angeles, California (through its HPOZs), have policy structures that afford such decentralized and community-based models for district oversight. In San Francisco's more recent cultural districts, "neighborhood-based community groups and their cultural values lead each District's efforts," and community members and municipal staff cowrite a three-year plan to guide action.[99] Co-management of heritage places and coproduction of heritage knowledge reach higher on Arnstein's ladder of citizen participation as forms of "partnership."[100] If these more public-empowered and just forms of participation are to proliferate within heritage policy, it will ultimately require preservation professionals to cede some of their control and reorient toward second-order preservation outcomes.

The discourse and practices of value-driven heritage planning and management over more than three decades sought to advance greater multidisciplinary and nonexpert engagement in decision-making about what to preserve and how. The ICOMOS Australia Burra Charter, which was adopted by the Australian government, served as an important touchstone for acknowledging how diverse values are ascribed to heritage places by different stakeholders or publics. But the intentions of these value-driven methodologies derive from the strategic end goal of conserving the heritage place. Participation is framed such that place, as object, is centered and paramount; planning for and managing the place are guided by how people ascribe interests and values to it—social, religious or spiritual, scientific, economic, and so on. As discussed in previous chapters, this positioning of publics as contextual to the object muddies the social-spatial dynamics that characterize place-based heritage and may veil alternative interventions. In other words, the exercising of people's values is in service to the heritage object through strategic planning that fundamentally limits options. Approaches rooted in scenario planning, which might engender more robust citizen participation and power, and thus more just decision-making, are underexplored.[101]

The second concern worth probing with regard to evangelizing preservation is the overwhelming focus on how preservation benefits people, with limited discussion of how it burdens or excludes people. Like any form of public policy, preservation *benefits* and *burdens,* and neither its benefits nor its burdens are always equitably distributed. Underlining the first-order, affirmative goal of saving the object means less examination of how various publics might be advantaged or disadvantaged by different scenarios of intervention—socially, economically, and/or environmentally—or how trade-offs across a spectrum of alternatives might be negotiated. This links directly to questions of distributive justice, which will be discussed in the following section, but it has procedural justice implications as well. Only advocating, researching, and deliberating about preservation's *benefits* means heritage institutions and professionals are not enabling publics to make informed choices when engaging in heritage decision-making. It's like encouraging people to play soccer by touting the wonderful physical and social benefits of the game but not informing them of the risks of heading the ball or the costs of playing in a league. The predominantly site-by-site nature of community engagement, even if value driven and participatory, can further obscure the systemic socioeconomic and environmental consequences of policy action. This harks back to Iris Marion Young's observation in chapter 1 about how unintended structural consequences can be obfuscated when lots of individuals are focused only on their business and on following the rules.[102] If the heritage enterprise is not actively interrogating and communicating how decisions across publics and geographies aggregate and function, how they fortify policy structurally, then individuals participate with limited knowledge of the broader implications of their respective decisions.

DISTRIBUTIVE JUSTICE

Several years ago, I met with officials from a municipal heritage agency to discuss possible policy research related to preservation's social outcomes. As the conversation progressed, I realized that our respective notions of *whom* government action affects or targets differed. A high-level staffer clarified that the work of the agency focused on the people who owned and lived in historic buildings and districts. This unsettled me. As a form of public policy, preservation intends, presumably, to improve conditions for all. But the first-order priorities of government action mean that target audiences are more often identified in ways that center the heritage place. The policy target audience is de facto socially constructed around the object, rather than understood as a more complex and diverse amalgam of publics with varying interests and rights in the social-spatial dynamics of a place. This influences who has agency or more power in preservation policy deliberations and who may be privileged or not by policy outcomes.[103]

When the preservation discourse pushes beyond these first-order stakeholders, it tends to focus on who experiences or encounters heritage. Although this presumably enlarges the target audience of publics, it still frames heritage in decidedly object-centric ways: who can visit or have access to a site, who can participate in a site's management, or who has the right to preserve or claim heritage. Returning to the soccer analogy, the distributive effects of policy are not simply about who engages directly with the ball. It is about how the broader rules of the game affect everyone: players, team owners, fans, school sports programs, other field users, investors, and all those in communities where the game takes place.

The distributive effects of preservation work, meaning how preservation benefits and burdens different publics, are also sorely underresearched. Following from the first-order premise of "save the place and other benefits will follow," these second-order concerns receive short shrift. The outcomes of heritage designation and investment are not always experienced evenly or positively; they may advantage some and disadvantage others. If and how the preservation enterprise produces knowledge about these benefits and burdens and incorporates it into ongoing policy reform are at the crux of distributive justice.

The aforementioned public policy rationales of municipal ordinances provide insight into the intentions of government action, how policy expects to perform, and thus serve as an important metric for interrogating preservation's outcomes and distributive effects. Social concerns regarding education, public welfare and enjoyment, and civic pride and social cohesion predominate among these policy intentions. Economic purposes likewise serve as prevalent public policy rationales across municipal preservation ordinances, from stabilizing and improving property values to spurring growth and investment to promoting tourism. Environmental aims are less common but no less important in the context of the climate crisis; these are interrogated in the next chapter.

Research about economic benefits preponderates in relation to preservation's distributive effects in the United States. Such analyses monetize the value of heritage and of preservation processes in an effort to demonstrate their benefits to society and individuals and to justify their worth in a market context. The field of cultural economics undergirds this research using a range of methodologies and metrics.[104] Per Rypkema, Cheong, and Mason, typical metrics include property values, job creation, heritage tourism, downtown (commercial) revitalization, and environment measurements.[105]

Property values serve as a core concern in the U.S. preservation enterprise. The U.S. Constitution expressly protects private property rights. And for most Americans, property ownership—specifically homeownership—constitutes their primary means of wealth creation, and the public and private benefits and burdens of listing or designation may be consequential. Although there is not agreement across all the literature, the majority of property value studies find that listing or designation has a neutral to positive effect on property values, with most indicating enhanced price premiums.[106] In 2010, Harvard economist Edward Glaeser, in a study of Manhattan south of Ninety-Sixth Street, estimated that the average price of a mid-size condominium in a historic district rose by $6,000 per year more than those outside a historic district in the period 1980–2002. Glaeser attributed this, in part, to the regulation of new construction in historic districts. Because historic districts have an aesthetic draw for potential residents, there is high demand, but low supply due to the restrictions on larger or higher-density infill buildings.[107]

Most of the property value studies focus on residential properties, with less research delving into the effects on commercial real estate. These findings suggest that designation has a potential value-added effect on private capital; aspects of this public–private dynamic have been examined through impact studies as well. Preservationists point to these residential and nonresidential property value studies as a positive benefit of listing and designation for those who own historic properties. But as Carol M. Rose notes, the value-added evidence makes "an uneasy companion" to preservationists' claims that it does not directly contribute to displacement or gentrification.[108] Logan pushes this interrogation of the "collective entitlements in urban places" further in his analysis of the preservation history of Washington, D.C. The regulatory measures that seek to preserve the form of historic neighborhoods and prevent indiscriminate development are intended as a public good but may ultimately "protect and promote the value of private property."[109]

The counterargument—that designation devalues a property by infringing on property rights—is the subject of important legal cases, mainly *Penn Central v. New York City* (1978) and *St. Bartholomew's Church v. City of New York* (1990).[110] The *Penn Central* case was a legislative milestone in which the rail company challenged the New York City Landmarks Preservation Commission (LPC) for denying a building permit to construct a fifty-five-story office tower atop the landmarked Grand Central Terminal. The suit claimed a "taking" of property without fair compensation and due process because it precluded the company from redeveloping the property for highest and best use and that the landmark designation of the terminal placed a discriminatory burden on Penn Central that was not required of other property owners. Though Penn Central made the claim that the terminal was currently operating at a loss, it could not prove that the terminal, in its physical state at the time, could not produce a reasonable rate of return in the future through improved management or that it met the conditions for economic hardship. Most preservation ordinances afford a hardship provision that allows a property owner to claim an economic hardship exemption with regard to rehabilitation (or demolition) of their historic property. The provision is meant to protect the owner's right to a reasonable return on his property investment and to prevent undue burden with regard to the cost of appropriate rehabilitation measures. Hardship provisions generally stipulate development of a plan to mitigate said burden and outline a range of options (e.g., tax exemptions, municipal loans, code waivers) in the event that the case for hardship is made.

The U.S. Supreme Court sided with the LPC, arguing that, in the case of landmarks, a reasonable rate of return does not necessarily hinge on highest and best use.[111] In the case of landmark designation, a property has been singled out for a reason; it is "special" because of the value—architectural, cultural, historical, and so on—that has been ascribed to the property through public policy. The presumed collective benefit to society that preservation provides is weighed against the individual rights and burdens of the property owner. In the case of Grand Central Terminal, the very public nature of the property as a railroad station worked to its advantage. Its financial success was largely contingent on a significant amount of public investment—in the railroads that terminated there, in the subways that stopped there, and so on. As such, the line between public and private burden, and public and private benefit, becomes rather blurry. As the New York State appellate decision noted,

> The massive and indistinguishable public, governmental, and private contributions to a landmark like Grand Central Terminal are inseparably joint. . . . It is exceedingly difficult but imperative, nevertheless, to sort out the merged ingredients and to assess the rights and responsibilities of owner and society. A fair return is

to be accorded the owner, but society is to receive its due for its share in the making of a once great railroad. The historical, cultural, and architectural resource that remains was neither created solely by the private owner nor solely by the society in which it was permitted to evolve.[112]

The *Penn Central* case continues to serve as an important touchstone in legal debates regarding property rights, and it spurred the transfer of development rights as a compensatory tool in landmarking in New York City, which will be examined further in the next section, on restorative justice.

Preceding *Penn Central,* however, was the aforementioned *Berman v. Parker* case, which redefined the taking of private property for public use and liberalized government power. Examined at the site level and through the lens of *process,* the decision was about empowering a community to improve quality of life by allowing government to claim and redevelop an area deemed "blighted." Pursuant scholarship analyzes the *outcomes* of this decision across time and multiple communities, finding that *Berman* has played a critical role in racial segregation and disparity through its urban renewal and revitalization applications.[113]

It is thus important to consider how the changing nature of individual versus government and collective heritage claims, codified by *Berman* and *Penn Central,* influences the distributive justice effects of preservation across scales and publics. Benefits and costs are accrued by historic property owners as well as by communities writ large. How those benefits and burdens are distributed—across populations and geographies—is likewise significant. The demographics of who owns historic properties or lives in historic districts is thus a critical question. Cross-sectional analyses of local historic districts[114] and National Register properties and districts[115] in New York City find populations that are Whiter, wealthier, and better educated than those in other areas of the city. Conversely, in Los Angeles, HPOZs have a higher percentage of BIPOC residents than the citywide average.[116] Examining differences and patterns is foundational to understanding how the costs and benefits of listing may be advantaging or disadvantaging publics.

National Register listing, for example, means a property owner can potentially access historic tax credits. The 1976 Tax Reform Act aimed to create greater parity with regard to the tax treatment of renovating older buildings and constructing anew. Until that point, real estate practices and tax structures favored replacement of older structures with new buildings. Again, under the premise that preservation provides collective benefits to the public writ large, the 1976 law provided for amortization and accelerated depreciation of renovated historic properties and removed some tax benefits associated with demolition of such properties. In this sense, the policy sought to ease property owners' burdens in maintaining older and historic buildings and to encourage investment in them.

These tax incentives were significantly improved with the passage of the Economic Recovery Tax Act of 1981. It established a 25 percent tax credit (straight line depreciation) for historic income-producing commercial properties and housing. A 15–20 percent credit was established for nonhistoric commercial buildings. Tax credits use a market-based approach to policy to engage the private sector in preserving downtowns, main streets, and urban neighborhoods and can make preservation and rehabilitation more profitable or viable in competitive and noncompetitive real estate markets. The ripple effects of such activities provide a rationale for continued public investment in private capital through the tax credit program. Continued amendments to the law reduced the federal historic credit to its current 20 percent and eliminated the credit for nonhistoric buildings, completing its transformation from a rehabilitation tax credit for *older* and *historic* buildings to just a historic tax credit. Many states have also established a state-level historic tax credit that can piggyback on the federal credit.

Who is able to avail themselves of the credit influences the distributive effects of this policy. Some state tax credit and other tax-reduction programs are available to homeowners (i.e., non-income-producing properties), sometimes targeting census tracts below a certain income threshold to focus support on publics in need, as in the case of New York State. But federal tax credits can be applied only to income-producing properties, and almost half of federal tax credit projects across the lifetime of the program have produced revenue-generating housing.[117]

Although tax credits can be used to offset a property owner's federal income tax liability, many cannot claim the credit because they have an insufficient tax liability or because their adjusted gross income exceeds Internal Revenue Service (IRS) limits.[118] To bypass these barriers, the credits can be "syndicated"—transferred to a third-party corporate investor in exchange for equity that can be used to finance the project in the early stages. The tax credits are essentially "sold" for a percentage on the dollar, meaning that the investor can offset their tax liability at a discount, and the property owner and tax credit investor form a limited partnership or limited liability company that owns or long-term leases the building. Syndication is especially beneficial to not-for-profit organizations that rehabilitate historic properties, as they do not have an income tax liability but can raise upfront project equity through syndication. Because significant overhead costs are incurred in setting up the legal entity and negotiating the financial arrangements, most investors will only syndicate deals with credits totaling more than $1 million—which, at the 20 percent tax credit rate, means that the qualified project costs must exceed $5 million. This may explain in part why tax credit projects have shifted in recent years from smaller rehabilitations to larger-scale revitalization and redevelopment projects.

These tax credits were conceived to ease the burden on historic property owners and incentivize rehabilitation. But syndication has redefined "property owners" as real estate developers and investors, complicating the landscape of who profits from tax credits, which ultimately are lost tax revenue to the government and thus a cost borne by the general populace. Although studies of their aggregated economic impacts have justified the programs based on returns on investment,[119] there is less analysis of community-level effects and how they are distributed. Stephanie Ryberg-Webster and Kelly Kinahan, in particular, have produced an important volume of research interrogating the use and effects of rehabilitation/historic tax credits (RTC), especially in postindustrial cities facing economic decline.[120] But as Kinahan notes, "understanding the full complexity of the relationship between RTC investments and racial, socioeconomic, and housing characteristics remains challenging."[121] Understanding community-level effects requires longitudinal studies that likewise account for the other types of investments and incentives at play in a locale.

Questions of how preservation policy influences neighborhood change over time—whether through tax credits, other forms of investment or incentives, or regulation—are on the whole complicated and underresearched. New studies, such as the National Trust's *Preserving African American Places: Growing Preservation's Potential as a Path for Equity,* explore important questions with regard to preservation and neighborhood change in historically Black neighborhoods.[122] The concerns over the potentially disparate impacts of preservation on marginalized publics, especially Indigenous peoples, Black and Brown peoples, and the economically disadvantaged, are building, but the call to address the potentially unjust distributive effects of preservation is not new, as noted in the compendium *Readings in Historic Preservation* in 1983:

> "Gentrification" is the normal sign of a successful rehabilitation program conventionally considered. . . . To note the problem is not to argue against a historic preservation program, but to consider the probable consequences thereof, and to prepare to deal with them. If nothing is done, those concerned with historic preservation should be prepared for the same sort of vigorous resistance that resulted from the minority clearance programs carried out in the name of slum clearance and urban renewal. Dealing with the problem later will not be any easier than facing it directly early in the process.[123]

Policies like the Federal Housing Act of 1954 and the Housing and Community Development Act of 1974, discussed in the previous chapter, codified displacement of marginalized populations as an acceptable, if not desired, outcome of neighborhood regeneration and preservation-oriented economic revitalization. U.S. preservationists have been well aware of this for decades. The aforementioned 1983 compendium dedicated an entire section to "A Major Problem, Often Overlooked: The Effect on the Poor and Minorities."[124] Authors and interviewees laid bare concerns regarding the largely White, middle-class interest in the urban rehabilitation movement:

> Robert Moore, Houston Housing Authority: "The renovation of old urban housing is called 'historic preservation,' but it is displacement."[125]
>
> David Prowler, San Francisco Human Rights Commission: "The big irony of gentrification is that today, in these traditionally poor black neighborhoods, [newcomers] won't rent to blacks. . . . I'm actually beginning to get discrimination cases there."[126]
>
> John P. Collins, Tucson Juvenile Court Judge: "The [Tucson] barrio has been a stable influence in an otherwise highly unstable community. . . . The Mexican-American nuclear family is being destroyed in the name of history—so that history's form will be retained as an empty form with no content."[127]

Arthur P. Zeigler, Pittsburgh History & Landmarks Foundation: "Community self-determination? Not exactly. We are bent on saving these buildings. To that end the Pittsburgh History & Landmarks Foundation, as an organization, pushes and prods, raises and spends funds and imposes on the neighborhood to the extent to which we own property and therefore control it and can present convincing ideas and plans to the residents and owners. But we try hard to be open minded and responsive to what advice the Mexican War Streets Neighborhood Association or individuals in the area offer to us. . . . Within the next few years, the area should be able to determine its own course, to go on its way—and we will then go ours."[128]

Michael deHaven Newsom, Chicago attorney: "The situation might be less obnoxious if preservationists showed some concern for relocation of the blacks, and put as much effort into that endeavor as they put into restoration. . . . A concern for social implications of a restoration project would compel the participation and involvement of blacks presently residing in historic neighborhoods in any preservation activities affecting that neighborhood. . . . Historic preservation work will confront black people who are tired of the things white people have done to them, and preservation activities will therefore have to change."[129]

The extent to which preservation activities have changed in the decades since these words of caution is arguable. One of the principal criticisms, particularly in urban contexts, is its association with displacement and gentrification, as the preceding quotations evidence. Researchers debate whether historic designation and investment cause or correlate to displacement, whether displacement is a consequence of larger market forces, or whether it is just part of a more complex set of factors driving gentrification.[130] As Brian McCabe and Ingrid Ellen conclude in their study of New York City, "on average, neighborhoods that comprise historic districts experience an increase in socioeconomic status relative to other nearby neighborhoods after designation. Some may welcome this result as offering new evidence that historic districts spur investment in neighborhoods. Yet others may view our findings as supporting the charge that the designation of historic districts can lead to gentrification and residential displacement."[131] Studies of multiple communities find that historic designation is but one of several factors regulating the positive physical qualities of neighborhoods that correlate to what Emily Talen refers to as "a pattern of loss of affordability, racial diversity, and economic diversity."[132]

Conversely, scholars are also exploring how historically marginalized communities embrace preservation as a potential tool to prevent displacement and counter neighborhood change.[133] And legal scholars caution how preservation, especially in the designation and management of historic districts (whether professionally directed, self-governed by communities, or both), constitutes a new form of exclusionary zoning when commissions prevent the introduction of low-income housing and not-in-my-backyard development within their borders, thereby privileging the district community over the needs of the larger community.[134]

Given the nuance of preservation policy at municipal levels, neighborhood change and distributive effects may vary significantly across localities. Benefits and burdens can differ, especially when examined at municipal, state, and national levels, and may not be consistent across communities and populations. But that does not preclude potential insights, even if not patterns or correlations, when viewed through the lens of publics.

A fair amount of the academic literature deals with the valuation of cultural resources given their public–private nature, again following object-centric priorities, and how the public–private and intergenerational nature of heritage places complicates their economic effects as *assets*. Heritage sites and historic buildings are not necessarily pure public goods in economic terms; they are generally nonrival but exclusive and can become rival (e.g., during peak visitation seasons). On the private end of the spectrum are those who see heritage places more like club goods and question whether the public provision of heritage sites is warranted, as true market failure has not been demonstrated.[135] On the public end are those who suggest that heritage sites are potentially a "merit good" or a "double public good" because of the combined effect of their market and nonmarket values.[136] Economic research also takes into account intergenerational equity and tends to frame heritage as nonrenewable resources, meaning resources that cannot be recovered or replenished at a rate that exceeds consumption. But people create heritage every day, listing and designating places the world over at increasing rates. These unchecked bequests of places incur burdens and potentially limit options for present and future generations, as well as potential benefits. There is decidedly less research, in economics and other social sciences, regarding the recursive nature of preservation policy and its effects on people so as to limit burdens and make benefits more equitable. A notable exception is Nir Mualam and Rachelle Alterman's insightful study of how private and public heritage interests are negotiated through planning inspection appeal processes in the United Kingdom and how inspectors often valorize protection of architectural and physical attributes (the object) over socioeconomic and proprietary issues, despite policy calling for more balanced consideration.[137] It speaks to how the procedural justice implications discussed in the previous section have potentially inequitable distributive effects.

In response to the long-standing and more contemporary critiques of unjust or uneven social impacts, U.S. heritage organizations and government institutions tend to take a protective stance. The case of the Americans with Disabilities Act of 1990 (ADA) illustrates how preservation institutions sought to underscore the collective social value of the heritage object as equally important to, if not more important than, accessibility. The ADA limited compliance exceptions for historic buildings, and they must meet a "threaten or destroy" standard. The NHPA implements an "adverse affect" standard in Section 106 review, and both the National Trust and the Advisory Council on Historic Preservation, at the time the ADA was under debate, advocated for reducing the stringency of the ADA and thus its impacts on historic buildings by using "adverse effect" instead of "threaten and destroy." Counteradvocates sought to ensure greater equity for those with disabilities, and the Department of Justice agreed that weakening the standard was inconsistent with congressional intent, which prioritized accessibility over historic integrity.[138] It is not unlikely that legislation advancing energy retrofits and climate adaptation, which likewise incurs similar distributive justice concerns, will force the preservation enterprise to cede control over how related impacts to historic properties are assessed and by whom.

Studies commissioned by preservation organizations often seek to counter negative claims and promote the positive outcomes of preservation, and thus protect the status quo. Economics is the primary language of these studies, with most analyzing the affirmative economic impact of preservation activities and revenues generated through construction, tourism, taxes, job creation, and more, using input–output modeling.[139] A growing number of statewide studies, evaluations of the Main Street program, and an eight-state study of the historic corridor of Route 66 assert quite resoundingly that preservation has a net positive effect on local and regional economies, thereby building a strong rationale for public intervention through the host of federal and state tax incentives; state grant, loan, and bond programs; and other local financing and tax-reduction tools.[140]

As noted, however, these studies tend to take advocacy positions, highlighting only positive outcomes and not necessarily examining the full range of costs and benefits incurred by public policy. The distributive effects of public financing of private capital, the cumulative impacts of racial disparities in listing and designation, how the privileges afforded properties on the National Register are disproportionately allocated across publics—these are some of the many ways in which distributive justice can and should be plumbed not merely to examine policy but to inform its ongoing evolution.

Beyond the United States, there are important efforts to measure outcomes and internalize policy evaluation within government agency remits. The United Kingdom is making notable strides through Historic England's Heritage Counts program, compiling data and producing annual and issue-focused reports that explore the economic, social, and environmental impacts of heritage.[141] It also produces a research agenda to facilitate collaboration with academia, the third and private sectors, and other government entities, the aims of which include to "demonstrate the impact of policy and provide evidence of where change is needed."[142] However, professional attitudes are still rife, for example, in how it frames its agenda for research, which asks that proposed projects make clear how they will contribute to a number of outcomes, the first being "the positive effect of the historic environment on society, the economy and individual."[143]

All too often, government preservation agencies and not-for-profit organizations, as well as many scholars, approach research with a priori assumptions about the value of heritage and the positive effects of policy. In doing so, they seek to bolster the status quo of operations rather than to investigate how their work benefits and burdens people, thereby skewing how publics are affected and how they can make informed choices. As many researchers contend, examining the outcomes of preservation policy is challenging and may not produce definitive or consistent results across publics and geographies. But the discourse clearly signals issues that can and should be anticipated in policy decision-making and reform. Policy cannot control the second-order entropy of preservation, but it can purposefully integrate the avoidance of unjust outcomes in its intentions and decision-making processes. Omitting or denying the sometimes inequitable consequences of preservation policy perpetuates injustice and makes the heritage enterprise complicit. As the 1983 volume quoted earlier cautions, "to note the problem is not to argue against a historic preservation program, but to consider the probable consequences thereof, and to prepare to deal with them."

RESTORATIVE JUSTICE

Any discussion of restorative justice should in theory be predicated on a robust understanding of injustice. It is therefore challenging to analyze preservation policy through the lens of restorative justice when other justice implications are still so understudied. Restorative justice is a form of remedy, and it is difficult to remedy a problem that is not yet sufficiently diagnosed. As discussed earlier in this volume, interrogating justice in the preservation enterprise undoubtedly begins with deeply interrogating what places conceal, how histories and practices in the built environment have served to embed exclusion and repeat trauma. But it also involves reckoning with how preservation policy itself has exacerbated and perpetuated those injustices, and how structural change must follow.

The concept of restorative justice derives as a counter or counterpart to punitive justice: rather than, or in addition to, punishing an offender, it seeks to compensate the victim(s), repair harm, and examine drivers of behavior. Within preservation laws and policies, there are long-standing examples of punitive justice, usually taking the form of fines or repairs, and sometimes imprisonment, when someone demolishes, vandalizes, or inappropriately alters a government-protected heritage place. In the United States, most municipalities with preservation ordinances require commissions to approve proposed modifications to a property; owners then receive a certificate of appropriateness or similar approval allowing them to proceed with the proposed work. This framing effectively makes the heritage object a potential victim of indiscriminate modification, along with the property owner who suffered a loss of or damage to property.

The framing of heritage as collectively "owned," and not just a matter of property rights, complicates concepts of both victim and perpetrator. Recent actions by the International Criminal Court (ICC) illustrate how the increasing interlinkage of cultural heritage and human rights, as seen through the Faro Convention, raises important issues for how preservation policy accounts for and activates restorative justice.

In 2016, the ICC convicted Ahmad Al Faqi Al Mahdi for the war crime of attacking cultural property in Timbuktu, Mali, and sentenced him to nine years in prison. He was a member of Ansar Dine, a group that, along with Al-Qaeda in the Islamic Maghreb, took control of Northern Mali in 2012. Al Mahdi led efforts to destroy fourteen sacred mausoleums that are part of the Timbuktu World Heritage site, designated in 1988. The Trial Chamber of the ICC identified three victim groups: the residents of Timbuktu, who were direct victims of the crime; the population of Mali; and the international community.[144] That all of humanity can be victimized by the loss of cultural heritage constituted a significant codification of preservation policy and more specifically how claims to place as heritage extend well beyond concepts of property ownership and geographic proximity (as discussed in chapter 2). The ICC has since issued a Policy on Cultural Heritage, to facilitate jurisprudence in the investigation and prosecution of future cases, noting that "crimes committed against cultural heritage constitute, first and foremost, an attack on a particular group's identity and practices, but in addition, an attack on an essential interest of the entire international community."[145]

In the case of Al Mahdi, the ICC prosecutor emphasized that the historic monuments were irreplaceable and that their destruction constituted an attack against a community and its beliefs. However, between 2013 and 2015, UNESCO sponsored a community-engaged project to reconstruct the mausoleums using traditional construction techniques, casting the effort as a form of restorative justice. In what Alberto Sanchez-Sanchez characterizes as the "Timbuktu Paradox," UNESCO publicly celebrated the reconstruction as the "cultural rebirth of the Timbuktu mausoleums," and a representative of the families that maintain the mausoleums noted that the rebuilding process "connects us back to our saints." Al Mahdi pled guilty to leading the attack before completion of the trial, and Sanchez-Sanchez ponders whether the reconstruction of these monuments might have served as evidence against their claimed irreplaceability. Although this does not lessen the crime itself, part of what distinguishes heritage places from other places is their perceived nonreplicability; this distinction underpins concepts of authenticity and allows the destruction of heritage to be elevated beyond the destruction of other property.[146]

This raises important questions regarding how publics whose heritage has been systematically or purposefully destroyed might collectively reclaim heritage places through reconstruction as a form of restorative justice. In practice, reconstruction is generally more acceptable directly following damage or loss by conflict or disaster and often predicated on documentary evidence, as discussed in the case of Monticello's replicated quarters of enslaved peoples. If such additive approaches were more widely considered as a form of restorative justice, the strict standards of reconstruction might be reimagined, allowing for spatial reclamations by publics whose ability to transfer heritage across generations has been structurally impeded.

The use of additive approaches to claim place as heritage is ubiquitously practiced through the use of historical markers and the erection of monuments and memorials. In lieu of or in addition to preserved buildings and structures, these new interventions and constructions claim a place for narratives, events, and people that the built environment does not effectively represent. But reconstruction must usually meet a higher standard. Professionals view documentary evidence and technical exactitude as safeguards against contrived reproduction, which could somehow misrepresent the past and thus skew social experiences and perceptions. Professional standards make justice not only secondary to the object but dependent on a certain way in which the object is physically and aesthetically presented. Authenticity claims thus trouble reconstruction debates; they suggest that the restorative process cannot heal or repair harm unless formal qualities are true to the original.

Restorative justice marked early preservation policy in the United States through the congressional designation of Civil War battlefields as national military parks. That the first of these, Chickamauga and Chattanooga (1890) and Shiloh (1894), were in the South, followed by Gettysburg (1895) in the North, underscores the way in which preservation policy served reconciliatory intentions. Though previously recognized as national war cemeteries, the claiming of these landscapes as cultural heritage, to recognize not only the people whose lives were lost but the cause for which they died—saving the union—set a profound nation-building precedent for the U.S. preservation enterprise.

Compensatory actions through public policy are also long-standing in U.S. preservation. The previously discussed *Penn Central* case established the transfer of development rights as a means of affording compensation to New York City landmark property owners with unused development rights. An owner with, say, a five-story historic building on a lot zoned for ten stories can sell the unbuilt air rights to a neighboring property. To help preserve historic Broadway theaters from redevelopment, a special Theater Subdistrict was established through zoning to allow owners to transfer air rights within the district. Transfers add square footage to hotels and other commercial redevelopment projects in the Times Square area. Buyers deposit a percentage of the air rights purchase into a special fund that supports theater development through grants. As an added dimension of restorative justice, many grants have focused on diversifying the theater community and training those from publics traditionally underrepresented in its trades.

Paradoxically, restorative justice in preservation policy can also be subtractive, through intentional demolitions and removals. Although averting loss is generally the default position of preservationists, relocation, deconstruction, and destruction represent critical frontiers for policy action, for justice- as well as climate-related reasons. Particularly for those subjugated by exclusionary and offensive representations in public space, subtractive approaches are important for counterclaiming heritage, place, narrative, and power.

First Nations peoples applied a subtractive approach to St. Michael's Indian Residential School in Alert Bay, British Columbia, which was ceremonially demolished. Canada's former residential schools, which operated from the 1880s to the 1990s, removed First Nations children from their families in an effort to assimilate them into the dominant Canadian culture.[147] The schools were scenes of horrible abuses and represent fractured familial ties, the loss of cultural identity, and stripped rights of self-determination. For survivors, demolition was an act of hope and healing. To confront and remember the residential school history, the Assembly of First Nations commissioned Indigenous artists to create markers and offered them to the communities whence children were taken, rather than placing them at the sites of schools.[148] In an act of restorative justice, this shifted spatial power, and with it narrative authority, from the institutions that perpetrated these offenses to the First Nations peoples.

Ridding objects from the landscape is a means through which to refute and dismantle both the physical structures and policy structures of injustice. The Berlin Wall serves as a poignant example of how destruction and preservation coexist in complex ways. After the Wall symbolically fell in 1989, pieces were auctioned by the government, gifted to dignitaries and heads of state, and salvaged by local residents, workers, and entrepreneurs; pieces still fetch considerable sums in the art market. Dismantled sections occupy landscapes and memorials across the globe.[149] Remnants in situ now form part of a formal memorial, or what Leo Schmidt refers to as a "landscape of memory." Their fragmented state compels visitors and new generations to interrogate the unfinished nature of memory-making and reconciliation.[150]

Across the United States, municipalities are removing monuments and statuary dedicated to White supremacists and other controversial figures, some of which were designated as landmarks or part of historic properties. Reimagining spaces to confront long-standing exclusion in the public sphere is an important means of not only renarrating history but reconciling how preservation policy has been complicit in perpetuating these spatial injustices. In Alabama, for example, in part to prevent the removal of Confederate monuments, the state legislature passed the Alabama Memorial Preservation Act of 2017, which "prohibits the relocation, removal, alteration, renaming, or other disturbance of any monument located on public property which has been in place for 40 years or more."[151]

But injustice in the historic built environment is not limited to monuments and statues. Architecture itself can be exclusionary, representing legacies of trauma and inhumanity, as in the case of the Canadian First Nations residential school. In the United States, the Federal Indian Boarding School Initiative was announced by secretary of the interior Deb Haaland in 2021. It seeks to research the problematic legacy of government-sponsored institutions that separated Native American children from their families and communities and spurred intergenerational trauma. A National Historic Landmark context study commissioned by the NPS is already under way to identify boarding school properties across the country and to update the documentation on four schools that are already National Historic Landmarks and one that is under nomination. Whether this preservation-focused study will engage with a range of potential scenarios for restorative justice in relation to this heritage—beyond the representational approach of National Historic Landmark listing—remains to be seen.

Occupied buildings and land are more problematic than statuary in public spaces, in the same way that their social-spatial dynamics complicate our claims to heritage places. But it is not beyond possibility that government preservation institutions will be confronted with issues of divestment or reclamation on the horizon. In the United States, many who oppose statue removal, for example, argue that reinterpretation, using signage and QR codes, could recontextualize controversial monuments. But the counterargument hinges on the reclamation of place and space as a means of restorative justice. Controversial government-owned properties, such as parks that forcibly removed Native Americans or plantations built by and perpetuated through the exploitation of enslaved people, are undertaking significant programs of reinterpretation to represent long-excluded publics in their narratives. Simply acknowledging and interpreting past wrongs may not be the only response or effectively redress social and spatial injustice.

There could likewise be calls to consider delisting or dedesignation so that structures and sites with problematic histories are not privileged or protected by preservation policy. At present, delisting is rarely used and mainly hinges on the failure of a heritage place to continue to perform aesthetically or formally; for example, it has been demolished or significantly altered. As of June 2022, the National Register included more than ninety-seven thousand properties, which constitute an estimated 1.4 million resources (a "property" can be an individual building or a complex or historic district made up of multiple buildings, which helps explain the disparity). To date, only twenty-three hundred properties have been removed from the National Register.[152] Of the more than eleven hundred World Heritage sites, only three have been delisted.

Such provocations suggest that the work of interrogating questions of structural justice in preservation policy is only beginning. Anticipating these polemics on the horizon is a critical gateway to actively examining how the preservation enterprise manages the duality of benefits and burdens and reforms policy toward justice.

4

Environmental Consequences

> If we fail to act soon, we will face an economic, social, and political crisis that will threaten our free institutions.
>
> —President Carter in his energy address to Congress,
> April 18, 1977

The preservation enterprise has a long history of victimizing and valorizing heritage in relation to environmental concerns. Chapter 2 discussed some of the fundamental linkages between cultural heritage and the concept of nature in the establishment of U.S. preservation policy and how wilderness-as-heritage helped to rationalize racism and land dispossession but, at the same time, enabled the protection of vast swaths of cultural landscapes through the creation of national parks and through monuments subsequently designated under the Antiquities Act. A century later, the oil crisis of the 1970s forged a new interplay between preservation and environmental conservation on the basis of energy and birthed the claims that older and historic buildings are inherently green. Preservationists capitalized on this energy-focused government action to advance policy in support of historic buildings. A now iconic 1980 poster produced by the National Trust morphed the images of an old building and a gasoline can, with the caption "It takes energy to construct a new building. It saves energy to preserve an old one." This assertion forged an indelible rhetoric in the U.S. preservation discourse, influencing the evolution of both the historic tax credits and the Secretary of the Interior's Standards.

During this same period, Congress started to appropriate monies to the Historic Preservation Fund (HPF), which was established through the NHPA to provide government grants and matching funds to SHPOs/THPOs and CLGs. Although Congress authorized $150 million per year, actual annual allocations vary, ranging from less than $20 million in 1977 to more than $118 million in 2020. Tax dollars do not finance the HPF; paradoxically, it is funded through the extraction of fossil fuels, namely, offshore oil and gas leasing.[1] This establishes a rather troubling dynamic between the U.S. preservation enterprise and climate change, muddying questions of accountability and victimization.

The positive energy benefits of reusing old buildings reemerged with new dynamism as the climate crisis evolved. Preservationists resuscitated energy arguments and attempted new, though limited, research on the avoided environmental impacts of rehabilitation versus new construction.[2] These renewed claims sought to position preservation as a means of climate mitigation. Mitigation fundamentally involves reducing and stabilizing greenhouse gas emissions—mostly carbon dioxide (carbon)—to avoid temperature overshoot and increasing carbon sinks, like forests and soil, which help to store these gases. Reduced energy consumption in the built environment, which is still chiefly dependent on fossil fuels, and/or transition to renewable energy results in less carbon emission.

In climate policy and discourse, the counterpart to mitigation is adaptation. It focuses on preparing and protecting people and places from the effects of climate change that are already under way, including the intensifying severity and frequency of flooding and storm surges, droughts and wildfires, and temperature extremes. There is a growing discourse around the intersection of preservation and adaptation. Calls for and proposed methods of assessing climate risk also characterize the body of literature, and philanthropic organizations and government institutions increasingly frame climate change as a threat to heritage places. The World Heritage Centre, ICCROM, and ICOMOS have undertaken numerous studies regarding climate-related risks. Preservation actors have mobilized advocacy efforts at the international level, for example, through the Climate Heritage Network, to ensure a place for cultural heritage and associated publics in climate action through more people-centered policymaking. These are significant efforts, focusing on how the loss of heritage places can fracture communities and prevent the freedom to transfer heritage across generations. This discourse dominates within the preservation enterprise, largely characterizing heritage—and those associated with it—as a victim of climate change. Policy dialogue and action that deeply examine how the climate crisis compels preservation policy reform, to meet these challenges, are less developed.[3]

The preservation enterprise is also asserting the role of heritage in

community resilience, thereby rationalizing the need for more government investment in protecting heritage places and communities
from climate impacts and supporting their recovery after severe climate events.[4] This emerging discourse acknowledges the significant
inequalities between the Global North and Global South that climate
impacts are exacerbating and how cumulative histories of carbon by
wealthier, highly industrialized countries place unjust burdens on less
industrialized countries, which did not substantially cause the crisis.
The United States, Canada, Japan, and much of Western Europe are
responsible for half of all the carbon emitted over the past 170 years
but constitute only 12 percent of the world's population.[5]

These inequities are further exacerbated by urban–rural disparities. Global urban population has quadrupled in the past half century,
and cities generate 70 percent of global carbon emissions.[6] In 2021,
UNESCO, ICOMOS, and the IPCC cosponsored efforts to advance
dialogue and knowledge about the role and importance of heritage
in climate action. The meetings and resulting reports had a decidedly
nonurban and anthropological bent, highlighting cultural landscapes,
traditional settlements, vernacular construction, and local knowledge.[7] The effort focused much-needed attention on the vulnerability
of these "heritage communities" and the injustice inherent in the climate burdens they bear due to the actions of industrialized nations.
The proceedings likewise championed the participatory role of local
publics in decision-making and how their diverse and time-tested
knowledge can inform adaptation and mitigation strategies.

This is vital work, important to ensuring justice in climate action.
However, in avoiding urban contexts, it allowed preservationists once
again to frame heritage in an almost exclusively positive light, emphasizing the benefits of heritage and characterizing burdens as the negative climate impacts experienced by heritage places and communities.
In examining the intersection of heritage and climate, there was little
interrogation of how preservation policies, especially in egregious
urban contexts, may be contributing to climate change and imped-
ing more just and effective mitigation and adaptation. Nor were the
complex challenges of mediating diverse, and often competing, public
concepts and practices of heritage in highly plural contexts like cities
addressed. More than 50 percent of people worldwide live in urban
areas, and that percentage is increasing due to both rural–urban migration and higher urban birthrates. Ninety percent of cities are coastal

and so at risk of rising sea levels and more severe storm surges.[8] In their 2011 publication *The City as Fulcrum of Global Sustainability,* Ernest Yanarella and Richard Levine proffer that grappling with economic, environmental, and social issues at the city-region level is the only way sustainability can be successfully undertaken. Though very normative in their approach, they make a compelling argument for why the city-region has the potential to be fertile ground for innovation:

> Our times are experiencing multiple crises on a variety of geographic scales that call for serious reconsideration and reevaluation of foundational values, social and economic institutions, political practices and visions of the good life and the good society. Such an era also calls for a serious rethinking of society's relationship with a natural world that is deeply implicated with the society and its built environment and in some ineliminable sense separate from it.[9]

Like the preservation enterprise's orientation toward justice, the first-order priorities of centering heritage-as-object in climate action has consequences. Preservation policy fundamentally seeks to privilege heritage places in relation to the rest of the built environment, affording protection from market forces, regulatory review, code exemptions, and incentives for conservation and rehabilitation. Both climate mitigation and adaptation require wholesale shifts in how the built environment is designed, constructed, and managed. In the same way that heritage cannot be divorced from the social-spatial dynamics of place and people, it cannot be disassociated from the climate-driven shifts in building and land use policies. It is important to plumb how the privileging of heritage, historically embedded and repeated in policy structures, and the first-order emphasis on preserving form and aesthetics may exacerbate existing injustices and create new ones.

This chapter examines key areas of climate action that involve the built environment—adaptation and migration; density, land use, and energy geographies; circular economies; and decarbonization—and situates the preservation enterprise within these evolving policies and practices to understand critical second-order dynamics. In contextualizing, rather than isolating, heritage intentions, I interrogate how preservation policy may contribute to and work against sustainability goals. In particular, I focus on how the climate vulnerability of publics is socially constructed, how preservation benefits and burdens may exacerbate vulnerability disparities, and how preservation policies influence more sustainable resource and land use.

ADAPTATION AND MIGRATION

A great deal of adaptation policy is dedicated to improving the resilience of communities in anticipation of more severe and frequent precipitation and storm surges, as well as rising sea levels, with decidedly less focus on fire, drought, and other climatic events. More than one-third of the global population, nearly 2.4 billion people, lives within sixty miles of an oceanic coast.[10] New calculations that incorporate sea level rise, rainfall, and flooding along smaller waterways estimate that more than 14 million properties in the United States are at risk from a hundred-year flood, with more risk being borne by minority and lower-income communities.[11] Similar research shows that 686,000 properties nationwide face a similar (1 percent) risk to fire, but warming conditions will increase that risk to 26 percent over thirty years.[12]

Universities and other research centers are cooperating in the collection of environmental data, to monitor trends and patterns and to better predict future conditions as well as identify vulnerabilities. Government-focused disaster preparedness and response programs are integrating climatic extremes and weather events into their scopes. States and municipalities are surveying their physical landscapes to identify areas of risk and develop strategies for preventing damage and destruction and to plan for change. As defined by the National Institute of Standards and Technology, "community resilience is the ability to prepare for anticipated hazards, adapt to changing conditions, and withstand and recover rapidly from disruptions."[13] Thus the primary outcomes of all of these adaptation-oriented initiatives are geared toward more responsive strategies for managing the built environment and protecting critical infrastructure (in addition to life and limb) in the face of climate events.

Central to these efforts are a host of indices and indicators for measuring risk and vulnerability, in terms of both geography and publics.[14] In the United States, regularized federal flood maps resulted from the National Flood Insurance Act of 1968, which sought to standardize the rules of the game in determining which properties were in flood zones and at risk and thus eligible for federally backed insurance.[15] The

U.S. Forest Service more recently began to map wildfire risk, particularly at wildfire–urban interfaces (WUI).[16] The Federal Emergency Management Agency (FEMA) in the last few years developed a Resilience Analysis and Planning Tool (RAPT), which aggregates a host of community resilience indicators from a broad body of literature and geospatializes risks to assist local governments in their climate planning.[17] It combines key population and community characteristics, infrastructure data, and hazard data to identify particularly vulnerable populations and geographies. There are more than twenty indicators in the RAPT tool, ranging from demographic attributes (such as single-parent households, people with disabilities, and limited-English-speaking people) to the presence of social institutions and houses of worship to the boundaries of flood and fire hazard zones.

These data support planning efforts to improve resilience, but they label publics and places, identifying those that are least resilient through gradient maps. They provide no longitudinal insight into how and why these people and places are made vulnerable. It is altogether possible that these data will be used much like flood hazard maps and have similar consequences, whereby those in areas of higher risk face decreases in property values and higher insurance rates.[18] This echoes the practices of government-endorsed redlining in U.S. cities that sought to reduce mortgage risks but effectively devalued areas populated largely by immigrants, people of color, and low-income publics, curtailing their opportunities to build wealth through property ownership. Across the United States, these disadvantaged communities, through exclusionary real estate and land use planning practices, were disproportionately relegated to land that is less desirable for construction and so already vulnerable.[19]

Similar to the ways in which urban renewal and revitalization hinged on government determinations of blight and slums, without historical reflection, the climate crisis raises the specter of repeating exclusionary policies that reinforce historical traumas and biases. As Tom Slater notes, "resilience pushes the emphasis back onto the victim as opposed to addressing issues of causation and questions of social (in)justice."[20] He goes on to cite Malini Ranganathan and Eve Bratman's observation that it privileges " 'climate proofing' the future, rather than ongoing and historical cause of harm."[21]

Andy Horowitz's account of Hurricane Katrina in New Orleans eloquently plumbs how, over the course of a century, seemingly positive decisions about land use, infrastructure, and community development created the historical conditions for the devastation and its disproportionate effects on marginalized publics:

> Disasters are less discrete events than they are contingent processes. Seemingly acute incidents . . . live on as the lessons they teach, the decisions they prompt, and the accommodations they oblige. Their causes and consequences stretch across much longer periods of time and space than we commonly imagine. Seeing disasters in history, and as history, demonstrates that the places we live, and the disasters that imperil them, are at once artifacts of state policy, cultural imagination, economic order, and environmental possibility.[22]

As Horowitz argues, the story did not start when the levees broke. Vulnerability was socially constructed over decades, and not just in New Orleans. The potentially disparate effects of climate change on diverse publics is the subject of equitable resilience, which seeks to account for "social vulnerability and differential access to power, knowledge, and resources," but it does not necessarily address structural injustice and its historical underpinnings.[23] Chapter 3 discussed some of the ways in which the preservation enterprise has been complicit in reproducing injustice by centering the heritage object and privileging publics and places that reflect Whiteness and wealth. Climate vulnerability adds a new layer of concern and complication to this policy foundation.

Because of the value it places on the object in context, the preservation enterprise tends to advocate more for in situ climate adaptation than relocation, and interventions range from building to site to community and district levels. For example, flood mitigation could take the form of elevating a building or retrofitting a basement to create a flood vent or cistern. The bulk of preservation guidance is at the building level, providing property owners with suggested options for minimizing impacts on historic fabric. The NPS published new Guidelines for Flood Adaptation in 2021 to supplement the Secretary of the Interior's Standards,[24] and preservation agencies in coastal states and municipalities are increasingly developing handbooks and design manuals for historic property owners.[25]

Climate-driven interventions compel new conversations about the issue of material integrity, as property owners face increasingly limited

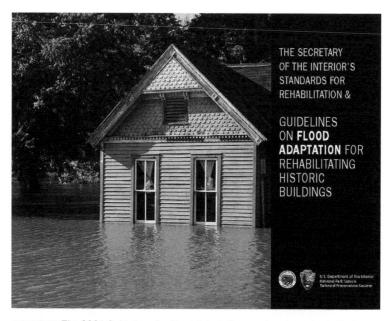

THE SECRETARY
OF THE INTERIOR'S
STANDARDS FOR
REHABILITATION &

GUIDELINES
ON **FLOOD
ADAPTATION** FOR
REHABILITATING
HISTORIC
BUILDINGS

U.S. Department of the Interior
National Park Service
Technical Preservation Services

FIGURE 16. The 2021 Guidelines for Flood Adaptation mark an important effort on the part of the NPS to address the effects of climate change on historic buildings. The dramatic environmental changes on the horizon compel significant investment in approaches that move beyond heritage-as-object and address the social-spatial implications of community-level adaptation and relocation.

options for preserving original form and fabric in the face of severe weather events. Whether those debates will extend beyond climate responses to confront the social justice implications of material integrity writ large has yet to be seen. But it certainly opens up new possibilities for challenging the potentially disparate application and effects of object-focused standards.

Site- and district-level interventions might include constructing flood berms around a property to control the influx of water or a seawall around a neighborhood to mitigate the impact of storm surges. Equity challenges pervade this decision-making, as diverting water from one locale (for example, with a seawall) can simply exacerbate flooding conditions for a nearby locale. This troubles questions already evoked by preservation regarding individual property rights versus collective claims to place. Historic streetscapes and districts rely heavily on aesthetic rationales of formal continuity in the design review of proposed interventions.[26] Problems like lollipopping—when some neighbors flood-elevate their buildings and others do not—complicate the interplay of individual property rights and standards of rehabilitation when aggregated to a multisite scale. As governments take decisions about where they will provide public assistance in adaptation, the triage process may prioritize historic districts because of their perceived collective value, legitimized by municipal designation or National Register listing.[27] Publics and their demographics cannot be ignored in such decisions, as this does not simply save important architecture; it privileges the owners and occupants of those properties.

The prioritizing of historic places likewise raises issues of infrastructure lock-in. The climate crisis will oblige new, adaptive patterns of land use and construction in the built environment. In valorizing historical forms and land use arrangements, the preservation enterprise is essentially trying to make the future conform to the past.[28] This may inhibit the speed and effectiveness of adaptation efforts and complicate debates regarding adapting in situ versus relocating.

In postdisaster situations, designation and listing can also work to the advantage of recovery and rebuilding for some.[29] One of the interesting take-away lessons from Hurricane Katrina for the preservation community was that many of the older homes and buildings throughout New Orleans could have been eligible for the National Register, but nominations and determinations of eligibility were never pursued. In some cases, buildings were listed locally, but not on the National Register. As a result, when federal monies supported redevelopment in the recovery process, preservation advocates could not invoke Section 106 review to protect these older structures from demolition or the adverse impacts of the redevelopment process. More sources of funding are available to owners of historic properties as opposed to nonhistoric properties, and historic property owners often have the added support and technical assistance of government agencies. Demographics again play an important role, for example, if historic districts in a locale are Whiter or wealthier. Research on the inequitable effects of FEMA funding demonstrates that White recipients of postdisaster funds tend to benefit financially, whereas Black, Latino/a, and Asian recipients experience a financial decline. In short, the distribution of federal assistance is exacerbating wealth inequality.[30] While FEMA is committed to rectifying these inequities in its procedures, it does not negate the historical harms that accrue. If the demographics of historic properties and districts in a locality lean Whiter and wealthier, it complicates inequalities further.

Some argue that historic districts may easily fall victim to climate gentrification. Designation may inherently valorize places that have stood the test of time and proven to be resilient. Historically, significant investment in architectural design and construction went hand in hand with siting on prime, buildable land.[31] This raises risks of displacement if and when, for example, real estate markets are squeezed in flood-prone places and wealthier inhabitants look for higher ground. This phenomenon of climate gentrification is already occurring in parts of Florida, largely affecting communities of color.[32] Place attachment might also cause publics to remain and reinvest in highly vulnerable geographies after disasters because of the values that have been ascribed and reinforced through preservation policy and action.[33] When property owners are in disagreement, for example, some want to rebuild whereas others want to retreat, or the uneven damage to properties precludes wholesale recovery, these publics and places are made even more vulnerable through potential population and infrastructure loss.

Climate-induced migration and displacement are and will continue to be significant challenges well beyond the competition for better land, as legal scholar Robin Bronen notes:

> In the United States, nearly 40% of the population lives in low-elevation coastal communities that continue to experience growth and development. Currently, sea level rise is causing a significant increase—anywhere from 300% to more than 900% since 1970—in the number of days when these communities are inundated with "sunny day" flooding caused by high tides, not storm surges. This type of flooding disrupts and damages coastal infrastructure, including homes, important transportation links, and storm and wastewater systems. As a result, without protective measures, as many as 13 million people could face permanent inundation and displacement.[34]

Whether forced or community led, the specter of relocation fundamentally troubles the social-spatial dynamics that define heritage places, and the preservation enterprise has yet to fully confront its position and agency in relation to it. It is not simply an object-focused question of whether a building can or should be moved or how the preservation enterprise confronts its aversion to loss.[35] The emerging concept of "adaptive release," which Caitlin DeSilvey and colleagues describe as "an active decision to accommodate and interpret the dynamic transformation of a heritage asset and its associated values and significance," serves as a compelling pathway for reimaging heritage adaptation in the face of climate change.[36] But this is about more than the loss or transformation of the heritage object or how the values people ascribe to it must evolve; it's about a fundamental fracturing of people and place.

Bronen reminds us that forced migration and resettlement is part of a pattern of repeated trauma for Native Americans, Alaska Native communities, and African Americans. These publics have been on the front line of climate vulnerability and forced relocation for decades. Recent announcements by the Biden administration to support the voluntary community-driven relocation of Tribal communities severely impacted by climate marks a watershed moment, and many hope that it signals more active leadership on the part of the federal government to coordinate climate-induced relocation while also addressing the systemic injustice that has characterized government action to date.[37] How displaced communities emplace elsewhere raises important questions for the heritage enterprise. If preservation professionals are not simply experts on the objects but experts in interrogating how social-spatial dynamics characterize heritage places and publics, what might be their potential role in mitigating the negative effects of relocation? How might they support displaced communities to claim space and reconstruct dimensions of those dynamics in new locales, particularly where new and existing communities are coming together? Negotiating these transforming place-based identities, not just transforming heritage objects, will be important considerations as climate increasingly compels migration.[38]

LAND USE AND DENSITY

Land consumption in urban areas worldwide is expanding at twice the rate of their populations.[39] The growth in per capita land consumption may in part be due to growth in per capita built square footage. In 1950, average residential floor space in the United States was 297 square feet per person; by 2000, it was 840 square feet per person.[40] And per capita retail space in the United States grew from four square feet in 1960 to thirty-eight square feet in 2005.[41] Increases in built-up and developed land can contribute to land degradation, diminish the areas of forests and soil that serve as carbon sinks, and compete with other land uses, such as agriculture and renewable energy generation.[42]

Density, as defined by people per square mile or kilometer, has significant benefits to reducing climate emissions and preserving land, especially greenfields. Denser urban neighborhoods are generally closer to downtowns or city centers, which can correlate to better access to public transit and less driving. Homes in denser geographies tend to be smaller, requiring less operational energy (though heat island effects can be an issue in many urban areas due to intersecting factors).[43] It is precisely because metropolitan areas are such egregious carbon emitters that urban land consumption and density are such critical areas of action, because more compact/less sprawling urban development is associated with lower carbon emissions in urban residential and transportation sectors.[44]

Research shows that infill development, which could bolster density and concentrate built-up land in urban areas, is underutilized; cities are mostly expanding outward. And this is complicated by the fact that, even prepandemic, the majority of Americans prefer single-family detached homes and large lots.[45] The housing and climate crisis compound the need for the densification of urban and suburban areas, and new legislation in U.S. states and municipalities is promoting this through incentivized low- and mid-scale infill development, accessory dwelling units (ADUs), and the elimination of single-family zoning. However, complex zoning laws across municipalities mean that localized issues around density are diverse, and effects are understudied. Sara C. Bronin's work on the *National Zoning Atlas* highlights the need for both concerted research and greater transparency in zoning regulations and how they affect communities.[46]

Preservation policies and attitudes can complicate these densification shifts. There are long-standing assertions regarding the positive role preservation can play in smart growth and preventing sprawl. David Listokin, in particular, noted the opportunities and challenges of policy advancement in the cases of Oregon and Florida. Wisconsin's 1999 Smart Growth legislation incorporated cultural resources in its comprehensive state planning, resulting in its *Guide to Smart Growth and Cultural Resource Planning.* Research like Daniel Bluestone's examination of the low-rise density achieved through Chicago's courtyard apartments demonstrates how historical inquiry can both rationalize preservation and assert an evidentiary basis for adapted forms of dense development.[47] Historically, there has been limited traction in the U.S. preservation enterprise around urban densification efforts, as engaging in the growth management discourse can mean embracing policies that potentially increase new development in historic areas.[48] This stands in contrast to the public policy rationales in U.S. preservation ordinances, as 27 percent underscore the role of preservation policy in managing urban growth and sustainable development.

Preservationists tend to focus on formal density, rather than population density, seeking to prevent out-of-scale development in historic neighborhoods. There is limited quantitative research demonstrating that low-scale buildings in urban historic districts equate to low population density, or conversely that new, tall buildings always create high population density. A study of Seattle, San Francisco, and Washington, D.C., by the National Trust Preservation Green Lab found that areas with a mix of new and old buildings had higher population densities than those with new buildings. And a study of New York City historic districts found that they had slightly higher population densities than similar, undesignated areas.[49] While such findings bode well for preservation, conflicting assertions and limited studies underscore the need for more and better data about urban historic districts and densities, particularly when land use tools—like upzoning—are involved.

New studies emerging from the United Kingdom and elsewhere in Europe suggest that densifying historic built environments is gaining traction, and preservationists in a number of U.S. localities are embracing densification, particularly as a means of promoting affordable housing.[50] Existing urban form and neighborhood character can significantly influence preservation positions. For example, adding new high-rise developments to a medium-rise historic center may be viewed as incompatible, while allowing ADUs in a single-family historic district may be viewed as an acceptable compromise that maintains neighborhood scale. The latter, however, is not without tensions, as there are also efforts on the part of preservationists to preserve single-family historic suburbs, despite their unsustainable land use and exclusionary history. Sustainability advocates and planners grapple with ways to densify suburbs and reduce sprawl, as well as reduce the long-standing injustices and racial segregation associated with the development of post–World War II U.S. suburbs. But suburban neighborhoods are a growing typology on the National Register as preservationists increasingly recognize and protect these developments as historic resources, using NPS-prepared guidance.[51]

Minneapolis, Minnesota, was the first major U.S. city to abolish single-family zoning and has allowed ADUs for years, but their promise has yet to be realized, as Jacque Randolph notes:

> Accessory dwelling units are an admittedly attractive solution to segregationist housing practices: they represent community-centered neighborhoods and allow proponents to reclaim the term "higher-density" living from its exclusionary history. However, there is continued opposition from more suburban neighborhoods seeking to maintain housing and resident aesthetics, primarily through ordinances regulating lot sizes, renter requirements, and even nitpicky decorative styles.[52]

Tensions are further exacerbated when the protection of low-rise historic centers plays a role in pushing development into open spaces beyond urban cores or when the transfer of development rights from landmarks to neighboring properties results in high rises looming over historic structures.[53] To engage more effectively in sustainable land use planning, preservationists need to better understand the extent to which preserving older buildings at low formal densities in the urban core or in historic suburbs may contribute to overall lower density development and sprawl and perpetuate exclusionary land use practices.

In my experience directing the World Monuments Watch, it was evident that cities with lower-density older buildings remain a battleground between preservation and growth, characterizing a repeating pattern of density versus preservation tensions. In Buenos Aires, Argentina, the 3.8-square-mile historic center is a vibrant hub of public, religious, cultural, and political activities; it includes approximately one hundred National Historic Monuments and an additional eight hundred listed historic properties. In 2007, the secretary of culture identified another twelve hundred buildings as having heritage value but provided no protection from alteration or demolition. Growth has fueled the demolition of many of the low-scale historic buildings in favor of more high-density replacements, the rationale being that the historic center of Buenos Aires should be a vibrant and growing hub of economic and political activity.

Kyoto is one of the few Japanese cities that survived World War II with limited damage. Heritage protections have been in place for decades in the areas surrounding listed monuments, and the city has been lauded for retaining its historic street pattern and buildings.[54] However, the traditional townhouses—or *machiya*—of Kyoto were included on the World Monuments Watch in both 2010 and 2012. These Edo period (1603–1867) structures originally functioned as both residences and workspaces; they incorporated interior gardens and fostered a culture that integrated urban living and commerce. However, as growth in the city intensified and planning policy separated commercial and residential uses, many *machiya* were demolished in favor of high-rise/high-density development; their surviving distribution across the city precluded the identification of a particular district that might be protected through typical preservation policy.

But even when effective legislation is in place to preserve large swaths of historic cities, problems ensue, as illustrated by World Monuments Watch sites in Spain. The World Heritage City of Avila has a designated core, bounded by its medieval ramparts. With protections in place for the historic center, new development instead has spread into the surrounding greenfields, increasing sprawl and land consumption. Heritage advocates protested the outlying low-density development, which was in many cases directly adjacent to the historic ramparts and destroyed view sheds. The negative impact on historic view sheds likewise rallied opposition to the construction of an office tower outside of the historic core of Sevilla. It became a cause célèbre for the World Heritage Committee, which voiced strong opposition and threatened to remove Sevilla's World Heritage status should the project proceed further. In both cases, development occurred *outside* the regulatory boundaries of the historic core, and in both Avila and Sevilla, preservationists argued the negative visual and aesthetic impact on the heritage resources.

The extent to which preservation regulations may contribute to pushing development outside historic city centers is underresearched but a worthy inquiry. Because of the first-order emphasis on the formal qualities of historic places, there is little interrogation of the second-order effects of designation and design review on broader patterns of land use and densification or the social and environmental consequences of thwarting development in historic cores.

ENERGY GEOGRAPHIES

Land use, heritage, and view shed concerns likewise characterize debates regarding the development of energy geographies, such as wind and solar farms, and hydroelectricity projects. Mitigation of climate change requires the large-scale reduction of fossil fuels and energy transitions to all-electric, or nearly all-electric, pathways in the building sector. This in turn requires significant investment in renewable energy generation. Mara Goff Prentiss provides a thorough examination of how development of the renewable energy sector is part of a long history of energy transitions and analyzes how various renewables influence land use and potentially meet energy demand in the United States.[55] Given their output potential and land availability in the United States, it is no doubt that wind and solar will continue to play a crucial role in the renewable energy sector (hydroelectricity, for example, could not alone meet the energy requirements of the United States) and in decarbonizing the power grid.

Heritage positions and policies nonetheless complicate the development and expansion of such renewable energy geographies, as energy farms require vast areas of open space (though building roofs can be used for solar), some degree of proximity to end users to ensure efficient transmission, and optimized locations with regard to wind and sun. This potentially impacts view sheds, damages natural resources, and disturbs cultural landscapes, creating community backlash. As Ted Nordhaus and Michael Shellenberger observe:

> landscapes, human and nonhuman, are always changing and evolving. When people describe something, whether it's new housing or a wind farm, as inappropriate to a particular place, what they are really saying is that it is inappropriate to a particular idea of that place.[56]

David A. Lewis provides a comprehensive analysis of some of the seemingly common aims of historic preservation and renewable energy generation in the United States, as well as the challenges created by historic preservation interests. He concludes that procedural reviews and existing legislation fail to effectively assess the relative public benefits of each and to resolve conflicts, and he calls for much-needed policy reform.[57] At the core of these debates are the typical visual and aesthetic concerns of the preservation enterprise, which opposes their perceived negative impact on the view sheds and experiences of proximate heritage places and/or the degradation of resources when such geographies are claimed as cultural landscapes themselves. And environmental conservationists have also been allies in some of this activism.

Several high-profile cases illustrate the tensions between these energy geographies and preservation policy. Cape Wind was a wind farm proposed for development off the eastern seaboard of the United States, near Cape Cod, Nantucket, and Martha's Vineyard. The proposal included the construction of 130 wind turbines across twenty-four square miles of Horseshoe Shoal. Despite the fact that it was an important clean energy project, Robert Kennedy, one of the country's renowned environmentalists and an attorney with the Natural Resources Defense Council, came out against it, noting a number of potential environmental hazards, from birds being killed in the turbines to impacts on fishing. (It should also be noted that Cape Wind would have been visible from Kennedy-owned properties nearby.) Indeed, many of its strongest opponents were moneyed families with compounds along the coast, while many local year-round residents were defenders of the project.[58]

The project went through nine years of review and challenges. Historic preservation groups opposed the wind farm and joined forces with Tribal communities with ancestral claims to the land, and the stretch of water was designated as a cultural landscape eligible for the National Register in an effort to thwart construction. This incurred Section 106 review, and in 2010, the Advisory Council on Historic Preservation (ACHP) recommended that secretary of the interior Ken Salazar deny or relocate the project because of the adverse impact on the view shed of thirty-four historic homes, the sunrise vista for the Mashpee Wampanoag Tribe and the Wampanoag Tribe of Gay Head. In late April 2010, however, Secretary Salazar approved the project and negotiated a large financial settlement with the Tribes, paid by Cape Wind and the state. Political and financial battles ensued, and the project was finally abandoned in 2017.

The Mojave Desert has long been a target area for wind and solar projects, some of which have been scuttled by a combination of congressional legislation, led by Senator Dianne Feinstein, and designation of the Mojave Trails National Monument, a portion of the desert in California, by President Barack Obama in 2016. Plans to build a sixty-eight-turbine wind farm on Nevada portions of the Mojave overlap with Tribal lands that include Avi Kwa Ame, the Mojave name for Spirit Mountain. Tribal groups have for years sought to protect the landscape, and in 1999, it was included as a TCP on the National Register. But that did not protect it from development. Potential impact of the wind farm on archaeological evidence, petroglyphs, and natural resources, and thus the site's spiritual and cultural significance, leveraged President Joseph Biden to designate the Avi Kwa Ame National Monument in 2023, comprising more than five hundred thousand acres that are now protected.

A battle over the Lava Ridge Wind Project is currently under way in southern Idaho. The proposed renewable energy development is planned for seventy-three thousand acres of land held by the federal government. The project site is adjacent to Minidoka National Historic Landmark, a World War II Japanese American incarceration camp. An estimated four hundred wind turbines and ancillary roads, transmission lines, and more will directly impact the original footprint and view sheds of the historic site. An environmental impact assessment is under way, with findings expected in 2024. Such reviews, required under the National Environmental Protection Act (NEPA), are intended to ensure that the potential impacts to heritage resources by federal undertakings are fully evaluated before a project's final approval. These processes constitute an important mode of procedural justice and are especially salient when undertakings potentially disproportionately impact historically marginalized publics. Nonetheless, the climate crisis compels more proactive planning for large-scale energy transitions, which will undoubtedly affect cultural landscapes and historic properties. Negotiating alternate ways forward, rather than relying on binary decisions about energy project versus heritage, will be critical to future decision-making and recognizing the second-order effects of prioritizing preservation over climate action.

Wind and solar opposition is not unique to the U.S. preservation enterprise. In October 2009, the landscape around the historic town of Trujillo in Spain was included on the World Monuments Watch

FIGURE 17. The Mojave Desert has long been a target area for the development of renewable energy facilities, such as the Tehachapi Pass wind farm in California. A recent battle over a proposed wind farm on Nevada portions of the desert resulted in the declaration of more than five hundred thousand acres of culturally significant Tribal lands as the Avi Kwa Ame (Mojave for Spirit Mountain, pictured in the second photograph above) National Monument in 2023. Such debates pit social justice–oriented preservation interests against climate action, complicating the seemingly shared goals of preservationists and environmentalists. Upper photograph courtesy of Paul Gipe under a Creative Commons Attribution-Share Alike 4.0 International license, via Wikimedia Commons. Lower photograph courtesy of Stan Shebs under a GNU Free Documentation License, Version 1.2, via Wikimedia Commons.

because of the construction of a solar farm several miles beyond the town, which was threatening view sheds. Proposed wind turbines near the UNESCO World Heritage site of Mont-Saint-Michel in France prompted considerable debate, and renewable energy facilities were included as one of the primary threats to World Heritage. The binary, conflict politics of procedural reviews and approvals, like Section 106 or NEPA in the United States, mean that preservationists tend to invest in opposing energy farms altogether, rather than in mitigating their potentially negative impacts. Policy structures are intended to empower local publics in preventing adverse and unjust distributive effects. That government systems, for example, are elevating the potential impacts on Native American sacred landscapes and view sheds and sites of Japanese American internment suggests that policy is to some extent serving just causes. However, the climate crisis incurs new and more complicated debates regarding equity trade-offs. The energy transition will likely continue to be at the core of these tensions, at the scale of landscapes as well as buildings, given the importance of carbon emissions mitigation. Policies around procedural and distributive justice will need to adapt, to afford more negotiation and allow for more second-order thinking and scenario exploration.

CIRCULAR ECONOMIES AND BUILDING LIFE CYCLES

The building and construction industry accounts for 6 percent of worldwide gross domestic product and more than 50 percent of national capital investment in most countries. Given the sector's continued dependence on fossil fuels, buildings are responsible for more than one-third of energy demand around the globe and for 37 percent of carbon emissions. The industry is also the world's largest consumer of raw materials. Only a small percentage of the waste generated by construction and demolition (C+D), which includes rehabilitation, is currently recycled or reused.[59] In the United States, C+D waste accounts for 600 million metric tons per year (as of 2018), more than double the amount of municipal solid waste.[60] In 2009, the U.S. Environmental Protection Agency estimated that 9 percent is generated by new construction, 42 percent by renovation, and 48 percent by demolition.[61]

Research to quantify the life cycles of buildings and how they consume energy and emit carbon began in the post–World War II era and continues to advance. Though models vary, in general, building life cycles involve the phases shown in Figure 18. All phases incur energy consumption, and because of the current dependence on fossil fuels, that energy consumption translates to carbon emissions. Accordingly, contemporary discourse refers to these emissions as *operational carbon, embodied carbon,* and *end-of-life carbon.* Operational carbon is associated with a building's use, including heating, cooling, ventilation, cooking, lighting, and so on. Embodied carbon is associated with the processes of manufacturing building materials and construction (*initial* embodied carbon, also referred to as "upfront" carbon), with renovations and retrofits (*recurrent* embodied carbon), and with demolition or deconstruction (end-of-life carbon).

Current research finds that operational carbon is most significant, constituting approximately 75–90 percent of a building's emissions over its lifetime.[62] Given the current rate at which carbon emissions are accumulating due to building use, reducing operational carbon in

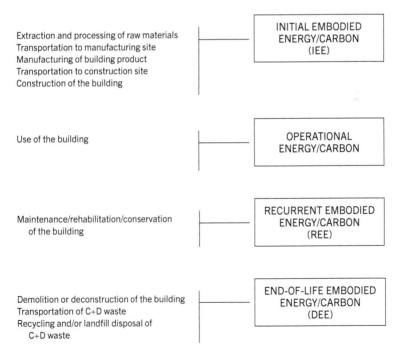

FIGURE 18. The phases of a building's life cycle involve energy consumption and carbon emissions. Adapted by the author from C40knowledgehub.org.

existing buildings—including historic ones—through electrification and improved energy efficiency is a critical and timely goal. However, as large-scale energy transitions occur, meaning that the power grid is converted to renewable energy and buildings are increasingly electrified, embodied carbon will take on more significance, constituting a higher ratio of life cycle emissions. Embodied carbon also plays a role in decision-making about how to retrofit for energy performance, as new materials and systems—such as insulation or a new HVAC unit—incur recurrent embodied carbon as part of their manufacture and installation, even if they are functioning to reduce operational carbon.

Circular economy thinking seeks to optimize building life cycles by minimizing the generation of C+D waste at the end of a building's life and shifting it toward reuse and recycling rather than landfills. This also works to avoid some of the initial embodied carbon associated with new construction, by reusing buildings and materials. To facilitate a more circular process, there are increasingly shifts in the design and construction of new buildings, whereby they are fabricated to eventually be adapted or deconstructed, with constituent materials repurposed or recycled. These changes push the industry from linear cradle-to-grave models to more circular cradle-to-cradle models.

The concept of a circular economy in the construction industry is preceded by long histories of salvaging materials for reuse from structures undergoing major renovation or removal. Contemporary practices of deconstruction, rather than mechanical demolition, build upon these traditions. Deconstruction likewise spurs new opportunities for heritage and C+D waste policies to intersect and mutually benefit through the development of regulations and markets for historic materials.[63] For example, in 2016, the city of Portland, Oregon, instituted a mandatory policy of deconstruction, rather than demolition, for any residential single- or two-family residence predating 1916. The ordinance was so successful that, in 2020, the requirement was revised to include homes built before 1940. In New York, the Circularity, Reuse, and Zero Waste Development (CR0WD) network was founded by a coalition of Cornell Research Labs and community-based planning, preservation, and environmental organizations to promote deconstruction. CR0WD argues not only for the economic and climate-related benefits of deconstruction but also for the social and cultural value of respecting historic materials and craftsmanship.[64]

Jennifer Minner's work and that of her Just Places Lab is integrating these concepts into community-based practices of preservation, reuse, and care, especially by reinforcing traditions of caring for buildings and thus extending their life cycles and avoiding the need for demolition or deconstruction.[65]

To inform decision-making during the design, rehabilitation, and retrofit of buildings, researchers and practitioners employ life cycle assessment (LCA) methodologies to analyze the anticipated energy use and carbon emissions of a new building or weigh options for renovation and retrofit that will minimize overall energy consumption and operational and embodied carbon emissions of an existing building. Performance modeling software, such as BIM, is likewise employed to examine how shifts in design, materials, and systems can optimize energy performance.

The preservation enterprise is contributing to these assessment efforts in important ways. One is through LCA-related tools that help design and engineering professionals determine the comparative benefits of rehabilitating an existing structure versus constructing anew. For example, the CARE Tool is an interactive estimator that calculates embodied, operational, and avoided carbon impacts across scenarios of new construction, retrofit of an existing building, and preserving a building as is. On average, CARE Tool data suggest that retrofitting an existing building results in greater overall carbon reduction over a building's anticipated life cycle than doing nothing or building a new structure.[66]

The U.S. preservation enterprise has long asserted claims of the *inherent* embodied energy, and now carbon, value of existing, specifically older, buildings as a rationale for preservation and adaptive reuse. Methods and data that more accurately account for the interplay of embodied, operational, and avoided carbon are challenging that assumption, as embodied carbon may not, in and of itself, counterbalance operational carbon costs over time without energy retrofits. This will likely weaken justifications of preservation on embodied carbon grounds alone and compel pathways toward deep retrofits that may involve significant changes to building forms and systems and thus challenge first-order notions of preservation. However, embodied carbon is still critical. The *reuse and retrofit* of existing buildings can avoid the generally more egregious initial embodied carbon associated with new construction while also reducing operational carbon.

Additionally, the fact that embodied carbon impacts can be avoided by deconstructing and recycling a building's materials, not simply by reusing a building in its entirety, in place, likewise challenges first-order intentions of preservation. The deconstruction of an older or historic property may seem a less desirable mode of conservation because it destroys encounters with place and thus the social-spatial dynamics that characterize heritage. However, from a second-order perspective, it represents an alternative scenario that challenges the binary of protected versus lost through compromise around shared goals. It confronts a strictly object-focused outcome of saving the building to engender a more systemic policy that reduces landfill and carbon emissions, creates new markets for labor and materials, and at least preserves architectural elements, if not spaces.

Applying second-order thinking to anticipate future implications of circular economies, it is important to anticipate the implications of design-for-deconstruction, meaning buildings are increasingly designed with eventual deconstruction in mind. If the built environment becomes progressively characterized by structures *intended* to be adapted, dismantled, and recycled, what effects will this have on the concept of place-based heritage and the work of the preservation enterprise? If a new climate era involves more mobility of both people and places (or at least the materials of place), preservationists will need to reconsider not only policy but the theoretical foundations of the enterprise.

DECARBONIZATION

In November 2022, the UNEP reported that energy consumption and carbon emissions from buildings across the globe reached "an all-time high" and that there is a widening gap between efforts to decarbonize the built environment and the growing reliance of the building and construction sector on fossil fuels.[67] Buildings comprise more than one-third of energy demand across the globe and 37 percent of carbon emissions.[68] Residential and commercial buildings accounted for 39 percent of U.S. energy consumption in 2021 and 36 percent of end-use carbon emissions from fossil fuels in 2020.[69] In some cities, the ratios are even higher: building energy use accounts for over 70 percent of all carbon emitted in New York City.[70]

Prevailing all-electric pathways to decarbonization will require large-scale conversion of power generation from coal and other fossil fuels to renewable energy, incurring significant shifts in land use. Energy transitions will likewise require the retrofitting of tens of millions of existing buildings currently reliant on fossil fuel combustion for heating and other power.[71]

The role historic buildings and the preservation enterprise play in this transition, and in carbon emissions, is complicated by an inconsistent policy history.[72] Preservation and energy, as noted previously, have a long-standing entanglement in the United States, stemming from the 1970s oil crisis. The oil embargo underscored the economic and national security issues associated with energy. Two primary avenues of research related to buildings emerged: the first examined embodied energy, or the energy required to produce the materials needed to construct a building; the second analyzed operational energy, or the energy required to heat, cool, light, and otherwise power a building's operations. The nascent research undergirded legislation that promoted the reuse and energy retrofit of older buildings as a means of reducing energy consumption, as opposed to new construction.

In the mid-1970s, buildings were estimated to account for nearly half of U.S. energy consumption, with 15 percent attributed to embodied energy and 34 percent to operational energy.[73] Research started in the 1960s monetized the embodied energy value of the materials needed to construct new buildings. To avoid these costs as energy demand and prices soared, the federal government passed legislation to incentivize the reuse of existing, older buildings. The aforementioned Housing and Community Development Act of 1974 sought to promote the revitalization of buildings in urban cores, as a means of saving energy and spurring economic growth. To encourage building-level rehabilitation, the 1976 Tax Act, discussed in chapter 3, was amended in 1979 to provide a 10 percent income tax credit on qualified expenditures to anyone who rehabilitated a building twenty years or older. By 1981, the legislation had a three-tiered system: 15 percent for buildings thirty to thirty-nine years old, 20 percent for buildings forty years old or older, and 25 percent for buildings deemed historic structures.

As these policies involved government-supported investment in private property, they required clear guidance about what was or was not acceptable in terms of rehabilitation. Think rules of the game: to have an equitable playing field, standards needed to be established. Several federal agencies developed energy-centric renovation and weatherization guidelines and handbooks to scaffold the various funding and incentive programs.[74] The preservation enterprise quickly capitalized on this energy-focused groundswell in support of older building rehabilitation. The NPS collaborated with the Department of Housing and Urban Development on rehabilitation principles for older buildings and neighborhoods, which was the precursor to the first version of the Secretary of the Interior's Standards in 1977. Neither of these documents, however, outlined energy-conserving strategies; with the participation of preservation professionals, all focus was on protecting historic features and materials, under the first-order presumption that preserving as much of the original building as possible would de facto save energy.[75]

These presumptions were underpinned by research sponsored by the ACHP, which claimed embodied energy as a rationale for conserving historic buildings, producing model cases to demonstrate the contributions of historic preservation to urban revitalization and the positive energy benefits of reuse over demolition and replacement:

> Once energy is embodied in a building, it cannot be recovered and used for another purpose—8 bricks embody energy equivalent to a gallon of gasoline but cannot fuel a car. Preservation saves energy by taking advantage of the nonrecoverable energy embodied in an existing building and extending the use of it.[76]

Parallel to this embodied energy research were a series of government-sponsored initiatives related to reducing operational energy. Primary focus was on the development of energy performance codes, which sought to make new and existing buildings more energy efficient, and the weatherization of existing buildings. Preservationists were particularly concerned about the implications of rehabilitation and energy codes given the potential effects of retrofits—such as adding insulation, replacing windows, and converting heating and cooling systems—on historic materials and structures. Through a series of position papers, studies, and collaborations with federal agencies, preservation professionals crafted a case to support special consideration and compliance waivers for historic buildings.[77] Baird Smith, historic architect with the NPS, made a persuasive first-order argument that positioned heritage aesthetics as equally if not more important to historic building performance as energy efficiency:

Society is now demanding that old buildings be retained because of their value as a physical resource and that important building features be preserved because of their contribution to our cultural and aesthetic heritage. For these reasons, historic preservation should be included as a performance attribute which must be achieved through a building code.[78]

While preservationists maintained that the aesthetic and material dimensions of heritage potentially outweighed the reduction of operational energy, evidence that older buildings actually consumed less operational energy proved more elusive. Multiple studies were also commissioned to investigate operational energy patterns and trends in existing buildings (in relation to age, materials, etc.), specifically office buildings, as they formed the core of many cities targeted for reinvestment by the 1974 Housing and Community Development Act. Most studies found that older buildings did *not* consistently consume less energy per square foot than newer ones.

One research report, a Department of Energy–sponsored study of existing New York City office buildings, however, identified a correlation between older age and lower energy consumption, identifying buildings put in service between 1941 and 1962 as the most energy consumptive. However, there were a number of issues with the findings: the study used only a forty-four-building sample, and although it found that, on average, older, pre–World War II buildings consumed less energy, there was high variability within the energy use data. Despite the limitations and variability of the data, this study served as an essential, and seemingly singular, source of evidence for preservationists at the time, and it formed a central theme of the preservation community's narrative about older buildings and energy performance. The findings were a primary focus of NPS publications, and the National Trust took up the mantle with a 1980 conference and pursuant volume, *New Energy from Old Buildings*; the findings of this one study—and no others—were cited by multiple contributors. Ann Webster Smith, deputy commissioner for historic preservation for the state of New York, boldly announced, "We now have proof that the buildings with the poorest energy efficiency are those that were built between 1941 and 1970."[79]

These claims of the energy-saving value of historic buildings influenced policy at the federal level, as model energy codes for both residential and commercial buildings—then and still today—provide exemptions for historic buildings, and this echoes across state- and municipal-level codes. These long-standing energy code exceptions have significant implications as U.S. municipalities and states enact new legislation to reduce carbon emissions from existing buildings. Emerging building performance standards use benchmarking data along with operational carbon reduction targets and/or energy use intensity limits to regulate buildings over time, whereas energy codes seek to improve energy efficiency at the time a building or renovation is designed. In theory, building performance standards and energy codes work in tandem to reduce operational carbon, but the still nascent development of building performance standards means that the intersections with energy codes are likely to evolve.

To understand the distributive effects of energy code exemptions and their intersection with operational carbon regulation, colleagues and I did a deep-dive analysis of New York City, where buildings account for 70 percent of the city's carbon emissions. In 2019, New York City passed groundbreaking legislation to reduce operational carbon in existing buildings, known as Local Law 97. Benchmarking, which is required for buildings over twenty-five thousand square feet in New York City, provided up-to-date data about energy consumption and carbon emissions. We used those data to test preservation's energy claims and whether building age, which was so central to the case made for the energy efficiency of older buildings in the 1970s, was potentially correlative to energy consumption and carbon emissions today. We applied the same methods used for that early New York City study to a data set of more than twenty-four hundred National Register buildings in New York City. Ironically, buildings constructed between 1941 and 1962—which were noted as the worst performers in the 1977 study—were the best energy performers on average today. But range data on energy consumption showed even more variability than in 1977, further underscoring that average consumption is an insufficient metric and that building age is an unreliable indicator. Additionally, analysis of the carbon emissions of buildings based on benchmarking data and targets set by Local Law 97 found historic buildings performing no better than nonhistoric buildings.

Because energy intensity is measured in British thermal units per square foot, we quantified the square footage of National Register properties that are exempt from energy codes. These exemptions affect

FIGURE 19. Skidmore, Owings, and Merrill's 1950 Lever House *(top left)* and Mies van der Rohe's 1956 Seagram Building *(top right)* are both exceeding their 2024 carbon emissions targets under New York City's climate law. One Chase Manhattan Plaza *(bottom left),* also designed by Skidmore, Owings, and Merrill in 1957, is meeting its targets. These differences illustrate how building age is an unreliable indicator of energy performance and challenge long-standing rhetoric about historic buildings being inherently green, as all of these are on the National Register of Historic Places. Upper photographs courtesy of the Gottscho–Schleisner Collection, Library of Congress, Prints and Photographs Division. Lower photograph courtesy of the New York World–Telegram and the Sun Newspaper Photograph Collection, Library of Congress, Prints and Photographs Division; photograph by Walter Albertin.

more than 847 million square feet distributed across 43,051 properties citywide, meaning that 16 percent of the built area of New York City is energy code exempt due to historic status. Most of this exempted built area is concentrated in Manhattan, where 32 percent of the borough's built area is energy code exempt.

To examine the distributive effects of these exemptions on various publics, we analyzed National Register built area by census tract. Demographic correlations suggest that the higher the concentration of National Register built area is, the more likely it is that the population is predominantly White and wealthier. From an energy justice perspective, this indicates that this more privileged population is bearing less burden in addressing energy efficiency and operational carbon reductions due to the code exemptions afforded historic properties.

Even with the introduction of Local Law 97 in New York City, more than thirty-nine thousand National Register structures are exempt from both the operational carbon regulation and energy codes. However, these historic buildings are now subject to the city's recently introduced green and cool roof laws. This raises another important aspect of decarbonization that continues to be an arena of debate for preservationists: solar panels. Alterations to most municipally designated historic buildings must be reviewed and approved by preservation agencies. Whereas some commissions are proactively supporting and guiding the installation of photovoltaics on historic properties, many property owners across the country are still denied approval or required to significantly reduce panel coverage, and thus output, to minimize aesthetic impact, because of the first-order priority of preserving the heritage object.[80] These debates were anticipated as early as the 1970s, though limited progress was made within the preservation community until the current climate crisis. One-third of the papers included in the aforementioned 1981 National Trust volume *New Energy from Old Buildings* were devoted to renewable energy and solar specifically, and the need to make design review more flexible was portended more than forty years ago:

> The historic preservation movement has not yet fully recognized the important role it can play in the national effort to conserve energy. . . . The methodology to determine which historic properties can withstand energy-related intervention without adverse effects is not flexible enough. Instead of resisting such interven-

tion, preservationists should become more actively involved in energy retrofit projects so that a more adequate methodology can be developed.[81]

In the more than four decades since the U.S. preservation enterprise first claimed its energy benefits, much has changed. Building age is not a reliable metric for operational energy performance, which undermines one aspect of preservation's green rhetoric: that older, historic buildings are inherently more energy efficient. The other aspect, embodied energy—or more specifically embodied carbon—raises important questions that are as yet underresearched, as suggested in the previous section. Embodied carbon analyses lack consistent data and methodological approaches.[82] And there is still much to learn about the intersection of recurrent embodied carbon and operational carbon in building retrofits and trade-offs with new construction.[83] Particularly germane to the preservation enterprise is that LCA methods largely calculate embodied carbon based on standardized replacement value estimates for construction materials, not the actual embodied carbon for specifically sourced materials at the time of construction.[84] Historic preservation lends a unique perspective to the question owing to the protracted, if not indefinite, life cycles of historic buildings, which are a subset of existing buildings. Historic buildings constitute a form of place investment and reinvestment—of energy, resources, time, and social attachments. As circular economies increasingly take hold in the construction industry, a fuller accounting of the cumulative investment in places, including actual embodied carbon as well as the labor associated with production and the human dimensions of heritage recognition and place attachment, has the potential to inform the complex trade-offs involved in retrofitting existing buildings versus deconstructing and building anew.

Bringing preservation insights and new research to bear on emerging carbon policies is particularly time sensitive. As noted, a growing body of research suggests that deeply retrofitting existing buildings incurs more carbon savings than new construction when both embodied and operational carbon are considered over a building's life cycle. However, most building performance standards in the United States, at municipal and state levels, focus almost exclusively on operational carbon. There is limited regulatory accounting for embodied carbon akin to the benchmarking for operational carbon and energy use intensity. For example, in New York City, property owners must meet increasingly stringent operational carbon reduction targets, leading to net zero in 2050, or face substantial fines. Although energy consumption and operational carbon emissions must be rigorously reported, embodied carbon is not considered. And there are no deconstruction or C+D recycling ordinances in the city. Thus property owners may be incentivized to demolish an existing building and construct a new, better-performing building, rather than deeply retrofit the existing one, because there are no consequences for the embodied carbon emissions of new construction.

For the preservation enterprise to influence this policy horizon, more research and second-order thinking about decarbonization are needed. There is too much reliance on cherry-picked data and recursive rhetoric about historic buildings being inherently sustainable. National Register criteria require a property to be fifty years old or older; *old* and *historic* are ever-moving targets. Building materials, forms, and systems will continue to evolve, especially in light of climate change. If part of the attachment to heritage places derives from their capacity to persist and adapt through time, then preservation policy may need to actively enable that, rather than seeking exemptions from the critical regulations needed to achieve decarbonization. The climate crisis is not only a justice issue; it is a survival issue. The emphasis of the preservation enterprise on the climate threats to heritage combined with the long-standing exemptions from energy codes perpetuate first-order notions of heritage-as-object. Buildings, including historic ones, are emitting carbon and contributing to the loss of places, livelihoods, and communities around the globe. Reforming preservation policy to actively promote the decarbonization of all existing buildings may allow the social-spatial dynamics of place to evolve and adapt in ways that serve not only immediate or proximate publics but humanity writ large.

Conclusion

WORK UNFINISHED

> Don't be stopped by the "if you can't define it and measure it,
> I don't have to pay attention to it" ploy. No one can define or
> measure justice, democracy, security, freedom, truth, or love.
> No one can define or measure any value. But if no one speaks
> up for them, if systems aren't designed to produce them, if we
> don't speak about them and point toward their presence or
> absence, they will cease to exist.
>
> —Donella Meadows, *Thinking in Systems*

I have tried to speak up for the values that the preservation enterprise
should produce, to consider how policy systems might be reformed.
I have centered justice and climate in this interrogation because the
global change we are experiencing inextricably links them and gives
them unparalleled significance; they are undoing ways of life. As I
stated earlier in the volume, preservation policy has always been
about social justice, about amplifying stories and squaring history
in the public realm though collective action. And the fundamentally
place-based nature of heritage means that it cannot be divorced from
the built environment or its role in the climate crisis. This collective,
government-sponsored act of preserving places generates benefits and
burdens distributed unevenly across populations, geographies, and
time. If we don't acknowledge and confront policy histories and their
consequences, and seek to learn from them, decision-making will continue to embed and repeat injustices in institutions, landscapes, and
communities.

The critiques of the preservation enterprise delineated herein are
not necessarily novel or unfamiliar, nor are they complete. Many of the
concerns about exclusion, lack of diversity, and risks of displacement
go back decades. Revisiting this ground helps to untangle the systemic

issues that enable injustice and recursively reinforce it. Focusing on policy's intersections with broader social and environmental agendas compels an understanding of how policy affects people and places beyond the heritage object and the dominant site-by-site praxis of preservation. This volume applies the concept of second-order thinking through a backward-focused inquiry of the rules of the game, asking, *where are the cracks in the foundational system, why are they there, and how are they affecting the structure as a whole?*

Facing forward, *how do we effectively integrate second-order thinking into heritage policy, by learning from that past and reiteratively integrating new knowledge into tools and frameworks for decision-making?*

CRITICAL ACTORS

Government agencies from the local to the national level are central to public policy reform. But similar to the early histories of heritage policy formation, they do not act independently. The interplay with civil society organizations as well as academia creates a crucial dynamic in understanding societal and environmental concerns and expounding the potential role of policy. Historically, these arenas mutually reinforced the tools in service today, from heritage lists to designation criteria to standards of treatment, and have the collective power to mobilize policy transformation. The landscape of heritage-oriented third-sector organizations in the United States is now vast, and dozens of undergraduate- and graduate-level university programs are dedicated to historic preservation. These networks of knowledge-based experts, or "epistemic communities" as described by Peter Hass, have a ripe opportunity to leverage their critical mass toward government action:

> Decision makers do not always recognize that their understanding of complex issues and linkages is limited, and it often takes a crisis or shock to overcome institutional inertia and habit and spur them to seek help from an epistemic community. In some cases, information generated by an epistemic community may in fact create a shock, as often occurs with scientific advances or reports that make their way into the news, simultaneously capturing the attention of the public and policymakers and pressuring them into action.[1]

Research is at the crux of any policy reform effort, and the preservation enterprise is challenged in that respect. Not-for-profits and philanthropic organizations largely sponsor work at discrete sites and often prioritize designation or physical interventions to preserve sites, interpret them, and make them more accessible. Support of such projects can provide the funder with tangible outcomes, easily documented in "before and after" photographs, and activities with direct public engagement. Although this is important work that can produce positive community effects, particularly at places representing underserved stories and marginalized populations, such site-by-site approaches do not change policy or its distributive effects.

Preservation policy research is much more challenging to fund, in government and the third sector, in part because it lacks the emotional victimizing–valorizing appeal of a site under threat or a community seeking to save their heritage. When policy-oriented research is supported, as noted previously, investment is all too often in advocacy-driven studies that perpetuate the status quo rather than interrogating and challenging structures of governance and decision-making. Heritage not-for-profits and government agencies are understandably hesitant to undertake research that may effectively expose preservation's shortcomings. These organizations are working with shoestring budgets and tend to invest in more advocacy-oriented research to help market their mission, demonstrate positive effect, and garner more resources.

This is in part why academia has a critical role to play in policy reform. University preservation programs have long served as fora for innovation. Public and social history found traction as a central mode of architectural and spatial interrogation through the evolution of preservation as a discipline. New frontiers in preservation discourse continue to be forged through universities as part of their training of the next generation of practitioners, including critical heritage studies, experimental preservation, and community-engaged practices. While some of this work moves beyond the heritage object, much is still site specific, because locality matters. It is what forms the social-spatial dynamics that compose heritage and attachment to place, and it is the milieu in which most preservation professionals will work.

But both pedagogy and research can push those boundaries. That is not to say that preservationists should abandon the object or locality; rather, learning in this first-order mode must be purposefully and directly put in dialogue with policy inquiry. It isn't enough simply to teach students the rules of the game; that only allows them to *navigate* the system. Emerging professionals need to learn how to question the rules and interrogate their implications from different perspectives if they are to effectively evolve the system to meet changing societal and environmental circumstances. This dialectical relationship between first- and second-order thinking can inform our understanding of how site-by-site approaches accumulate into patterns and are complicit in reinforcing them. Returning to the public health analogy, most doctors are not public health researchers; they are treating patients as opposed to undertaking population and policy studies. However, as clinicians, they are encouraged, if not trained, to understand and consider public health research, to incorporate the latest findings and changing guidance into their patient care, and to report their on-the-ground outcomes to centralized repositories and policy institutions. Professional education has an affirmative obligation to anticipate the evolution of the field; that in itself is a form of second-order preservation. Teaching to where the field is going, rather than where it is, means we are equipping students to adapt and explore alternative scenarios, rather than simply to integrate into the status quo. Whether interrogating invisible histories or studying embodied and operational carbon in existing buildings, different demands are being made of the heritage enterprise, and emerging professionals should be grappling with these challenges. This also involves preparing students to understand the implications of policy, undertake policy-related research, and engage in policy reform so that they more critically question how object-focused work scales up, aggregates, and affects different publics.

One of the biggest barriers to introducing students to policy research, and undertaking it writ large, is the lack of systematic data collection and analysis by government preservation agencies.[2] This is a conundrum in a field that so meticulously relies on historical rigor and accuracy. Part of this stems from the site-by-site, "battle won, move on to the next" mentality as well as the first-order focus on the object. Much of the research emerging from the preservation enterprise is case based, but the landscape of policy literature is growing. To cultivate this further, there is a crucial codependency among government agencies, universities, and third-sector funders.

The NPS, SHPOs, and municipal agencies should be critical repositories of policy-relevant data that are accessible and usable. In other fields, like community development and housing, the need for government investment in collecting and maintaining accessible data for the purposes of policy research is inherently recognized. HUD User is an example of how a federal agency, the Department of Housing and Urban Development (HUD), actively undertakes and supports policy-related research, enabling longitudinal and latitudinal studies to inform how public policy related to housing and community development is performing.[3]

The vast amount of data collection that occurs in government preservation agencies, federal to municipal, tends to comprise object-centric inventories. Although geospatial platforms are improving access to data and allowing for greater usability on the part of researchers, information is still uneven and disjointed, like the National Register database. The NPS has an Office of Policy, but it functions quite differently from HUD's Office of Policy Development and Research and does not have a clear mandate to share data and support external and public-facing policy research. The ACHP has a distinct policy mandate and a history of policy studies, for example, those around embodied energy, but much of its work centers on Section 106 review, responding to site-by-site concerns over adverse impacts and issuing statements about what policy should do. The latter are not so unlike the many international charters produced by ICOMOS and similar organizations declaring aspirational policy intentions without necessarily undertaking research to understand the effects of existing policy on people as evidence for guiding reform.

There is a clear need for a federal hub for policy-related preservation data and research. This is critical infrastructure that would acknowledge the undeniable responsibility of government to invest in understanding how policy is performing, to identify emerging issues, and to engage in modes of reform. The federal government may not undertake all of the research, but by making data available and maintaining a hub of resources, it would establish a platform to allow academia and the third sector to engage more readily in policy research. It would likewise establish a model for other levels of government: by integrating policy research into its ongoing operations, the federal government could set a precedent for state- and municipal-level agencies to advance second-order preservation.

The NPS could house such a policy data and research hub, but this may not afford the degree of perspective and intersection required to understand people- and justice-oriented issues and effects more broadly. Thinking back to the soccer analogy, soccer is not the only game in town. Accounting for how preservation overlaps with other policy agendas, from affordable housing to energy retrofits to economic development, is a critical means of making preservation policy more just. We cannot simply advocate for incorporating object-focused preservation interests in other policy realms; we need to robustly examine negotiated outcomes and trade-offs to achieve common purpose. The ACHP could serve as an innovative hub for preservation policy research, not only because of its mandate and history, but because of its diverse composition and the varied interests represented by council members. Current ACHP chair (2022–25) the Honorable Sara C. Bronin is exploring this potential. Because the ACHP includes heads of multiple federal agencies, representatives from multiple levels of governance (a governor, a mayor, and a member of a Native American or Hawaiian Native community), preservation experts, and members of the general public, it may be uniquely positioned to interrogate preservation policy from multiple perspectives.[4]

Funding is a consistent challenge, and reorienting resources toward policy-related projects involves government, universities, and third-sector organizations. Federal grants to SHPOs and CLG funding to municipalities include a range of supported projects, including surveys, tax incentives, and planning efforts. But there is no clear program area related to policy, and specifically to analyses of who is benefiting from or being burdened by existing policy. Nor do the projects that received grants reflect an orientation toward policy concerns; most are fairly first order focused.[5] Explicitly stating policy research as a legitimate government grant–funded program area would go a long way toward seeding policy efforts at state and local levels.

Universities have long engaged with government and not-for-profits to produce policy research in the past, often through studies commissioned by the NPS or the ACHP in the United States. But recent decades have also seen an increase in independent academic research that more freely examines benefits and burdens. Scholars have opportunities to expand this research landscape through interdisciplinary projects, for example, engaging scholars in data sciences, public policy, community development, climate, and law. Academic researchers often have greater capacity to innovatively position such research and engage teams from across university departments. Third-sector organizations likewise have opportunities to draw project collaborators from beyond traditional preservation entities. For example, funders interested in social justice and climate action may support policy-oriented preservation research when contextualized through these overlapping concerns. Pursuing these intersectional inquiries affords legitimacy to such research, like a prompt from an epistemic community, which can influence both government actors and more traditional preservation funders, pushing them beyond first-order preservation of heritage places to second-order policy interrogation.

TOWARD SOCIAL JUSTICE

The preservation enterprise has done considerable work to further representational justice and correct what Ned Kaufman termed the field's "diversity deficit."[6] To expand who is represented by the stories told in the built environment, government agencies are undertaking theme studies to identify places associated with underrepresented publics and are advancing related research, surveys, and listings/designations. New types of recognition and policy tools, like legacy businesses and cultural districts, redefine the role of government vis-à-vis expanding typologies of heritage that more directly acknowledge the social-spatial dimensions of heritage places. For heritage that has been erased or compromised, government agencies and third-sector organizations are supporting more commemorative action and counter-narration through interpretive signage and installations, performative events, plaques and markers, community-engaged listening and learning, and online platforms for storytelling. Alternative approaches for the stories historically decentered by or excluded from the preservation enterprise are garnering new lines of funding through heritage-oriented not-for-profits and philanthropic institutions. These are significant and laudable advances, but they are insufficient.

There is an overreliance on these additive, site-by-site approaches to addressing the multifaceted dimensions of justice, beyond representation. There is likewise limited systemic effect, as more diverse places on heritage rosters does not change policy structure. An important avenue already being pursued and warranting expansion is audits of existing heritage rosters. For example, municipal, state, and federal agencies can further invest in evidence-based demographic research and heritage audits that examine *existing* designations and listings, and how they center or decenter certain publics, narratives, and geographies, to help identify factors and patterns in potential underrepresentation. This is a form of backward-facing second-order policy research that can inform where a locality might focus community-based support or prioritize designations moving forward, especially when coupled with distributive justice concerns, discussed later.

Academia has a role to play not only in helping to undertake such research and audits but also in preparing professionals who can do the work. Students are regularly trained in how to do a windscreen survey through visual assessment and to undertake archive-researched inventories or in how to prepare National Register nominations and historic structure reports. There is less emphasis on how to collect and use social and geospatial data as part of policy tool analyses and decision-making and how to interrogate loss and survivorship bias and their implications in understanding place identity, memory, and attachment. These are skills fundamental to addressing systemic underrepresentation in preservation policy and in the built environment as a whole.

The last decades are also marked by important advances in procedural justice within the preservation enterprise. Community engagement, public participation, and bottom-up approaches increasingly characterize place-based preservation and contribute to innovation in heritage-making, especially through interpretation, participatory data collection, and storytelling. At the same time, community-driven preservation activism can fuel a dialectical relationship of government and civil society. As noted previously, these dynamics too frequently play out as a binary struggle of designate versus not designate, save versus lose, framing policy decision-making as conflict politics. More evidence-based policy research has the potential to elucidate how preservation influences communities over time, which can in turn inform publics and institutions and promote negotiated processes of establishing shared goals.

Values-driven heritage planning works to better account for diverse publics and interests in conservation and management at the site-by-site level and likewise marks important advances with regard to procedural justice. It nonetheless centers places a priori deemed heritage as the object of decision-making. Returning to the soccer analogy, it presumes that soccer is the primary game and that the ball and interaction with it are the priorities. How publics engage with each other and how they may be advantaged or disadvantaged in terms of policy processes and outcomes cannot be understood if the eye is only on the ball.

Universities, again, have a particular responsibility in educating the next generation of preservation professionals in how to conduct research with people, facilitate community-driven processes, and co-produce knowledge. Students emerge from historic preservation programs with intricate knowledge of how to research and document buildings and landscapes, assess conditions, and design interventions. Relatively fewer courses address the ethics and processes of conducting interviews, people-based surveys, and observational studies or working in reciprocal, nonextractive ways with publics to empower their participation and decision-making.

Improving participatory research skills and community engagement processes may help to promote access to and use of the existing policy toolbox, but it does not fundamentally change the policy tools themselves. Revising designation and listing criteria, as well as standards and guidelines for intervention, constitutes a critical arena of second-order preservation investment. This work is happening at a number of levels, for example, the flood adaptation guidelines prepared by the NPS and by an increasing number of flood-prone states and municipalities. But there is less evidence of, for example, revised standards of documentation, criteria for designation, approaches to research and survey work, and standards of intervention that more inclusively recognize different forms of evidence and knowledge and varying aspirations for the use of preservation policy tools.

A primary concern is the reform of listing and designation evaluation criteria to better accommodate values beyond formal aesthetics and material integrity. It is time to challenge the binary qualification that heritage places either retain integrity or do not.[7] Creating new typologies of heritage, like traditional cultural properties, or calling systematically erased or excluded heritage "intangible" does not account for the historic barriers that prevented the survival of original forms and materials. Nor does it allow for more robust acknowledgment of the legacies of disadvantaged publics and their narratives and of how survivorship bias makes the preservation enterprise complicit in recursive exclusion. Deciding whether to invoke public policy to protect a place should be informed by how heritage is intended to perform on behalf of people and their relationship to it, not simply based on physical attributes and how they materially demonstrate associated histories.

Similarly, standards of intervention should not be based solely on how they affect existing fabric and form but on how they advance—or not—valued social-spatial dynamics and the freedom to transfer heritage across generations. The Secretary of the Interior's Standards have been revised and updated multiple times and augmented with varying guidelines. Debates over both their inadequacies for addressing more inclusive heritage conservation and their inconsistent application by SHPOs and the NPS continue to evolve, marked recently by a 2023 American Institute of Architects colloquium focused on questions of revising the Standards and a public comment process initiated by the ACHP to understand concerns with the Standards on the part of local preservation agencies and organizations. As they stand, the Standards and the municipal design review guidelines they have informed have a fundamental orientation toward first-order preservation, relying heavily on the notion that any benefit derived is a consequence of retaining the original form and materiality of the object to the extent possible.

Second-order preservation seeks more conscious explication of preservation's higher purposes, an articulation of its aspirations. Although legal texts convey a range of public policy rationales, these have been distorted in the translation from law to functional governance and skewed toward professional, first-order interests. This constitutes a critical pathway toward addressing both procedural and distributive justice concerns.

Following on Donella Meadows's advice at the start of this chapter, *what do we want the system of preservation to produce?* I have made a case for social justice and climate action, but not to the exclusion of other or additional intentions. And just like the existing municipal ordinances, those intentions—which are public policy rationales—may vary from locale to locale. Some intentions may already be articulated, like the "energy benefits" added to the NHPA, but not effectively supported through policy. Revisiting the expectations of policy is a potential means of spurring dialogue within epistemic communities and government toward distributive justice.

Intentions are themselves a metric; they establish a baseline against which processes and outcomes can be evaluated. If the public policy rationale of a given city's preservation ordinance notes economic goals of tourism development, or civic education goals, how are these policy

·

intentions incorporated into decisions about what to designate, how to preserve, and for how long? Imagine, as a possibility, if heritage designation were only temporary or for discrete timeframes—say, twenty years. At the time of designation, a plan of intentions—meaning a case for listing that stems from public policy rationales and articulates how a property will serve the public—is proffered, adding to the historical associations and to the architectural and cultural significance documentation already required. That plan of intentions thus becomes a metric by which to measure the performance of policy and inform future alterations or decisions to renew designation.

Research already suggests a wide range of motivations behind seeking heritage recognition, from preventing displacement to accessing tax credits for redevelopment. Municipalities especially, because of the power they wield in shaping built environments through land use regulation, are poised to revisit their public policy rationales in light of distributive justice concerns. Such review can aid in determining if those intentions need to be revised and how municipalities might incorporate them into their operations and regulatory processes for designation and design review.

Revisiting intentions forces us to orient toward the future in policy and establish expectations of how we want the system to perform in relation to people and in terms of processes and outcomes. Carving space and time for reviewing public policy rationales and determining how to effectively incorporate them into decision-making is challenging for often underfunded and understaffed preservation commissions and organizations. But maybe there is cause to consider, for example, a moratorium on listing for a discrete period of time to prioritize these kinds of policy efforts and structural analyses (such hiatuses are not unprecedented; a nearly two-year moratorium on local designations in New York City helped to inform a 1973 amendment to the Landmarks Law to include interiors and scenic landscapes). Another possibility could involve institutional restrictions to allow listing only in known underserved neighborhoods until more research can be done on representation and distributive effects and on how questions of integrity, or a lack thereof, might be confronted with respect to designation and design review.

What may be most important to note is that communities are often seeking distributive justice through preservation policy. Whether to prevent displacement or gentrification, or challenge new zoning or proposed developments, or encourage economic revitalization, the use of preservation policy tools, like designation or tax credits or transfer of development rights, is perceived to provide some form of neighborhood protection and investment extending well beyond aesthetics.[8] Instead, because of how policy is operationalized, the preservation enterprise offers mostly representational justice through listing, interpretation, and commemoration. This is especially troubling in neighborhoods with histories of exclusion, which may struggle to meet material integrity standards due to recursive policies that promoted disinvestment. They are seeking equity but find that the rules of the game are rigged against them.

Second-order preservation calls for addressing how these cracks in the policy structure—these intersecting representational, procedural, and distributive injustices reinforced and reproduced by the system—can be mended. In this sense, second-order preservation is conceptually a form of restorative justice. It calls the existing policy toolbox to account, seeking an understanding of how the enterprise privileges and disprivileges publics as a first step in developing compensatory action. The ideas suggested herein, from revising designation criteria and intervention standards to revisiting and operationalizing municipal ordinance public policy rationales, are compelled by a need for restorative justice that seeks to prevent future harm, not just account for past harm.

TOWARD CLIMATE

The obligation to prevent future harm associated with the preservation enterprise is poignantly exemplified by the climate crisis, which will only compound injustice if it is not decidedly addressed. Adaptation and migration realities force preservationists to embrace the fact that its intentions may not always center on saving places. Frontline communities, including those in urban locales and especially those historically marginalized, remain an important public for whom the preservation enterprise should be working. Not all place-based heritage can be saved or relocated in the face of extreme and more frequent weather events. As noted previously, the preservation enterprise has much to offer with regard to triage and decision-making about what and how to adapt in the built environment, extending well beyond places officially recognized as heritage. People do not attach to places simply because they are on a historic register or designated as a land-mark, and not all places valued by people are formally recognized as heritage. Place attachment may complicate decision-making about climate-related adaptation and displacement in any existing built envi-ronment or community. While preservationists focus on the discrete subset of historic places, methodologically, they work with commu-nities and engage questions of social history and context, cultural sig-nificance, place attachment, and more, as well as the technical, design, and policy dimensions of intervening in and adapting existing, older buildings.

This research and teaching on the existing built environment is surprisingly unique within the academy. University architecture and engineering programs in the United States focus primarily on new de-sign and construction in curricula; limited attention is devoted to ex-isting buildings. In this sense, the preservation field has the potential to bring important knowledge to bear in the adaptation and decarboni-zation of the existing built environment and in working with com-munities toward climate action in ways that acknowledge and seek to preserve important social-spatial dynamics. Even in the context of climate-related displacement, the fundamental preservation focus on people–place relationships might present important pathways to de-termining how community-significant social-spatial dynamics can be reproduced through emplacement.

Climate adaptation and migration are fundamentally influenced by long histories of socially constructing vulnerability. Understanding histories of who laid claim to place, or who could not, and how poli-cies regarding land use, built infrastructure, and even preservation in-creased risk will be crucial to more just decision-making about where to invest in climate-response infrastructure, where to promote relo-cation, or where to encourage building-level adaptation. Again, the methodological approaches of the preservation enterprise have the potential to forge important insights into how deep histories of in-justice are embedded in landscapes and built environments and how climate policy can not only account for them but potentially seek to remedy them.

Using preservation methods and tools to advance climate actions will undoubtedly challenge first-order priorities of retaining form and materiality but pose innovative avenues for rethinking how preser-vation policy contributes to second-order social and environmental aims. This is likewise the case with density. The long-standing conflict politics of density, pitting preservation against new development, has not been conducive to creating processes for negotiating how and where to effectively densify existing urban and suburban areas. Important to reducing carbon in both the building and transportation sectors, infill development and denser zoning are increasingly being addressed through new legislation that, for example, prohibits single-family housing or allows ADUs. More pressing equity concerns, such as affordable housing and sustainable land use, are taking precedence over preservation policy. Like the 1990 ADA, repeated calls for the importance of first-order object-focused materiality and aesthetics do not carry the day in the face of the existential threat posed by the climate crisis.

How preservation policy itself adapts and shifts will determine whether it continues to be marginalized or integrated into decision-making. For example, rather than simply reviewing (and potentially opposing) new development, municipal preservation agencies could undertake land use research and neighborhood-based community engagement processes to identify areas conducive to low-, medium-, or high-density infill or redevelopment, both within historic districts and not. Overall, this would reduce more indiscriminate policymaking and provide greater predictability for developers seeking redevelopment or infill opportunities. More importantly, in the spirit of second-order preservation, such scenario planning would allow for evaluating the distributive effects of potential redevelopment or infill on historic versus nonhistoric neighborhoods, thereby anticipating who might be advantaged or disadvantaged and how more equitable outcomes might be achieved. A similar approach could be applied to identifying landscapes conducive to renewable energy infrastructure and urban/suburban areas conducive to neighborhood-scale energy development, for example, collective solar rooftops. By taking a proactive approach to finding common ground, and scenario planning rather than simply reacting to proposed developments, the preservation enterprise could better leverage issues of justice and equity in policy.

Previously discussed research into and mobilization around deconstruction policy illustrate second-order preservation already in motion. By negotiating how goals of a circular construction economy can intersect with those of preservation, rather than simply opposing the loss of older buildings, municipalities are forging new policy arenas, and industry networks are helping to create new markets and modes of practice. Similar proactive approaches are warranted in decarbonizing historic buildings. That the federal HPF is financed by offshore oil and gas leasing and that historic buildings are largely exempt from energy performance codes constitute a doubly egregious policy injustice that cannot hold. As discussed, the ADA did not exempt historic buildings from complying with accessibility requirements, because justice outweighed historic and material integrity. New building performance standards and carbon reduction laws, like the New York City Climate Mobilization Act (Local Law 97), do not provide waivers for historic buildings. In comparing climate-oriented legislation to the ADA, legal scholar Sara Bronin noted that the preservation field has a choice to engage proactively in policy reform, but it will "happen with us or without us."[9]

Rather than trying to prove that historic buildings are inherently green, preservation agencies, academia, and third-sector organizations should be anticipating energy transitions and seeking pathways to decarbonize existing buildings, again, historic or otherwise. We should be actively phasing out energy code waivers and embracing the opportunity to demonstrate how retrofitting can be accomplished in the existing built environment, by showcasing the creative adaptability of historic structures as models. And we can no longer rest on the laurels of embodied energy/carbon claims; the climate crisis must be met with continued development of analytical tools and research that more accurately quantifies embodied and operating carbon in historic building retrofits and characterizes also the qualitative dimensions of energy, such as human labor, collective action, and government investment.

The climate crisis is not contained within geopolitical borders and is inequitably affecting vulnerable populations and thereby fundamentally altering multilateral politics and governance. The equation of heritage with human rights at the international level poses new avenues of policy for the preservation enterprise that may complicate individual and collective rights.[10] The rules of the game are changing around the preservation enterprise, compelling reform that is as much about reckoning as it is about charting new possibilities. Now more than ever, preservation is not simply a movement motivated by collective interest in saving places and telling their stories. It is a dimension of an increasingly complex climate-responsive policy toolbox that is fundamentally altering the built environment and how publics claim space. The preservation enterprise can choose to engage second-order thinking, anticipate these shifts, and inform more just futures through reflexive analysis, or it can seek to protect the status quo and risk increasing marginalization in the policy discourse about the built environment and the publics who inhabit it.

TOWARD THE FUTURE

I raise issues and concerns to which many preservationists might take exception and purposefully ask questions in ways that disrupt traditional perspectives on the heritage enterprise. In doing so, I hope to provoke self-reflection, including my own, on the structural deficits of heritage policy and how we, as preservationists, can do the difficult things ahead. Most importantly, I seek to emphasize that preservation is accountable to people and, as a form of public policy, that accountability is long overdue. In untangling the recursive structures of policy, I have critically examined some foundational concepts of professional theory and practice that warrant some reflective commentary.

Aesthetics received particularly demanding treatment in the context of first-order preservation approaches. That does not negate the significance of heritage-as-object nor dismiss the critical dimension aesthetics brings to the experience, valuing, and social-spatial dynamics of heritage places. Many places may be worthy of preservation simply because of their unique artistry or inimitable visual appeal. Rather, it seeks to expose how, when utilizing "beauty-based" polices for preservation, we must be mindful of the potential to center particular ideals and exclude others.[11]

Authenticity and material integrity were likewise prodded to expose their inherent relativism and implications for procedural injustice. There is nevertheless a draw and temporal solace in material accuracy that may allow people to more acutely locate themselves within the arc of history. But I believe heritage can speak truth in many different ways, giving agency to those who seek to realize their own truths through heritage-making in their own ways. The opposite of *authentic* is not *inauthentic*; it is *indefinite*. Consciously allowing space for the unknown, for the provisional, in the heritage enterprise affords more open-ended and just avenues for scenario planning and participatory policy.

The focus on largely urban contexts neither prioritizes the places and peoples of cities nor diminishes rural heritage or less built-up or industrialized contexts. Rather, as palimpsests of occupation, hubs of pluralism, and critical spaces of capital flows, cities can readily reveal the political nature of the heritage enterprise. Returning to the soccer analogy and the desire to prioritize soccer over other games, in urban environments, the heritage enterprise regularly competes with interests that seek to claim place for other agendas—affordable housing, tourism, commercial development, and so on. This unending competition incurs complex negotiation and squarely situates preservation as public policy with dynamic social, environmental, and economic implications. It likewise emphasizes the need to recognize preservation as not strictly a humanities-based or scientific discipline but one that warrants the perspectives and skills of the social sciences, particularly in how it engages with people and seeks to understand who may be burdened and/or privileged by preservation policy's direct and indirect effects.

The role of professionals received considerable attention in this volume with regard to expert and nonexpert agency. This does not discount the importance of professional knowledge and leadership within the heritage policy arena. But it does seek to illuminate how some professional norms and standards discount publics and the social dimensions of heritage places and thus impede policy reform.

The concept of second-order preservation builds on the notion that heritage is used by various publics toward different ends. This is not new; heritage has always been performative, and history bears repeated witness to the many political, social, economic, and other uses of heritage across time and geographies. Rather, I am intentionally challenging the inherent notion that heritage first *is* and then *does*, to push the policy gaze toward the future and not just the past. Through designation and design review, so much of regulation orients decision-making around what has been instead of around what could be. How can we develop policy models that activate the regenerative dimensions of heritage—that is, not regenerative like revitalization or renewal, but rather regenerative as opposed to consumptive or accumulated?

Focusing on second-order thinking and centering climate and justice neither negates nor diminishes the importance of first-order preservation. Saving places still matters. Across the United States and the globe are examples of heritage places that are adapting in the face of climate change, transitioning to renewable energy, interpreting underrepresented histories and counternarrating centered stories, advancing human rights and restorative justice, and robustly engaging local communities in collaborative decision-making. Like the diversity of municipal-level preservation policies, these localized and site-focused projects illustrate the power and potential of heritage as a medium of collective, bottom-up action. But site-by-site action does not aggregate into policy reform, nor does it alone change systemic bias. Concerns of justice and climate transcend spatial boundaries and remind us that increased or more diverse participation in heritage decision-making will not solve structural injustice; just processes do not ensure just outcomes. Likewise, building-by-building retrofits will not aggregate to a sustainable built environment. The top-down purview of government is still crucial for ensuring intra- and intergenerational equity.[12] And it does so by considering and reconsidering policy intentions, processes, and outcomes with respect to publics and their environments.

The avoidance of significant policy reflection may in part arise from the perception that the preservation enterprise lacks power. This is particularly the case in the United States. Caught between a profession and a social movement, focus is more easily drawn to the object and site-by-site concerns. Each building saved from the wrecking ball or from indiscriminate alterations is a battle won, another victim rescued; the next battle ensues. But the preservation enterprise doesn't necessarily lack power; its institutions and regulations have considerable effect. It may simply lack legitimacy. In response to the long-standing and more contemporary critiques of unjust or uneven social impacts, U.S. heritage organizations and government institutions tend to take a defensive stance, commissioning studies that seek to counter negative claims and promote the positive outcomes of preservation. If the enterprise only communicates the positive rhetoric of cobenefits and does not deeply interrogate burdens and unintended consequences, its capacity to serve as an effective agent of public policy is compromised.

The stewardship position of the heritage enterprise, that deeply engrained moral certitude that preservationists must convince publics about why (their) heritage is important and worth saving, may also prevent the preservation enterprise from more just power sharing and thus greater legitimacy. Prioritizing heritage over other societal concerns—economic, social, and environmental—can further marginalize the preservation enterprise in the context of competing interests. How the preservation enterprise chooses to address and reform its own policies will be a critical factor in determining its power and positionality in the broader urban policy arena of the future.

This interrogation and its second-order orientation stem from Lindblom's premise that "policy is not made once and for all; it is made and re-made endlessly. . . . A wise policy-maker consequently expects that his policies will achieve only part of what he hopes and at the same time will produce unanticipated consequences he would have preferred to avoid. If he proceeds through a succession of incremental changes, he avoids serious lasting mistakes in several ways."[13] In an ever-changing world, to adapt is to reform, to consistently incorporate new knowledge into behavior and systems of action. As preservationists, we are acutely aware of the importance of history and the significance of time in producing new knowledges and ways of knowing. A focus of our gaze on our own past and the implications of our work on people—and over time—is long overdue. To inform and sustain our collective future, it must be instituted as an ongoing dimension of our very public enterprise.

As a child, I had a penchant for sneaking into the attic or basement and rummaging through dusty boxes, albums of faded photographs, and old dressers filled with tokens of previous lives and worlds. My mother would call it "rooting," meaning I was digging up the past by rifling through things that were long ago packed away. But I was rooting in other ways. I was piecing together my heritage and identity, by understanding what came before me and led to my existence. Like a tree extending its roots deep into the soil, that foundation anchored me and allowed me to grow. I am still rooting, now cheering for the transformative potential of heritage, not to moor us to the past but to enable us to chart alternative futures.

Preservation and its collective power reminds us of things bigger than ourselves, that our stories are but chapters in the arc of history. There is a human instinct to find ourselves in that arc, in those stories.

Policy is the primary vehicle through which that agency is made manifest and just. There is a profound accountability to *people* in heritage work that has yet to be internalized in governance structures, policy tools and legal frameworks, academic pedagogy and scholarship, and professional practice. We need to run toward this making and remaking of policy if the preservation enterprise is to weather this crucible of change.

Acknowledgments

I would like to see a building, say, the Empire State, I would
like to see on one side of it a foot-wide strip from top to
bottom with the name of every bricklayer, the name of every
electrician, with all the names. So when a guy walked by, he
could take his son and say, "See, that's me over there on the
forty-fifth floor. I put the steel beam in."

— Mike Lefevre, interview in Studs Terkel, *Working:*
People Talk about What They Do All Day and How
They Feel about What They Do

In penning this reflection and call to action, I am inherently seeking to
raise my voice. Yet so much of this volume is a result of learning with
and from others and an attempt to raise their voices as well. Historic
preservation is a decidedly collective act. Many people over multiple
decades helped me develop my thinking and in effect coproduced so
many of the ideas in these pages.

My students at Columbia University and in other educational contexts over the years remain my driving inspiration. I am indebted to
them for consistently reaffirming my hope in the preservation enterprise, by seeking new knowledge, asking challenging questions, and
exploring alternative futures.

This volume would not have been possible without the support
and counsel of numerous colleagues at Columbia. I am forever grateful to Andrew Dolkart, for creating a place for me and for policy in the
Historic Preservation Program, and to Jorge Otero-Pailos, for always
encouraging me to experiment. Deans Mark Wigley, Amale Andraos,
Weiping Wu, and Andrés Jaque gave me time and space to frame these
ideas within the broader context of built environment scholarship and
practice. Mabel Wilson forged the ground for me and so many others
to interrogate questions of justice. Janet Foster advocated for introducing sustainability into the preservation curriculum. Elliott Sclar,

Jacqueline Klopp, and Kate Orff readily recognized the integral links among preservation, climate, and justice and helped me position my work across traditional disciplinary boundaries. Bob Beauregard reminded me of our responsibility to people *through* the built environment, as an object of action. And I am indebted to all of my studio cofaculty for teaming with me to test ideas in the classroom and the field, especially Will Raynolds, Morgan O'Hara, Shreya Ghoshal, and Tim Michiels for their intrepid and coconspiratorial curiosity. That debt extends to our studio collaborators in New York City and beyond who generously embraced colearning and coproductive research to our educational benefit.

After conceiving and in parallel to developing this manuscript, I curated a series of roundtables as integrative platforms to help elevate a diversity of preservation voices around questions of policy. I organized these cocreative dialogues through my research project "Urban Heritage, Sustainability, and Social Inclusion," generously funded by the New York Community Trust. Each resulted in a hybrid volume of scholarly and community-based research, interviews, and commentaries; these volumes originated the Issues in Preservation Policy series published by Columbia Books on Architecture and the City. Promoting second-order thinking in preservation requires integrative discourse that develops critical collaborative processes and spaces for threaded dialogue about policy reform; this series was a strategic effort to seed the ground and build a network for policy reform. These roundtables and publications expanded my thinking and helped me find my voice, and I want to acknowledge the incredible colleagues who contributed to these volumes and dialogues, and who all can claim a stake in advancing preservation policy, including Fallon Samuels Aidoo, Lisa T. Alexander, Allison Arlotta, Louise Bedsworth, Ken Bernstein, Ciere Boatright, Robin Bronen, Sara Bronin, Vanilson Burégio, Sangita Chari, Caroline Cheong, Marco Castro Cosio, Sara Delgadillo Cruz, Andrew Dolkart, Jenna Dublin, Ingrid Gould Ellen, Anna Gasha, Shreya Ghoshal, Scott Goodwin, Donna Graves, Claudia Guerra, Nicholas Hamilton, Matt Hampel, Janet Hansen, Cory Herrala, Victoria Herrmann, Lisa Kersavage, Kelly L. Kinahan, Brent Leggs, Rinaldo Lima, James Lindberg, Michelle Magalong, Randall Mason, Brian J. McCabe, Jennifer Minner, Jennifer L. Most, Douglas Noonan, Tetsuharu Oba, Emma Osore, Michael Powe, Andrea Roberts, Marcy Rockman, Eduardo Rojas, Maria Rosario Jackson, Alicia Rouault,

Stephanie Ryberg-Webster, A. R. Siders, Mark Silberman, Mark J. Stern, Emily Talen, Gerard Torrats-Espinosa, Daniel Watts, Amanda Webb, Vicki Weiner, Jeremy C. Wells, and Chris Whong.

This project is the result of an amazing team at University of Minnesota Press and especially editor Pieter Martin. Three reviewers commissioned by the Press provided invaluable feedback on the manuscript, as did Marla Miller. I am grateful for the investment of their time and acumen.

My work with the Getty Conservation Institute and World Monuments Fund laid a critical foundation of professional experience that stoked many of my policy queries and gave me the opportunity to interrogate them through research and field projects. These institutions likewise afforded me the privilege to engage with colleagues and communities across the globe; their insights and perspectives educated me and compelled me to see heritage and its conservation through varied lenses. I wish to thank the many mentors, coworkers, and collaborators who invested in me and my ideas with their time and wisdom. In particular, I am forever indebted to Marta de la Torre for guiding me as a person and a professional and for looking beyond heritage as an object. Gustavo Araoz exemplified the importance of institutions and systems to the work of heritage. Jeanne Marie Teutonico continues to remind me that preservationists can and should be good "doctors," along with their policy responsibilities. Lisa Ackerman gave me license to weave policy questions into heritage advocacy. Martha Demas, Molly Lambert, and Michael Devonshire keep me honest about how the on-the-ground work of preservation remains central to the enterprise. Christina Cameron underscored the importance of collective dialogue in examining policy and shifting discourse. With Hugo Houben and Alejandro Alva, I experienced the tremendous power of collaboration, listening, and mutual respect at individual and institutional levels; their memories serve as constant guideposts.

My interrogation of the preservation enterprise is in large part due to my education at Columbia and Rutgers and the dedicated professors who encouraged me to ask questions and challenge the status quo. I am especially grateful to Daniel Bluestone for centering social history as a shaping force of the built environment and a critical dimension of preservation inquiry. Bob Lake helped me hone my social justice thinking and reinforced the critical role of government in ensuring equity. David Listokin both forged and introduced me to the growing landscape of preservation policy research. And Clint Andrews helped me understand the systemic nature of the built environment and its intersections with climate and heritage.

I have benefited from many mentors over the course of my career, but I especially want to thank three early ones for their enduring guidance and friendship. Allen Kopelson taught me the humanity of architecture and introduced me to the influential power of land use and regulatory review. Waveney Jenkins celebrated the beauty and diversity of cultures and how the built world reflects difference and meaning. Frances Resheske exemplified the public-facing responsibilities of government and the obligation to work with communities.

Numerous colleagues and friends have helped me work through and exercise ideas over many years, and I am indebted to them for both their critical input and their positive reinforcement, especially Vicki Weiner, for always keeping justice in the crosshairs, and Randy Mason, for his unwavering support and belief in the value of my inquiries. Carolina Castellanos is a steadfast confidante and adviser and continues to see me through the dark days of self-doubt.

Family and friends tolerated my angst over years as this book came to fruition and buoyed me along the way. I am thankful to Tina, Morgan, Katrina, and Kristin, for reinforcing the shared joy in experiencing heritage places; to Darryl, for never doubting the value of investing in old buildings and the people who inhabit them; to Maggie, for always reminding me of the power our bodies have to define space and tell stories; to Heather, for having the patience, even at age six, to "walk the walls" with me; to my siblings Nicole and Lou, for co-enduring all those childhood visits to military heritage sites and making them memorable, and holding me up ever since; and most important, to my son, Harry, for always inspiring me, abiding me, and just being a rock.

Notes

PREFACE

1. My choice to capitalize *White* is in support of those who argue that not capitalizing it "frames Whiteness as both neutral and the standard." Thúy Nguyễn and Maya Pendleton, "Recognizing Race in Language: Why We Capitalize 'Black' and 'White,'" Center for the Study of Social Policy, March 23, 2020, https://cssp.org/. As sociologist Eve L. Ewing argues, "when we ignore the specificity and significance of Whiteness—the things that it is, the things that it does—we contribute to its seeming neutrality and thereby grant it power to maintain its invisibility." Ewing, "I'm a Black Scholar Who Studies Race. Here's Why I Capitalize 'White,'" *Zora*, July 2, 2020, https://zora.medium.com/.

2. Laurajane Smith, *Uses of Heritage* (New York: Routledge, 2006).

3. *Miriam-Webster*, s.v. "enterprise" (n.), https://www.merriam-webster.com/dictionary/enterprise.

4. *Miriam-Webster*, s.v. "enterprise" (n.), https://www.merriam-webster.com/dictionary/enterprise.

5. David Lowenthal, *The Past Is a Foreign Country* (New York: Cambridge University Press, 1985), 385.

INTRODUCTION

1. House of Commons Rebuilding, HC Deb, October 28, 1943, vol. 393, cc403–73, https://api.parliament.uk/historic-hansard/commons/1943/oct/28/house-of-commons-rebuilding.

2. Hannah Arendt, *The Human Condition* (Chicago: University of Chicago Press, 1958), as cited in William Lipe, "Value and Meaning in Cultural Resources," in *Approaches to the Archaeological Heritage: A Comparative Study of World Cultural Resources Management Systems,* ed. Henry Cleere (New York: Cambridge University Press, 1984), 1.

3. Ian Hodder, *Entangled: An Archaeology of the Relationships between Humans and Things* (Malden, Mass.: Wiley-Blackwell, 2012).

4. Jorge Otero-Pailos, "Experimental Preservation," *Places Journal,* September 2016. See also Michel Serres, *The Parasite,* trans. Lawrence R. Schehr (Baltimore: Johns Hopkins University Press, 1982).

5. A total of 195 states parties had ratified the UNESCO World Heritage Convention as of August 2023.

6. Iris Marion Young, *Responsibility for Justice* (Oxford: Oxford University Press, 2011).

7. Global Alliance for Buildings and Construction, International Energy Agency, and United Nations Environment Programme, *2019 Global Status Report for Buildings and Construction: Towards a Zero-Emission, Efficient and Resilient Buildings and Construction Sector* (Nairobi: UNEP, 2019).

8. Daniel Bluestone, "Conservation's Curatorial Conundrum," *Change over Time* 7, no. 2 (2018): 235.

9. Erica Avrami, Cherie-Nicole Leo, and Alberto Sanchez-Sanchez, "Confronting Exclusion: Redefining the Intended Outcomes of Historic Preservation," *Change over Time* 8, no. 1 (2018): 102–20.

10. Young, *Responsibility for Justice*, 63.

11. My use of the public health analogy is rooted in several sources and snowballed over time. In 1998–2000, my son's father, an orthopedic surgeon, pursued a master's degree in public health at UCLA. One of his research projects looked at racial disparities in the treatment of broken arms in children. I was working at the Getty Conservation Institute at the time and already asking questions related to heritage policy and publics. Daily exposure to his work made me think about how heritage professionals behave like doctors treating individual patients and that the preservation enterprise did not have anything equivalent to public health as a way of thinking beyond individual sites and aggregating data to understand systemic effects. The comparative association was reinforced when I pursued my doctorate in planning and public policy at Rutgers's Bloustein School, as I was assigned to serve as a teaching assistant for an undergraduate policy course, Introduction to Public Health, taught by adjunct professor Kevin Breen, in fall 2006. My decision to transition from a career in the not-for-profit sector to full-time academia was predicated on my desire to pursue policy research, and in a meeting with Professor Reinhold Martin in December 2019, we discussed how I might better explain my research agenda using an analogy to another field, such as public health. During the Covid-19 pandemic, public health resonated yet again as a comparative illustration for systemic policy analysis and to help articulate first- and second-order preservation. It should be noted that I later discovered that Professor Michael Holleran gave a guest lecture at the University of Pennsylvania on September 25, 2014, titled "Public Health as a Paradigm for Preservation," though the lecture content was not published. That we independently arrived at the same preservation–public health analogy is not surprising, as it is an apt comparison. But I want to acknowledge that I am not the only person to have drawn the analogy.

12. Vin Bhalerao, "Beyond First Principles Thinking Lies Second Order Thinking," *Medium,* June 10, 2022, https://medium.com/; Howard Marks, *The Most Important Thing: Uncommon Sense for the Thoughtful Investor* (New York: Columbia University Press, 2011); Ray Dalio, *Principles* (New York: Simon and Schuster, 2017).

13. Karl H. Müller and Alexander Riegler, "Second-Order Science: A Vast and Largely Unexplored Science Frontier," *Constructivist Foundations* 10, no. 1 (2014): 10.

14. Michael Lissack, "What Second Order Science Reveals about Scientific Claims: Incommensurability, Doubt, and a Lack of Explication," *Foundations of Science* 22, no. 3 (2017): 575–93.

15. There is a growing body of literature regarding critical heritage theory, but some early and elucidating references included Smith, *Uses of Heritage,* and Tim Winter, "Clarifying the Critical in Critical Heritage Studies," *International Journal of Heritage Studies* 19, no. 6 (2013): 532–45.

16. For a discussion of instrumental approaches to heritage conservation, see Erica Avrami and Randall Mason, "Mapping the Issue of Values," in *Values in Heritage Management,* edited by Erica Avrami, Susan Macdonald, Randall Mason, and David Myers, 9–33 (Los Angeles, Calif.: J. Paul Getty Trust, 2019).

17. Isabelle Wilkerson, "America's Enduring Caste System," *New York Times,* July 1, 2020, https://www.nytimes.com/2020/07/01/magazine/isabel-wilkerson-caste.html.

18. Young, *Responsibility for Justice,* 109.

19. Charles E. Lindblom, "The Science of 'Muddling Through,' " *Public Administration Review* 19, no. 2 (1959): 86.

1. HERITAGE AS PLACE AND POLICY

1. Michael A. Di Giovine, *The Heritage-Scape: UNESCO, World Heritage, and Tourism* (Lanham, Md.: Lexington Books, 2009).

2. James Marston Fitch, *Historic Preservation: Curatorial Management of the Built World* (New York: McGraw-Hill, 1982).

3. For more information on the "I Have a Dream" marker, see https://www.nps.gov/places/000/lincoln-memorial-i-have-a-dream-marker.htm. For more information about the Mississippi Delta National Heritage Area, see https://www.msdeltaheritage.com/. For more information on the Cliff of Bandiagara, see https://whc.unesco.org/en/list/516.

4. Francesco Bandarin and Ron van Oers, *The Historic Urban Landscape: Managing Heritage in an Urban Century* (Hoboken, N.J.: Wiley-Blackwell, 2012).

5. See Lynn Meskell, *A Future in Ruins: UNESCO, World Heritage, and*

the Dream of Peace (New York: Oxford University Press, 2018), 220–21, for a discussion of the challenges posed by separating intangible and tangible in the context of UNESCO World Heritage. For reflections on intangible heritage in the U.S. context, see the National Trust for Historic Preservation Leadership Forum blog on intangible heritage in *Forum Journal* 32, no. 4 (2020).

6. Columbia University Graduate School of Architecture, Planning, and Preservation, *Heritage and Sustainable Urbanization: Freetown, Sierra Leone* (New York: World Monuments Fund, 2021).

7. Columbia University Graduate School of Architecture, Planning, and Preservation, "Yangon at a Turning Point: Progress, Heritage, and Community" (unpublished report, 2014).

8. Columbia University Graduate School of Architecture, Planning, and Preservation, *Heritage, Education, and Urban Resilience: Building Alternative Futures in Port-au-Prince, Haiti* (New York: World Monuments Fund, 2018); Columbia University Graduate School of Architecture, Planning, and Preservation, *Post-disaster Resilience in the Gingerbread Neighborhood of Port-au-Prince, Haiti* (New York: World Monuments Fund, 2016).

9. For helpful reviews, see Thomas F. Gieryn, "A Space for Place in Sociology," *Annual Review of Sociology* 26 (2000): 463–96, and Carla Koons Trentelman, "Place Attachment and Community Attachment: A Primer Grounded in the Lived Experience of a Community Sociologist," *Society and Natural Resources* 22, no. 3 (2009): 191–210.

10. Gieryn, "A Space for Place in Sociology," 464–65.

11. For reviews of the literature, see Maria Lewicka, "Place Attachment: How Far Have We Come in the Last 40 Years?," *Journal of Environmental Psychology* 31, no. 3 (2011): 207–30, and Trentelman, "Place Attachment and Community Attachment."

12. Dan Abramson, Lynn Manzo, and Jeffrey Hou, "From Ethnic Enclave to Multi-ethnic Translocal Community: Contested Identities and Urban Design in Seattle's Chinatown-International District," *Journal of Architectural and Planning Research* 23, no. 4 (2006): 341–60.

13. W. Neil Adger, Jon Barnett, F. S. Chapin III, and Heidi Ellemor, "This Must Be the Place: Underrepresentation of Identity and Meaning in Climate Change Decision-Making," *Global Environmental Politics* 11, no. 2 (2011): 1–25; A. R. Siders and Marcy Rockman, "Connecting Cultural Heritage and Urban Climate Change Adaptation," in *Preservation, Sustainability, and Equity*, ed. Erica Avrami, 21–30 (New York: Columbia Books on Architecture and the City, 2021).

14. Erica Avrami, Jennifer L. Most, Anna Gasha, and Shreya Ghoshal, "Energy and Historic Buildings: Toward Evidence-Based Policy Reform," *Journal of Cultural Heritage Management and Sustainable Development* 13, no. 2 (2023): 379–404.

15. Anthony Giddens, "Space, Time and Politics in Social Theory," *Environment and Planning D: Society and Space* 2 (1984): 123–32; William Sewell Jr., "A Theory of Structure: Duality, Agency and Transformation," *American Journal of Sociology* 98 (1992): 1–29.

16. Henri Lefebvre, *The Production of Space* (Oxford: Blackwell, 1991); David Harvey, *Social Justice and the City* (Baltimore: Johns Hopkins University Press, 1973); Harvey, *Justice, Nature and the Geography of Difference* (Cambridge, Mass.: Blackwell, 1996); Edward W. Soja, *Postmodern Geographies* (London: Verso, 1989); Soja, *Seeking Spatial Justice* (Minneapolis: University of Minnesota Press, 2010); Dolores Hayden, *The Power of Place* (Cambridge, Mass.: MIT Press, 1995).

17. Soja, *Postmodern Geographies*, 6.

18. Fernando Armstrong-Fumero and Julio Hoil Gutierrez, introduction to *Legacies of Space and Intangible Heritage: Archaeology, Ethnohistory, and the Politics of Cultural Continuity in the Americas,* ed. Fernando Armstrong-Fumero and Julio Hoil Gutierrez, 3–14 (Boulder: University Press of Colorado, 2017).

19. Thomas F. Gieryn, "What Buildings Do," *Theory and Society* 31, no. 1 (2002): 35–74.

20. Susan Kemp, "Environment through a Gendered Lens: From Person-in-Environment to Woman-in-Environment," *Affilia* 16, no. 1 (2001): 7–30.

21. Siders and Rockman, "Connecting Cultural Heritage and Urban Climate Change Adaptation."

22. Leonie Sandercock, *Cosmopolis II: Mongrel Cities of the 21st Century* (New York: Continuum, 2003), 37.

23. Keith H. Basso, *Wisdom Sits in Places: Landscape and Language among the Western Apache* (Albuquerque: University of New Mexico Press, 1996), 6.

24. Elizabeth Kamarck Minnich, *Transforming Knowledge* (Philadelphia: Temple University Press, 1990), 274.

25. G. R. Elton and Diarmaid MacCulloch, *England under the Tudors* (New York: Routledge, 2018).

26. Joseph L. Sax, "Heritage Preservation as a Public Duty: The Abbé Grégoire and the Origins of an Idea," *Michigan Law Review* 88, no. 5 (1990): 1142–69.

27. Stefan Fisch, "National Approaches to the Governance of Historical Heritage: A Comparative Report," in *National Approaches to the Governance of Historical Heritage,* ed. S. Fisch, 1–13 (Amsterdam: IOS Press, 2008).

28. U.S. Conference of Mayors, *With Heritage So Rich*, 1st ed. (New York: Random House, 1966).

29. For more information on ICOMOS-related charters, see https://www.icomos.org/en/resources/charters-and-texts.

30. For more information, see Convention on the Value of Cultural Heritage for Society (Faro Convention, 2005), Council of Europe, https://www.coe.int/en/web/culture-and-heritage/faro-convention.

31. J. de Monchaux and J. M. Schuster, "Five Things to Do," in *Preserving the Built Heritage: Tools for Implementation,* ed. J. M. Schuster, J. de Monchaux, and C. A. Riley II, 1–12 (Hanover, N.H.: University Press of New England, 1997).

32. Avrami et al., "Confronting Exclusion."

33. As an example, see the model preservation law developed for New York State municipalities by the New York State Historic Preservation Office (governmental) and the Preservation League of New York State (not-for-profit): https://www.preservenys.org/model-preservation-law.

34. War-related treaties like the Hague Convention offer additional avenues of recourse when damage or destruction of heritage results from transnational armed conflict. International criminal law has also been applied to cultural heritage–based offenses in a few cases. Although these policy tools are not within the purview of the UNESCO World Heritage Convention, they speak to other international policy regimes that intersect with heritage. For additional examination, see Anne-Marie Carstens and Elizabeth Varner, eds., *Intersections in International Cultural Heritage Law* (Oxford: Oxford University Press, 2020), online ed.

2. VICTIMIZING AND VALORIZING

1. Virginia Lee Burton, *The Little House* (Boston: Houghton Mifflin, 1942).

2. Emerging discourse on the affect of heritage further explores these emotional drivers; see D. P. Tolia-Kelly, E. Waterton, and S. Watson, *Heritage, Affect and Emotion: Politics, Practices and Infrastructures* (New York: Routledge, 2016).

3. For further examination of risk in heritage conservation, see Trinidad Rico, "The Limits of a 'Heritage at Risk' Framework: The Construction of Post-disaster Cultural Heritage in Banda Aceh, Indonesia," *Journal of Social Archaeology* 14, no. 2 (2014): 157–76; Rico, "Heritage at Risk: The Authority and Autonomy of a Dominant Preservation Framework," in *Heritage Keywords: Rhetoric and Redescription in Cultural Heritage,* ed. Kathryn Lafrenz Samuels and Trinidad Rico, 147–62 (Boulder: University of Colorado Press, 2015); Scott Goodwin, " 'Red Listing' Heritage: Endangerment as Policy and Collective Action" (master's thesis, Columbia University, 2020); Cornelius Holtorf, "Averting Loss Aversion in Cultural Heritage," *International Journal of Heritage Studies* 21, no. 4 (2015): 405–21; Holtorf, "Why Cultural Heritage Is Not 'at Risk' (in Syria

or Anywhere)," *Heritage for Transformation* (blog), April 4, 2016, https://heritagefortransformation.wordpress.com/; Holtorf and Oscar Ortman, "Endangerment and Conservation Ethos in Natural and Cultural Heritage: The Case of Zoos and Archaeological Sites," *International Journal of Heritage Studies* 14, no. 1 (2008): 14–90.

4. National Historic Preservation Act of 1966, Pub. L. No. 89-665, as amended by Pub. L. No. 96-515.

5. UN Educational, Scientific, and Cultural Organization, Convention Concerning the Protection of the World Cultural and Natural Heritage, November 16, 1972.

6. For more information on the fourteen primary factors affecting UNESCO World Heritage, see https://whc.unesco.org/en/factors/.

7. Iris Marion Young, *Inclusion and Democracy* (New York: Oxford University Press, 2000), 261.

8. Caitlin DeSilvey, *Curated Decay: Heritage beyond Saving* (Minneapolis: University of Minnesota Press, 2017), 3.

9. DeSilvey.

10. J. Mark Schuster, "Making a List: Information as a Tool for Historic Preservation," in *Economics of the Arts and Culture, Invited Papers of the 12th International Conference of the Association of Cultural Economics International,* ed. Victor Ginsburgh, 221–40 (Amsterdam: Elsevier, 2004).

11. U.S. Department of the Interior, National Park Service, *The Secretary of the Interior's Standards for the Treatment of Historic Properties with Guidelines for Preserving, Rehabilitating, Restoring and Reconstructing Historic Buildings* (Washington, D.C.: U.S. Department of the Interior, 2017).

12. Cass R. Sunstein and Edna Ullmann-Margalit, "Second-Order Decisions" (Working Paper 57, University of Virginia School of Law, 1998), 9.

13. For a discussion of scenario planning as applied to preservation decision-making, see Cherie-Nicole Leo, "'When I'm Dead, Demolish It': Contradictions and Compromises in Preserving Values at Lee Kuan Yew's Oxley Road Home, Singapore" (master's thesis, Columbia University, 2016).

14. John J. Costonis, *Icons and Aliens: Law, Aesthetics, and Environmental Change* (Chicago: University of Illinois Press, 1989).

15. For a detailed account of these early preservation projects, see Charles Hosmer, *The Presence of the Past* (New York: Putnam's, 1965).

16. Hosmer, 270.

17. Peri E. Arnold, "American Heritage and the Development of Historic Preservation Policy in the United States," in Fisch, *National Approaches to the Governance of Historical Heritage,* 201–17; Roderick Nash, *Wilderness and the American Mind* (New Haven, Conn.: Yale University Press, 1982); Lary M. Dilsaver, ed., *America's National Park System: The Critical*

Documents (New York: Rowman and Littlefield, 1994), https://www.nps .gov/parkhistory/online_books/anps/anps_index.htm.

18. Dilsaver, *America's National Park System.*

19. Dilsaver, reprinted from *Landscape Architecture* 43 (1952): 12–25.

20. Mark David Spence, *Dispossessing the Wilderness: Indian Removal and the Making of the National Parks* (New York: Oxford University Press, 1999).

21. Spence, 67–68.

22. Spence, 109.

23. Marie Bridonneau, *Lalibela, une ville éthiopienne dans la mondialisation: Recomposition d'un espace sacré, patrimonial et touristique* (Paris: Karthala, 2014); World Bank, *Ethiopia: Tourism Development Project* (Washington, D.C.: World Bank, 2008); World Bank, *Resettlement Policy Framework* (Washington, D.C.: World Bank, 2009); World Bank, *Resettlement Action Plan for Lalibela Town,* vol. 1 (Washington, D.C.: World Bank, 2011); Columbia University's Graduate School of Architecture, Planning, and Preservation and Addis Ababa University—Ethiopian Institute of Architecture, Building Construction, and City Development, *Heritage, Tourism, and Urbanization: The Landscape and Development of Lalibela, Ethiopia* (New York: World Monuments Fund, 2017).

24. Report of the UNESCO/ICOMOS/ICCROM Advisory Mission to Rock-Hewn Churches, Lalibela (Ethiopia), May 20–25, 2018, https:// whc.unesco.org/en/documents/169702/.

25. Erica Avrami, Gina Haney, Jeff Allen, and William Raynolds, *New Gourna Village: Conservation and Community* (New York: World Monuments Fund, 2011). This report summarizes conflicting values associated with New Gourna and Fathy's legacy (15–17) and includes an annotated bibliography of relevant scholarship (92–99).

26. UNESCO, preliminary phase document, safeguarding project of Hassan Fathy's New Gourna Village, April 2011.

27. UNESCO, *Safeguarding Hassan Fathy's Architectural Legacy in New Gourna* (Paris: UNESCO, 2022).

28. Karen Engle, *The Elusive Promise of Indigenous Development: Rights, Culture, Strategy* (Durham, N.C.: Duke University Press, 2010).

29. George Perkins Marsh, *Man and Nature,* ed. David Lowenthal (1864; repr., Cambridge, Mass.: Belknap Press of Harvard University Press, 1965).

30. Theodore Roosevelt, *A Book-Lover's Holidays in the Open* (New York: Scribner's, 1916), 299–300.

31. A. Berle Clemensen, *Casa Grande Ruins National Monument, Arizona: A Centennial History of the First Prehistoric Reserve 1892–1992* (Washington, D.C.: U.S. National Park Service, 1992).

32. Chip Colwell-Chanthaphonh, "Cultural Extermination and Archaeo-

logical Protection: Native Americans and the Development of the Antiquities Act of 1906," paper presented at the annual conference of the Society for American Archaeology, April 2, 2005, https://www.nps.gov/archeology/sites/antiquities/activities/saacoch.htm.

33. Norms of Quito, https://www.icomos.org/en/resources/charters-and-texts/179-articles-en-francais/ressources/charters-and-standards/168-the-norms-of-quito.

34. Francesca Russello Ammon, *Bulldozer: Demolition and Clearance of the Postwar Landscape* (New Haven, Conn.: Yale University Press, 2016).

35. Stephanie R. Ryberg, "Historic Preservation's Urban Renewal Roots: Preservation and Planning in Midcentury Philadelphia," *Journal of Urban History* 39, no. 2 (2013): 193–213; G. W. Born, "Urban Preservation and Renewal: Designating the Historic Beacon Hill District in 1950s Boston," *Journal of Planning History* 16, no. 4 (2017): 285–304.

36. New York City Landmarks Law of 1965, Title 25, chapter 3.

37. Avrami et al., "Confronting Exclusion."

38. Housing and Community Development Act of 1974, Pub. L. No. 93-383.

39. Avrami et al., "Energy and Historic Buildings."

40. Raynor M. Warner, Sibyl M. Groff, Ranne P. Warner, and Frank Stella, *Business and Preservation: A Survey of Business Conservation of Buildings and Neighborhoods* (New York: INFORM, 1978).

41. Sharon Zukin, *The Cultures of Cities* (Malden, Mass.: Blackwell, 2005), 23–24.

42. Steven Erlanger, "What Does UNESCO Recognition Mean, Exactly?," *New York Times*, January 8, 2012.

43. Young, *Inclusion and Democracy*, 261.

44. For a robust examination of these human–nature debates, see Steven Vogel, *Thinking Like a Mall: Environmental Philosophy after the End of Nature* (Cambridge, Mass.: MIT Press, 2005).

45. Charles Hosmer, *Preservation Comes of Age: From Williamsburg to the National Trust, 1926–1949*, 2 vols. (Charlottesville: University Press of Virginia, 1981).

46. Dilsaver, *America's National Park System*.

47. Robert E. Stipe, *A Richer Heritage* (Chapel Hill: University of North Carolina Press, 2003), 470, and 492–93.

48. Ted Nordhaus and Michael Shellenberger, *Break Through: From the Death of Environmentalism to the Politics of Possibility* (New York: Houghton Mifflin, 2007).

49. World Commission on the Environment and Development, *Our Common Future* (London: Oxford University Press, 1987).

50. Elizabeth Dowdeswell and Steve Charnovitz, "Globalization, Trade, and Interdependence," in *Thinking Ecologically: The Next Generation of Environmental Policy,* ed. Marian R. Chertow and Daniel C. Esty, 91–102 (New Haven, Conn.: Yale University Press, 1997).

51. International Council for Research and Innovation in Building and Construction, *Agenda 21 on Sustainable Construction,* CIB Report Publication 237 (Rotterdam: CIB, 1999), 18.

52. International Council for Research and Innovation in Building and Construction and United Nations Environment Programme, International Environmental Technology Centre, *Agenda 21 for Sustainable Construction in Developing Countries: A Discussion Document,* prepared by Chrisna du Plessis (Pretoria: CSIR Building and Construction Technology, 2002).

53. For the reports on the 2021 IPCC, UNESCO, and ICOMOS meeting, see https://www.cultureclimatemeeting.org/ and especially Nick Shepherd, Benjamin Joshua Cohen, William Carmen, Moses Chundu, Christian Ernsten, Oscar Guevara, Franziska Haas et al., "ICSM CHC White Paper III: The role of cultural and natural heritage for climate action: Contribution of Impacts Group III to the International Co-sponsored Meeting on Culture, Heritage and Climate Change" (discussion paper, ICOMOS/ISCM CHC, 2022).

54. Arnold, "American Heritage," 202.

55. United States v. Gettysburg Elec. Ry. Co., 160 U.S. at 680–82 (1896).

56. Carol M. Rose, "Preservation and Community: New Directions in the Law of Historic Preservation," *Stanford Law Review* 33, no. 3 (1981): 483.

57. Colwell-Chanthaphonh, "Cultural Extermination and Archaeological Protection."

58. Joe E. Watkins, "The Antiquities Act at 100 Years: Then, Now, and Tomorrow," paper presented at the annual meeting of the American Association of Museums, May 3, 2005.

59. UNESCO World Heritage Convention.

60. John Henry Merryman, "Two Ways of Thinking about Cultural Property," *American Journal of International Law* 80, no. 4 (1986): 831–53; Ashley Mullen, "Note: International Cultural Heritage Law: The Link between Cultural Nationalism, Internationalism, and the Concept of Cultural Genocide," *Cornell Law Review* 105, no. 1489 (2020), https://www.cornelllawreview.org/2020/07/15/international-cultural-heritage-law-the-link-between-cultural-nationalism-internationalism-and-the-concept-of-cultural-genocide/.

61. Matthew S. Weinert, "Grounding World Society: Spatiality, Cultural Heritage, and Our World as Shared Geographies," *Review of International Studies* 43, no. 3 (2017): 409–29.

62. Tim Winter, "Heritage Diplomacy," *International Journal of Heritage Studies* 21, no. 10 (2015): 997–1015.

63. Smith, *Uses of Heritage*; Meskell, *A Future in Ruins*; Rodney Harrison, *Heritage: Critical Approaches* (New York: Routledge, 2013).

64. Lior Jacob Strahilevitz, "The Right to Destroy," *Yale Law Journal* 114, no. 4 (2005): 781–854; E. Bissell Perot V, "Monuments to the Confederacy and the Right to Destroy in Cultural-Property Law," *Yale Law Journal* 128, no. 4 (2019): 1130–72.

65. Rose, "Preservation and Community."

66. M. Langfield, W. Logan, and M. N. Craith, eds., *Cultural Diversity, Heritage and Human Rights: Intersections in Theory and Practice* (London: Routledge, 2009); Helaine Silverman and D. Fairchild Ruggles, eds., *Cultural Heritage and Human Rights* (New York: Springer, 2007). In many respects, the heritage-as-human-rights discourse intersects with that examining the right to the city, including David Harvey, "The Right to the City," *International Journal of Urban and Regional Research* 27, no. 4 (2003): 939–41; Lefebvre, *Production of Space*; Harvey, *Social Justice and the City*; Soja, *Seeking Spatial Justice*; and Hayden, *Power of Place*.

67. Anne-Marie Carstens and Elizabeth Varner, "Intersections in Public International Law for Protecting Cultural Heritage Law: Past, Present, and Future," in *Intersections in International Cultural Heritage Law*, ed. Anne-Marie Carstens and Elizabeth Varner (Oxford: Oxford University Press, 2020), online ed.

68. Council of Europe, Framework Convention on the Value of Cultural Heritage for Society (Faro Convention), European Treaty Series 199, 2005, http://conventions.coe.int/Treaty/EN/Treaties/Html/199.htm.

3. SOCIAL CONSEQUENCES

1. "Sustainability, Equity, and Preservation: A Conversation with Dr. Erica Avrami," interview by Nicholas Redding, March 14, 2022, podcast produced by PreserveCast, episode 220, 39:15.

2. For compilations of charters and declarations, see https://web .archive.org/web/20231115185833; https://www.getty.edu/conservation /publications_resources/research_resources/charters.html; and https:// www.icomos.org/en/resources/charters-and-texts.

3. Thomas F. Gieryn, "What Buildings Do," *Theory and Society* 31, no. 1 (2002): 35–74, http://www.jstor.org/stable/658136.

4. These illustrations were inspired and informed by those who participated in developing "Building a Foundation for Action: Anti-racist Historic Preservation Resources," https://academiccommons.columbia.edu /doi/10.7916/2va5-xz66.

5. Cameron Logan, *Historic Capital: Preservation, Race, and Real Estate in Washington, D.C.* (Minneapolis: University of Minnesota Press, 2017); Dennis E. Gale, *The Misunderstood History of Gentrification: People, Planning, Preservation, and Urban Renewal, 1915–2020* (Philadelphia: Temple University Press, 2021).

6. Michael deHaven Newsom, "Blacks and Historic Preservation," *Law and Contemporary Problems* 36, no. 3 (1971): 423–31.

7. The lack of representation of histories of enslaved people in Montgomery is now countered by the since completed Legacy Museum.

8. Hayden, *Power of Place*; Gail Lee Dubrow and Jennifer B. Goodman, eds., *Restoring Women's History through Historic Preservation* (Baltimore: Johns Hopkins University Press, 2003); Dubrow, with Donna Graves, *Sento at Sixth and Main: Preserving Landmarks of Japanese American Heritage* (Seattle: University of Washington Press, 2002); Ned Kaufman, *Race, Place, and Story* (New York: Routledge, 2009).

9. Casey Cep, "The Fight to Preserve African-American History," *New Yorker,* January 27, 2020, https://www.newyorker.com/.

10. California Department of Parks and Recreation, Office of Historic Preservation, "Five Views: An Ethnic Historic Site Survey for California" (December 1988), https://www.nps.gov/parkhistory/online_books /5views/5views.htm; Donna Graves, "Achieving Equity through Heritage Preservation: Lessons from the Margin for the Center," in Avrami, *Preservation and Social Inclusion,* 85–96.

11. For a list of Los Angeles historic contexts, see https://planning .lacity.org/preservation-design/historic-resources/historic-themes; for San Francisco, see https://sfplanning.org/project/citywide-historic -context-statement.

12. For a list of NHL theme studies, see https://www.nps.gov/subjects /nationalhistoriclandmarks/full-list-of-theme-studies.htm.

13. For more information about the New York City LGBT Sites Project, see https://www.nyclgbtsites.org/. For more information about the African American Cultural Heritage Action Fund, see https://savingplaces.org /african-american-cultural-heritage.

14. For discussion of the policy challenges of increasing rosters, see Françoise Benhamou, "Conserving Historic Monuments in France: A Critique of Official Policies," in *Economic Perspectives on Cultural Heritage,* ed. Michael Hutter and Ilde Rizzo, 196–210 (New York: St. Martin's Press, 1997); Françoise Benhamou, "Is Increased Public Spending for the Preservation of Historic Monuments Inevitable? The French Case," *Journal of Cultural Economics* 20, no. 2 (1996): 115–31.

15. Janet Hansen and Sara Delgadillo Cruz, "Los Angeles's Historic

Contexts: Pathways to Inclusion in Preservation," in Avrami, *Preservation and Social Inclusion,* 71–83.

16. Winter, "Heritage Diplomacy."

17. Fekri A. Hassan, "The Aswan High Dam and the International Rescue Nubia Campaign," *African Archaeological Review* 24, no. 3/4 (2007): 73–94, http://www.jstor.org/stable/40743449.

18. Not all of which have been viewed in a positive light; see Meskell, *A Future in Ruins.*

19. Knut Einer Larsen, ed., *Nara Conference on Authenticity, Nara, Japan, 1–6 November 1994* (Paris: UNESCO World Heritage Centre, 1995).

20. M. Ishizawa and C. Westrik, *Analysis of the Global Strategy for a Representative, Balanced and Credible World Heritage List, 1994–2020* (Paris: World Heritage Centre, 2021), https://whc.unesco.org/en/documents/187906.

21. These estimates are compiled from the UNESCO World Heritage "search the list" function at https://whc.unesco.org/en/list/ from November 2022 and from the 2020 data on religion from Gina A. Zurlo, *World Religion Database* (Leiden, Netherlands: Brill, 2024).

22. Andrea Roberts, "The End of Bootstraps and Good Masters: Fostering Social Inclusion by Creating Counternarratives," in Avrami, *Preservation and Social Inclusion,* 109–21.

23. Smith, *Uses of Heritage.*

24. Joe Watkins, "From the Inside Looking Out: Indigenous Perspectives on Heritage Values," in Avrami et al., *Values in Heritage Management,* 210–22.

25. The Venice Charter, https://www.icomos.org/en/participer/179 -articles-en-francais/ressources/charters-and-standards/157-thevenice -charter.

26. U.S. Conference of Mayors, *With Heritage So Rich.*

27. Cep, "Fight to Preserve African-American History"; Sangita Chari, "Serving All Americans: The Case for Relevancy, Diversity, and Inclusion in the National Park Service," in Avrami, *Preservation and Social Inclusion,* 65–70.

28. Lucas Lixinski, *International Heritage Law for Communities: Exclusion and Re-imagination, Cultural Heritage Law and Policy* (London: Oxford University Press, 2019), 253.

29. Memorandum from NPS director Arno Cammerer, May 19, 1937, included in Appendix 2 of Harlan D. Unrau and G. Frank Williss, *Administrative History: Expansion of the National Park Service in the 1930s* (Denver, Colo.: Denver Service Center, National Park Service, September 1983).

30. Cameron Logan, "Beyond a Boundary: Washington's Historic

Districts and Their Racial Contents," *Urban History Review* 41, no. 1 (2012): 57–58.

31. Hayden, *Power of Place,* 8.

32. For an illustrative example of the bias of surveys and related criteria, see Stephanie Ryberg-Webster, "Toward an Inclusion Preservation: Lessons from Cleveland," in Avrami, *Preservation and Social Inclusion,* 23–34, and Hansen and Delgadillo Cruz, "Los Angeles's Historic Contexts."

33. For a report of the 2021 studio, "The Harlem Renaissance: Preservation, Spatial Encounter, and Anti-racism," see https://www.filepicker.io /api/file/cYL99bQSQkK2qEqmuAYl.

34. Herb Stovel, "Origins and Influence of the Nara Document on Authenticity," *APT Bulletin: Journal of Preservation Technology* 39, no. 2–3 (2008): 9–17.

35. National Register of Historic Places, *How to Apply the National Register Criteria for Evaluation* (Washington, D.C.: U.S. Department of the Interior, National Park Service, Cultural Resources, 1997).

36. National Register of Historic Places, *Guidelines for Completing National Register of Historic Places Forms* (Washington, D.C.: U.S. Department of the Interior, National Park Service, Cultural Resources, 1986), 42.

37. As noted in chapter 1, the sampling from the Avrami et al., "Confronting Exclusion," study suggested that more than 85 percent of municipal ordinances conform to or cite National Register criteria.

38. Michael Henry Adams, "Harlem at a Glance: Looking Back to Move Forward" panel discussion, Save Harlem Now! Preservation Conference, November 3, 2022, Ford Foundation, New York.

39. John Freeman Gill, "Preserving New York's Ties to the Underground Railroad," *New York Times,* January 8, 2021, https://www.nytimes.com/.

40. Costonis, *Icons and Aliens*; Baird M. Smith, "Information Structure of Building Codes and Standards for the Needs of Existing Buildings," in *Selected Papers Dealing with Regulatory Concerns of Building Rehabilitation,* ed. P. W. Cooke, 17–54 (Washington, D.C.: U.S. Department of Commerce, National Bureau of Standards, 1979).

41. Hansen and Delgadillo Cruz, "Los Angeles's Historic Contexts."

42. National Park Service, "The Secretary of the Interior's Standards for the Treatment of Historic Properties: Reconstruction as a Treatment and Standards for Reconstruction," https://www.nps.gov/articles/000 /treatment-standards-reconstruction.htm.

43. National Register of Historic Places, *How to Apply the National Register Criteria,* 2.

44. Edward S. Rutsch and Kim M. Peters, "Forty Years of Archaeological Research at Morristown National Historical Park, Morristown, New Jersey," *Historical Archaeology* 11 (1977): 15–38; Mathew Grubel, "Building

the Log Hut City: An Analysis Using the Tools Issued at Morristown, New Jersey," in *Historical Archaeology of the Revolutionary War Encampments of Washington's Army*, ed. Cosimo A. Sgarlata, David G. Orr, and Bethany A. Morrison (Gainesville: Florida Scholarship Online, 2019), online ed.; Jesse West-Rosenthal, " 'We Are All Going into Log Huts—a Sweet Life after a Most Fatiguing Campaign': The Evolution and Archaeology of American Military Encampments of the Revolutionary War" (Temple University, 2019).

45. A. B. Wilkinson, "Slave Life at Thomas Jefferson's Monticello," *American Quarterly* 71, no. 1 (2019): 247–64, https://doi.org/10.1353 /aq.2019.0017.

46. Charlotte Adams, "Beyond Preservation: Reconstructing Sites of Slavery, Reconstruction, and Segregation" (thesis, University of South Carolina, 2018), 19–20.

47. Hannah Knowles, "As Plantations Talk More Honestly about Slavery, Some Visitors Are Pushing Back," *Washington Post*, September 8, 2019.

48. Laurajane Smith, "Heritage, the Power of the Past, and the Politics of (Mis)recognition," *Journal for the Theory of Social Behaviour* 52, no. 4 (2022): 623–42, https://doi.org/10.1111/jtsb.12353.

49. Stovel, "Origins and Influence of the Nara Document," 12.

50. The Nara Document on Authenticity, https://whc.unesco.org /document/116018.

51. The Nara Document on Authenticity, https://whc.unesco.org /document/116018.

52. Dawson Muneri, "The Notions of Integrity and Authenticity: The Emerging Patterns in Africa," in *Authenticity and Integrity in an African Context*, ed. Galia Saouma-Forero (Paris: UNESCO, 2021), 18.

53. UNESCO World Heritage Centre, *Operational Guidelines for the Implementation of the World Heritage Convention*, WHC.21/01, July 31, 2021.

54. Senate Report 101-85, as summarized in *Keepers of the Treasures: Protecting Historic Properties and Cultural Traditions on Indian Lands* (Washington, D.C.: U.S. Department of the Interior, National Park Service, 1990).

55. U.S. Forest Service and National Park Service, "Traditional Cultural Properties: Questions and Answers," http://npshistory.com/publications /tcp-qa.pdf. See also National Register of Historic Places, *Guidelines for Evaluating Traditional Cultural Properties*, Bulletin 38 (Washington, D.C.: U.S. Department of the Interior, National Park Service, Cultural Resources, 1992).

56. Patricia L. Parker, "Traditional Cultural Properties: What You Do and How We Think," *CRM Bulletin* 16 (1993): 3, http://npshistory.com /newsletters/crm/crm-v16-special.pdf.

57. Elizabeth Morton, "Legacy Business Programs: Emerging Directions" (PAS Memo 109, American Planning Association, January 1, 2022).

58. For more information on San Francisco cultural districts, see https://sf.gov/information/cultural-districts-program.

59. Donna Graves, "Achieving Equity through Heritage Preservation: Lessons from the Margin to the Center," in Avrami, *Preservation and Social Inclusion,* 85–96.

60. Anthony C. Wood, *Preserving New York: Winning the Right to Protect a City's Landmarks* (New York: Routledge, 2008).

61. Adele Chatfield-Taylor, "From Ruskin to Rouse," in *Historic Preservation: Forging a Discipline,* ed. Beth Sullebarger (New York: Preservation Alumni Inc., 1986), 27.

62. Antoinette Lee, "Historians as Managers of the Nation's Cultural Heritage," *American Studies International* 42, no. 2&3 (2004): 131.

63. Ned Kaufman, "Moving Forward: Futures for a Preservation Movement," in *Giving Preservation a History: Histories of Historic Preservation in the United States,* ed. Max Page and Randall Mason (New York: Routledge, 2004), 313.

64. For a list of university historic preservation programs, see the National Council for Preservation Education: https://www.ncpe.us/program-list/.

65. Patrick W. Andrus, Michael J. Auer, Caroline R. Berlinger, Susan L. Henry, Stephen A. Morris, and John W. Renaud, *Manual for State Historic Preservation Review Boards* (Washington, D.C.: U.S. Department of the Interior, National Park Service, Interagency Resources Division, 1992), 7.

66. For commission information, see https://sfplanning.org/historic-preservation-commission.

67. For commission information, see https://www.townofmorristown .org/.

68. World Heritage Convention, article 14; UNESCO, "Operational Guidelines" (WHC.21/01, 2001), paras. 30–37, https://whc.unesco.org /en/guidelines/.

69. This is not unlike the concept of outstanding universal value (OUV), which all World Heritage sites must demonstrate by meeting one or more of ten OUV nomination criteria, meeting conditions of integrity and/or authenticity, and having an adequate protection and management system. OUV suggests that the significance of a place is "so exceptional as to transcend national boundaries and to be of common importance for present and future generations of all humanity." See UNESCO, "Operational Guidelines," paras. 49 and 78.

70. For analysis of how this has played out in the United Kingdom, see Nir Mualam and Rachelle Alterman, "Looking into the 'Black Box' of Heritage Protection: Analysis of Conservation Area Disputes in London through the Eyes of Planning Inspectors," *International Journal of Heritage Studies* 24, no. 6 (2018): 599–618. For discussions of frameworks to

confront expert versus nonexpert biases, see Nir Mualam and Rachelle Alterman, "Architecture Is Not Everything: A Multifaceted Conceptual Framework for Evaluating Heritage Protection Policies and Disputes," *International Journal of Cultural Policy* 26, no. 3 (2020): 291–311.

71. Avrami et al., "Confronting Exclusion," 110–12.

72. Avrami et al., 112–13.

73. Avrami et al., 114–16.

74. Parker, "Traditional Cultural Properties," 5.

75. New York City Mayor's Office of Immigrant Affairs, *2021 Report*, 2, https://www.nyc.gov/.

76. Pew Research Center, "Modern Immigration Wave Brings 59 Million to U.S., Driving Population Growth and Change through 2065: Views of Immigration's Impact on U.S. Society Mixed" (September 2015), https://www.pewresearch.org/.

77. Each states party develops and maintains its own tentative list, which includes properties the states party seeks to potentially nominate once full dossiers are prepared. Not all properties, however, move beyond a tentative list, and tentative lists are often updated after several years.

78. UNESCO, "Operational Guidelines," para. 12.

79. UNESCO, para. 123.

80. NHPA 54 U.S.C. §307101(d).

81. Jess Theodore, "Over My Dead Property! Why the Owner Consent Provisions of the National Historic Preservation Act Strike the Wrong Balance between Private Property and Preservation" (Georgetown University Law Center, 2008), http://scholarship.law.georgetown.edu/hpps_papers/30.

82. Julia Hatch Miller, "Owner Consent Provisions in Historic Preservation Ordinances: Are They Legal?," *Preservation Law Reporter*, February 1991, 1019–39.

83. Rose, "Preservation and Community," 500.

84. Conn. Gen. Stat. Ann. §7–147, chapter 97a*, "Historic Districts and Historic Properties"; Sarah N. Conde, "Striking a Match in the Historic District: Opposition to Historic Preservation and Responsive Community Building" (Georgetown University Law Center, 2007), 29–30, https://scholarship.law.georgetown.edu/hpps_papers/24/.

85. Conde, "Striking a Match," 30–32.

86. Elizabeth Durfee Hengen and Carolyn Baldwin, *Neighborhood Heritage Districts: A Handbook for New Hampshire Municipalities* (Concord: New Hampshire Division of Historical Resources, December 2008), 10, https://www.nh.gov/nhdhr/publications/documents/nh_neighborhood_heritage_handbook.pdf.

87. Conde, "Striking a Match," 30–31.

88. Conde, 26–28.

89. Miller, "Owner Consent Provisions," 1021.

90. Miller, 1021.

91. Joseph L. Sax, "Heritage Preservation as a Public Duty: The Abbé Grégoire and the Origins of an Idea," *Michigan Law Review* 88, no. 5 (1990): 1142–69.

92. Sax, 111.

93. Smith, *Uses of Heritage*; Lynn Meskell, "Human Rights and Heritage Ethics," *Anthropological Quarterly* 83, no. 4 (2010): 839–59.

94. Jeremy C. Wells and Barry L. Stiefel, eds., *Human-Centered Built Environment Heritage Preservation: Theory and Evidence-Based Practice* (New York: Routledge, 2018); Jeremy C. Wells, "Does Intra-disciplinary Historic Preservation Scholarship Address the Exigent Issues of Practice? Exploring the Character and Impact of Preservation Knowledge Production in Relation to Critical Heritage Studies, Equity, and Social Justice," *International Journal of Heritage Studies* 27, no. 5 (2021): 449–69; Barry L. Stiefel and Jeremy C. Wells, eds., *Preservation Education: Sharing Best Practices and Finding Common Ground* (Lebanon, N.H.: University Press of New England, 2014).

95. Council of Europe Framework Convention on the Value of Cultural Heritage for Society (Faro Convention, 27.X.2005), https://www.coe.int/en/web/conventions/full-list?module=treaty-detail&treatynum=199.

96. Faro Convention.

97. Aaron Passell, *Preserving Neighborhoods: How Urban Policy and Community Strategy Shape Baltimore and Brooklyn* (New York: Columbia University Press, 2021).

98. Sherry R. Arnstein, "A Ladder of Citizen Participation," *Journal of the American Institute of Planners* 35, no. 4 (1969): 216–24.

99. See https://sf.gov/information/cultural-districts-program.

100. Arnstein, "A Ladder of Citizen Participation."

101. For an applied examination of the use of scenario planning, see Leo, "When I'm Dead, Demolish It."

102. See quote in chapter 1 from Young, *Responsibility for Justice*, 63.

103. For further discussion of the social and political issues associated with target populations in public policy, see Anne Schneider and Helen Ingram, "Social Construction of Target Populations: Implications for Politics and Policy," *American Political Science Review* 87, no. 2 (1993): 334–47.

104. For an overview of the economics and preservation literature, see Randall F. Mason, "Economics and Historic Preservation: A Guide and Review of the Literature," discussion paper, Brookings Institution Metropolitan Policy Program, 2005, and the annotated bibliography in Donovan R. Rypkema, Caroline Cheong, and Randall F. Mason, *Measuring Economic Impacts of Historic Preservation*, 2nd ed., a report to the Advisory Council

on Historic Preservation (Washington, D.C.: PlaceEconomics, September 2013).

105. Rypkema et al., *Measuring Economic Impacts of Historic Preservation.*

106. N. E. Coulson and M. Lahr, "Gracing the Land of Elvis and Beale Street: Historic Designation and Property Values in Memphis," *Real Estate Economics* 33, no. 3 (2005): 487–507; New York City Independent Budget Office, "The Impact of Historic Districts on Residential Property Values," background paper, 2003; R. Leichenko, N. E. Coulson, and D. Listokin, "Historic Preservation and Residential Property Values: An Analysis of Texas Cities," *Urban Studies* 38, no. 11 (2001): 1973–87.

107. Edward Glaeser, "Preservation Follies," *City Journal* 20, no. 2 (2010), https://www.city-journal.org/html/preservation-follies-13279.html.

108. Rose, "Preservation and Community," 514.

109. Logan, *Historic Capital,* 101–2.

110. Penn Central Transportation Co. v. New York City, 438 U.S. 104 (1978); St. Bartholomew's Church v. City of New York, 728 F. Supp. 958 (S.D.N.Y. 1990).

111. John J. Costonis, "The Disparity Issue: A Context for the Grand Central Terminal Decision," *Harvard Law Review* 91 (December 1977): 402–27; Daniel Carvarello, "From *Penn Central* to *United Artists' I & II*: The Rise to Immunity of Historic Preservation," *Boston College Environmental Affairs Law Review* 22 (Spring 1995): 593–623; Andrew J. Miller, "Transferable Development Rights in the Constitutional Landscape: Has *Penn Central* Failed to Weather the Storm?," *Natural Resources Journal* 39, no. 3 (1999): 459–517.

112. Penn Central Transportation Company v. City of New York, Court of Appeals of New York, v. 366 N.E.2d 1271-79 (June 23, 1977), 1276.

113. Wendell E. Pritchett, "The 'Public Menace' of Blight: Urban Renewal and the Private Uses of Eminent Domain" (Faculty Scholarship at Penn Law 1199, 2003), https://scholarship.law.upenn.edu/faculty_scholarship/1199.

114. Brian J. McCabe and Ingrid Gould Ellen, "Does Preservation Accelerate Neighborhood Change? Examining the Impact of Historic Preservation in New York City," *Journal of the American Planning Association* 82, no. 2 (2016): 134–46.

115. Avrami et al., "Energy and Historic Buildings."

116. Louise Bedsworth and Ken Bernstein, "Balancing Sustainable Growth, Preservation, and Equity: Lessons from California," in Avrami, *Preservation, Sustainability, and Equity,* 71–83.

117. Kelly L. Kinahan, "The Neighborhood Effects of Federal Historic Tax Credits in Six Legacy Cities," *Housing Policy Debate* 29, no. 1 (2019): 166–80.

118. Other IRS passive activity rules, alternative minimum tax regulations, and business tax credit considerations also limit the claiming of tax credits, but these are the most common.

119. David Listokin, Michael L. Lahr, and Charles Heydt, *Third Annual Report on the Economic Impact of the Federal Historic Tax Credit* (Washington, D.C.: Historic Tax Credit Coalition, 2012); David Listokin, Michael L. Lahr, Charles Heydt, and David Stanek, *Second Annual Report on the Economic Impact of the Federal Historic Tax Credit* (New Brunswick, N.J.: Rutgers University, Edward J. Bloustein School of Planning and Public Policy, 2011).

120. Stephanie Ryberg-Webster, "Preserving Downtown America: Federal Rehabilitation Tax Credits and the Transformation of U.S. Cities," *Journal of the American Planning Association* 79, no. 4 (2013): 266–79; Ryberg-Webster, "The Landscape of Urban Preservation: A Spatial Analysis of Federal Rehabilitation Tax Credits in Richmond, Virginia," *Journal of Urban Affairs* 37, no. 4 (2014): 410–35; Ryberg-Webster, "Urban Policy in Disguise: A History of the Federal Historic Rehabilitation Tax Credit," *Journal of Planning History* 14, no. 3 (2015): 204–23; Ryberg-Webster and Kelly L. Kinahan, "Historic Preservation and Urban Revitalization in the Twenty-First Century," *Journal of Planning Literature* 29, no. 2 (2014): 119–39; Ryberg-Webster and Kinahan, "Historic Preservation in Declining City Neighbourhoods: Analysing Rehabilitation Tax Credit Investments in Six U.S. Cities," *Urban Studies* 54, no. 7 (2017): 1673–91.

121. Kinahan, "Neighborhood Effects of Federal Historic Tax Credits."

122. National Trust for Historic Preservation, *Preserving African American Places: Growing Preservation's Potential as a Path for Equity* (Washington, D.C.: African American Cultural Heritage Action Fund, October 2020).

123. Norman Williams Jr., Edmund H. Kellogg, and Frank B. Gilbert, *Readings in Historic Preservation: Why? What? How?* (New Brunswick, N.J.: Center for Urban Policy Research, 1983), 292.

124. Williams et al., 291–312.

125. Williams et al., 296, excerpted from Robert Lindsey, "Urban Revival Poses Some Hard Choices," *New York Times,* April 21, 1978, sec. D, 15.

126. Williams et al., 298.

127. Williams et al., 300, excerpted from "Designation Forcing Out Families: Barrio Discovers Its History Can Hurt," *Arizona Daily Star,* March 1, 1977.

128. Williams et al., 307–8, excerpted from Arthur P. Ziegler, "Implications of Urban Social Policy: The Quest for Community Self-Determination," in National Trust for Historic Preservation, *Legal Techniques in Historic Preservation* (Washington, D.C.: National Trust for Historic Preservation, 1972), 36–37.

129. Williams et al., 294, excerpted from Newsom, "Blacks and Historic Preservation."

130. McCabe and Ellen, "Does Preservation Accelerate Neighborhood Change?"; Vicki Been, Ingrid Gould Ellen, Michael Gedal, Edward Glaeser, and Brian J. McCabe, "Preserving History or Restricting Development? The Heterogeneous Effects of Historic Districts on Local Housing Markets in New York City," *Journal of Urban Economics* 92 (2016): 16–30; Ryberg-Webster, "Preserving Downtown America"; Kinahan, "Neighborhood Effects of Federal Historic Tax Credits"; J. Chusid, "Preservation in the Progressive City: Debating History and Gentrification in Austin," *Next American City* 12 (2006): 23–27; Glaeser, "Preservation Follies"; Edward L. Glaeser, *Triumph of the City: How Our Greatest Invention Makes Us Richer, Smarter, Greener, Healthier, and Happier* (New York: Penguin, 2011); Neil Smith, "Market, State and Ideology: Society Hill," in *The New Urban Frontier: Gentrification and the Revanchist City*, 116–35 (New York: Routledge, 1996).

131. McCabe and Ellen, "Does Preservation Accelerate Neighborhood Change?"

132. Emily Talen, Sunny Menozzi, and Chloe Schaefer, "What Is a 'Great Neighborhood'? An Analysis of APA's Top-Rated Places," *Journal of the American Planning Association* 81, no. 2 (2015): 131.

133. Francesca Russello Ammon, "Resisting Gentrification amid Historic Preservation: Society Hill, Philadelphia, and the Fight for Low-Income Housing," *Change over Time* 8, no. 1 (2018): 8–31; Passell, *Preserving Neighborhoods*; Malo André Hutson, *The Urban Struggle for Economic, Environmental and Social Justice: Deepening Their Roots* (New York: Routledge, 2016); Jenna Dublin, "The Spatial Politics of Urban Character: Analyzing the Roles of Historic Districts in Neighborhood Land Use Activism to Resist Displacement, New York City and Los Angeles, 2000–2020" (PhD diss., Columbia University, 2022).

134. Rose, "Preservation and Community"; John Mangin, "Exclusionary Zoning," *Stanford Law and Policy Review* 25, no. 1 (2014): 91–120.

135. Robert W. Turner, "Market Failures and the Rationale for National Parks," *Journal of Economic Education* (Fall 2002): 347–56; Turner, "The Optimal Provision of Services in National Parks," *Topics in Economic Analysis and Policy* 2, no. 1 (2002).

136. Karin A. Sable and Robert W. Kling, "The Double Public Good: A Conceptual Framework for 'Shared Experience' Values Associated with Heritage Conservation," *Journal of Cultural Economics* 25 (2001): 77–89.

137. Mualam and Alterman, "Looking into the 'Black Box.'"

138. Grant P. Fondo, "Access Reigns Supreme: Title III of the Americans with Disabilities Act and Historic Preservation," *BYU Journal of Public Law* 8, no. 1 (1994): 99.

139. Mason, "Economics and Historic Preservation"; Rypkema et al., *Measuring Economic Impacts of Historic Preservation*.

140. See the literature review in Rypkema et al., *Measuring Economic Impacts of Historic Preservation*; David Listokin, *Route 66 Economic Impact Study—Synthesis of Findings*, 2 vols. (New York: World Monuments Fund, 2012).

141. For more information on Historic England's Heritage Counts program, see https://historicengland.org.uk/research/heritage-counts/.

142. Historic England, "Research Strategy" (December 1, 2016), 6, https://historicengland.org.uk/images-books/publications/research -strategy/.

143. Historic England, "Research Agenda" (July 21, 2017), 3, https:// historicengland.org.uk/images-books/publications/he-research-agenda /research-agenda/.

144. Simona Pinton, "The ICC Judgement in Al Mahdi: Heritage Communities and Restorative Justice in the International Criminal Protection of Cultural Heritage," *Seattle Journal for Social Justice* 19, no. 1 (2020).

145. International Criminal Court, Office of the Prosecutor, *Policy on Cultural Heritage*, June 2021, article 17, 8.

146. Alberto Sanchez-Sanchez, " 'The Timbuktu Paradox' (or the Side Effects of Post-conflict Reconstruction)," in *From Conservation to Reconstruction: How World Heritage Is Changing Theory and Practice*, ed. Christina Cameron and Mallory Wilson, Round Table 2016, organized by the Canada Research Chair on Built Heritage Faculty of Environmental Design (Montreal: Université de Montréal, 2016), 175–77. For additional examination of the Al Mahdi case, see A. F. Vrdoljak, "Prosecutor v. Ahmad Al Faqi Al Mahdi: Judgment and Sentence and Reparations Order (Int'l Crim. Ct.)," *International Legal Materials* 57, no. 1 (2018): 17–79; Oumar Ba, "Contested Meanings: Timbuktu and the Prosecution of Destruction of Cultural Heritage as War Crimes," *African Studies Review* 63, no. 4 (2020): 743–62; T. Joffroy and B. Essayouti, "Lessons Learnt from the Reconstruction of the Destroyed Mausoleums of Timbuktu, Mali," *International Archives of the Photogrammetry, Remote Sensing and Spatial Information Sciences* XLIV-M-1 (2020): 913–20; Michelle Moore Apotsos, "Timbuktu in Terror: Architecture and Iconoclasm in Contemporary Africa," *International Journal of Islamic Architecture* 6, no. 1 (2017): 97–120; Mark A. Drumbl, "From Timbuktu to The Hague and Beyond: The War Crime of Intentionally Attacking Cultural Property," *Journal of International Criminal Justice* 17, no. 1 (2019): 77–99.

147. Truth and Reconciliation Commission of Canada, *Honouring the Truth, Reconciling the Future: Summary of the Final Report of the Truth and*

Reconciliation Commission of Canada (Saskatoon: Truth and Reconciliation Commission of Canada, 2015), http://www.trc.ca/.

148. Pieta Woolley, "Grim Reminders: What Should Be Done with Canada's Remaining Indian Residential School Buildings?," *United Church Observer,* June 2015, https://www.ucobserver.org/.

149. Elizabeth Della Zazzera, "Where Have All the Fragments Gone? The Afterlives of the Berlin Wall," *Lapham's Quarterly,* November 5, 2019, https://www.laphamsquarterly.org/; http://en.the-wall-net.org/.

150. Leo Schmidt, "Commemorating the Berlin Wall and Its Victims: Controversies and Pitfalls," *Journal of Human Security* 5, no. 3 (2009).

151. For more information, see https://ahc.alabama.gov/Monument Preservation.aspx/PDF/legislativeupdates.aspx.

152. For data sources, see https://www.nps.gov/subjects/nationalregister /data-downloads.htm.

4. ENVIRONMENTAL CONSEQUENCES

1. For information about the Historic Preservation Fund, see https:// ncshpo.org/ and https://revenuedata.doi.gov/.

2. National Trust for Historic Preservation, Preservation Green Lab, *The Greenest Building: Quantifying the Environmental Value of Building Reuse* (Washington, D.C.: National Trust for Historic Preservation, 2011); S. Agbonkhese, R. Hughes, M. Tucker, and A. H. Yu, *Greendeavor Carbon Calculator* (Newport, R.I.: 1772 Foundation, 2010).

3. Elena Sesana, Alexandre S. Gagnon, Chiara Ciantelli, JoAnn Cassar, and John J. Hughes, "Climate Change Impacts on Cultural Heritage: A Literature Review," *WIREs Climate Change* 12 (2021): e710; Scott Allan Orr, Jenny Richards, and Sandra Fatorić, "Climate Change and Cultural Heritage: A Systematic Literature Review: 2016–2020," *Historic Environment: Policy and Practice* 12, no. 3–4 (2021): 434–77; Sandra Fatorić and Erin Seekamp, "A Measurement Framework to Increase Transparency in Historic Preservation Decision-Making under Changing Climate Conditions," *Journal of Cultural Heritage* 30 (2018): 168–79; ICOMOS Climate Change and Heritage Working Group, *The Future of Our Pasts: Engaging Cultural Heritage in Climate Action* (Paris: ICOMOS, 2019); UNESCO World Heritage Centre, *World Heritage Reports n°22— Climate Change and World Heritage* (Paris: UNESCO World Heritage Centre, May 2007); UNESCO World Heritage Centre, *Case Studies on Climate Change and World Heritage* (Paris: UNESCO World Heritage Centre, 2007).

4. ICOMOS, *Future of Our Pasts.*

5. Nadja Popovich and Brad Plumer, "Who Has the Most Historical Responsibility for Climate Change?," *New York Times,* November 12, 2021; Jason Hickel, "Quantifying National Responsibility for Climate Breakdown: An Equality-Based Attribution Approach for Carbon Dioxide Emissions in Excess of the Planetary Boundary," *The Lancet Planetary Health* 4, no. 9 (2020): 399–404.

6. Megha Mukimand and Mark Roberts, eds., *Thriving: Making Cities Green, Resilient, and Inclusive in a Changing Climate* (Washington, D.C.: World Bank, 2023).

7. For reports related to the meetings and research, see https://www.cultureclimatemeeting.org/.

8. Hannah Ritchie and Max Roser, "Urbanization" (rev. 2024), https://ourworldindata.org/urbanization.

9. Ernest J. Yanarella and Richard S. Levine, *The City as Fulcrum of Global Sustainability* (New York: Anthem Press, 2011), 230–31.

10. NASA Science, "Living Ocean," https://science.nasa.gov/earth-science/oceanography/living-ocean.

11. First Street Foundation, "The First National Flood Risk Assessment Defining America's Growing Risk" (2020), https://firststreet.org/.

12. Volker C. Radeloff, David P. Helmers, Miranda H. Mockrin, Amanda R. Carlson, Todd J. Hawbaker, and Sebastián Martinuzzi, *The 1990–2020 Wildland–Urban Interface of the Conterminous United States—Geospatial Data,* 3rd ed. (Fort Collins, Colo.: Forest Service Research Data Archive, 2022); First Street Foundation, "The 5th National Risk Assessment: Fueling the Flames" (2022), https://firststreet.org/.

13. National Institute of Science and Technology, "Resilience," https://www.nist.gov/community-resilience.

14. National Academies of Sciences, Engineering, and Medicine, *Building and Measuring Community Resilience: Actions for Communities and the Gulf Research Program* (Washington, D.C.: National Academies Press, 2019).

15. Brian Rumsey, "From Flood Flows to Flood Maps: The Understanding of Flood Probabilities in the United States," *Historical Social Research/Historische Sozialforschung* 40, no. 2 (152) (2015): 134–50.

16. See U.S. Forest Service mapping at https://wildfirerisk.org/.

17. See FEMA's RAPT at https://www.fema.gov/.

18. Evelyn G. Shu, Jeremy R. Porter, Bradley Wilson, Mark Bauer, and Mariah L. Pope, "The Economic Impact of Flood Zone Designations on Residential Property Valuation in Miami-Dade County," *Journal of Risk and Financial Management* 15 (2022): 434.

19. Fallon S. Aidoo, "Architectures of Mis/managed Retreat: Black Land

Loss to Green Housing Gains," *Journal of Environmental Studies and Sciences* 11 (2021): 451–64.

20. Tom Slater, *Shaking Up the City: Ignorance, Inequality, and the Urban Question* (Oakland: University of California Press, 2021), 46.

21. Malini Ranganathan and Eve Bratman, "From Urban Resilience to Abolitionist Climate Justice In Washington, DC," *Antipode* 53, no. 1 (2021): 115–37, as cited in Slater, 46.

22. Andrew Horowitz, *Katrina: A History 1915–2015* (Cambridge, Mass.: Harvard University Press, 2020), 3.

23. Nilufar Matin, John Forrester, and Jonathan Ensor, "What Is Equitable Resilience?," *World Development* 109 (2018): 197–205.

24. The NPS Flood Adaptation Guidelines were illustrated, updated, and reissued in June 2021. See https://www.nps.gov/orgs/1739/upload/flood-adaptation-guidelines-2021.pdf; Ann D. Horowitz, "Planning before Disaster Strikes: An Introduction to Adaptation Strategies," *APT Bulletin: The Journal of Preservation Technology* 47, no. 1 (2016): 40–48.

25. The state of Maryland and its capital, Annapolis, have been at the forefront of flood mitigation in relation to historic buildings; see Dominique M. Hawkins, *Flood Mitigation Guide: Maryland's Historic Buildings* (Crownsville: Maryland Historic Trust, 2018). Connecticut produced a guide for planners: R. Christopher Goodwin and Associates, *Resilient Historic Resources: Best Practices for Planners—Guidance for Connecticut Municipalities in an Era of Climate Change* (Hamden: Connecticut State Historic Preservation Office, May 2019). Newport, Rhode Island, was among the first municipalities to issue standards for elevating historic buildings in response to flooding; see its "Policy Statement and Design Guidelines for Elevating Historic Buildings," https://www.cityofnewport.com/getattachment/City-Hall/Boards-Commissions/Commissions/Historic-District-Commission/HDC-Policy-Statement-Design-Guidelines-for-Elevating-Historic-Buildings-with-App-A-Sep-19-2023-UPDATED-and-APPROVED.pdf. Charleston, South Carolina, adopted similar "Design Guidelines for Elevating Historic Buildings" in 2019.

26. Ziming Wang, "Living above the Street: Flood Retrofitting and Adaptive Streetscape of New York City's Historic Districts" (master's thesis, Columbia University, 2022).

27. Siders and Rockman, "Connecting Cultural Heritage and Urban Climate Change Adaptation"; W. Neil Adger, Jon Barnett, Katrina Brown, Nadine Marshall, and Karen O'Brien, "Cultural Dimensions of Climate Change Impacts and Adaptation," *Nature Climate Change* 3 (2012): 112–17.

28. William C. Baer, "The Impact of 'Historical Significance' on the

Future," in *Preservation of What, for Whom?*, ed. M. Tomlan, 73–83 (Ithaca, N.Y.: National Council for Preservation Education, 1998).

29. Federal Emergency Management Agency, *Integrating Historic Property and Cultural Resource Considerations into Hazard Mitigation Planning: State and Local Mitigation Planning How-To Guide* (Washington, D.C.: FEMA, 2005).

30. Julia Howell and J. R. Elliott, "As Disaster Costs Rise, So Does Inequality," *Socius,* January 2018; National Advisory Council, *National Advisory Council Report to the FEMA Administrator* (Washington, D.C.: National Advisory Council, November 2020), https://www.fema.gov/sites/default/files/documents/fema_nac-report_11-2020.pdf.

31. Meredith Wiggins, "Eroding Paradigms: Heritage in an Age of Climate Gentrification," *Change over Time* 8, no. 1 (2018): 122–30.

32. William Butler, Tisha Holmes, April Jackson, Zechariah Lange, Bertram Melix, and Anthony Milordis, *Addressing Climate Driven Displacement: Planning for Sea Level Rise in Florida's Coastal Communities and Affordable Housing in Inland Communities in the Face of Climate Gentrification—a Research Report for the Leroy Collins Institute at Florida State University* (Tallahassee: LeRoy Collins Institute, Florida State University, 2022), https://lci.fsu.edu//wp-content/uploads/sites/28/2022/02/Butler-Jackson-Holmes-et-al.-2021-Final-LCI-Report-Climate-Gentrification-Updated-min.pdf.

33. Siders and Rockman, "Connecting Cultural Heritage and Urban Climate Change Adaptation."

34. Robin Bronen, "Rights, Resilience and Community-Led Relocation: Creating a National Governance Framework," *The Harbinger—NYU Review of Law and Social Change* 45 (2021), https://socialchangenyu.com/harbinger/rights-resilience-and-community-led-relocation/.

35. Cornelius Holtorf, "Averting Loss Aversion in Cultural Heritage," *International Journal of Heritage Studies* 21, no. 4 (2015): 405–21.

36. Caitlin DeSilvey, Harald Fredheim, Hannah Fluck, Rosemary Hails, Rodney Harrison, Ingrid Samuel, and Amber Blundell, "When Loss Is More: From Managed Decline to Adaptive Release," *Historic Environment: Policy and Practice* 12, no. 3–4 (2021): 418–33.

37. U.S. Department of the Interior, "Biden–Harris Administration Makes $135 Million Commitment to Support Relocation of Tribal Communities Affected by Climate Change" (press release, November 30, 2022), https://www.doi.gov/pressreleases.

38. Victoria Herrmann, "New Residents, New Heritage, New Policy: Planning for Climate Change Displacement, Migration, and Emplacement into America's Cities," in Avrami, *Preservation, Sustainability, and Equity*, 31–43.

39. Karen C. Seto, Burak Güneralpa, and Lucy R. Hutyra, "Global Forecasts of Urban Expansion to 2030 and Direct Impacts on Biodiversity and Carbon Pools," *Proceedings of the National Academy of Sciences of the United States of America* 109 (2012): 16083–88.

40. U.S. Census; National Association of Home Builders, "Housing Facts, Figures, and Trends for 2006," https://www.nahb.org/.

41. Stacy Mitchell, *Big-Box Swindle: The True Cost of Mega-retailers and the Fight for America's Independent Businesses* (Boston: Beacon Press, 2006).

42. Intergovernmental Science-Policy Platform on Biodiversity and Ecosystem Services, *2018 Assessment Report on Land Degradation and Restoration* (Bonn: IPBES, 2018).

43. David Garcia, Muhammad Alameldin, Ben Metcalf, and William Fulton, "Unlocking the Potential of Missing Middle Housing" (brief, Terner Center for Housing Innovation, University of California, December 2022), https://ternercenter.berkeley.edu/research-and-policy/unlocking-missing-middle/; Christopher M. Jones, "Consumption Based Greenhouse Gas Inventory of San Francisco from 1990 to 2015" (Berkeley Energy and Climate Institute, 2020); Brad Plumer, "Your Neighborhood's Emissions," *New York Times,* December 16, 2022, https://www.nytimes.com/.

44. Mukimand and Roberts, *Thriving.*

45. K. Chapple, *Planning Sustainable Cities and Regions* (London: Routledge, 2015); Belden Russonello and Stewart, *The 2011 Community Preference Survey: What Americans Are Looking for When Deciding Where to Live* (Washington, D.C.: Belden Russonello and Stewart LLC, 2011).

46. Sarah C. Bronin, "Zoning by a Thousand Cuts," *Pepperdine Law Review* 50 (February 24, 2021): 719–84; see also http://zoningatlas.org/.

47. Daniel Bluestone, "Framing Landscape While Building Density," *Journal of the Society of Architectural Historians* 76, no. 4 (2017): 506–31.

48. Constance Beaumont, *Smart States, Better Communities: How State Governments Can Help Citizens Preserve Their Communities* (Washington, D.C.: National Trust for Historic Preservation, 1996); David Listokin, "Growth Management and Historic Preservation: Best Practices for Synthesis," *Urban Lawyer* 29, no. 2 (1997): 199–213; Alexander J. Reichl, "Historic Preservation and Progrowth Politics in U.S. Cities," *Urban Affairs Review* 32, no. 4 (1997): 513–35; Anthony Downs, "Smart Growth: Why We Discuss It More Than We Do It," *Journal of the American Planning Association* 71, no. 4 (2005): 367–79.

49. National Trust Preservation Green Lab, *Older, Smaller, Better: Measuring How the Character of Buildings and Blocks Influences Urban Vitality* (Washington, D.C.: National Trust for Historic Preservation, 2014); Ingrid Gould

Ellen, Brian McCabe, and Eric Stern, "Fifty Years of Preservation in New York City" (NYU Furman Center, March 2016), https://furmancenter.org/.

50. Arup, "Increasing Residential Density in Historic Environments: A Literature Review" (commissioned by Historic England, 2018); Elisa Conticelli, Stefania Proli, and Simona Tondelli, "Integrating Energy Efficiency and Urban Densification Policies: Two Italian Case Studies," *Energy and Buildings* 155 (2017): 308–23; Rikke Stenbro, Aga Skorupka, Kirsten Østensjø Kørte, Erik Bjørnson Lunke, and Hege Hellvik, "Suburban Densification in Oslo through the Lens of Social and Cultural Sustainability," *Articulo—Journal of Urban Research* 13 (2016); John D. Landis, "The End of Sprawl? Not so Fast," *Housing Policy Debate* 27, no. 5 (2017): 659–97.

51. National Park Service, *Historic Residential Suburbs Guidelines for Evaluation and Documentation for the National Register of Historic Places* (Washington, D.C.: National Park Service, 2002).

52. Jacque Randolph, "Not-So-Affordable Housing: Regulatory Blocks on Accessory Dwelling Units in the Twin Cities," *Inequality Inquiry* (blog), March 3, 2023, https://lawandinequality.org/inequality-inquiry/.

53. Emily Talen, *City Rule: How Regulations Affect Urban Form* (Washington, D.C.: Island Press, 2012).

54. Anthony Tung, *Preserving the World's Great Cities: The Destruction and Renewal of the Historic Metropolis* (New York: Clarkson Potter, 2001).

55. Mara Goff Prentiss, *Energy Revolution: The Physics and the Promise of Efficient Technology* (Cambridge, Mass.: Harvard University Press, 2015).

56. Nordhaus and Shellenberger, *Break Through*, 96.

57. David A. Lewis, "Identifying and Avoiding Conflicts between Historic Preservation and the Development of Renewable Energy," *New York University Environmental Law Journal* 22, no. 3 (2015): 274–362.

58. Nordhaus and Shellenberger, *Break Through*.

59. United Nations Environment Programme, *2022 Global Status Report for Buildings and Construction* (Nairobi: Efficient and Resilient Buildings and Construction Sector, UNEP, 2022).

60. U.S. Environmental Protection Agency, "Advancing Sustainable Materials Management: 2018 Fact Sheet, Assessing Trends in Materials Generation and Management in the United States" (December 2020).

61. U.S. Environmental Protection Agency, "Municipal Solid Waste Generation, Recycling, and Disposal in the United States: Facts and Figures for 2009" (2009).

62. T. Ramesh, Ravi Prakash, and K. K. Shukla, "Life Cycle Energy Analysis of Buildings: An Overview," *Energy and Buildings* 42, no. 10 (2010): 1592–1600; V. Venkatraj and M. K. Dixit, "Challenges in Implementing Data-Driven Approaches for Building Life Cycle Energy Assess-

ment: A Review," *Renewable and Sustainable Energy Reviews* 160 (2022): 112327.

63. Susan Ross and Victoria Angel, "Heritage and Waste: Introduction," *Journal of Cultural Heritage Management and Sustainable Development* 10, no. 1 (2020.): 1–5; Tina McCarthy and Eleni Glekas, "Deconstructing Heritage: Enabling a Dynamic Materials Practice," *Journal of Cultural Heritage Management and Sustainable Development* 10, no. 1 (2020): 16–28; G. K. C. Ding, "Embodied Carbon in Construction, Maintenance and Demolition in Buildings," in *Embodied Carbon in Buildings,* ed. Francesco Pomponi, Catherine De Wolf, and Alice Moncaster, 217–45 (Cham, Switzerland: Springer, 2018); Alison Arlotta, "Locating Heritage Value in the Reciprocal Relationship between Preservation and Waste Management" (master's thesis, Columbia University, 2018).

64. Circularity, Reuse, and Zero Waste Development Network, *Toward Building Sustainable Communities and Circular Economies: A Local Government Policy Guide to Alternatives to Demolition through Deconstruction and Building Reuse* (Ithaca, N.Y.: Just Places Lab/CR0WD, 2023).

65. Gretchen Worth, Anthea Fernandes, Felix Heisel, Jennifer Minner, and Christine O'Malley, "The Case for Deconstruction: How Cities Can Stop Wasting Buildings," In *Building Better—Less—Different: Circular Construction and Circular Economy,* 32–37 (Basel, Switzerland: Birkhäuser, 2022); Jennifer Minner, "A Pattern Assemblage: Art, Craft, and Conservation," *Change Over Time* 10, no. 1 (2021): 26–45; Minner, "More than Repairing Cracks in the Façade: Building Systemic Change in Times of Crisis," in Avrami, *Preservation, Sustainability, and Equity,* 149–64.

66. See http://caretool.org/.

67. Portions of this section are summarized and excerpted from Avrami et al., "Energy and Historic Buildings."

68. United Nations Environment Programme, *2022 Global Status Report for Buildings and Construction.*

69. Energy consumption is for 2021 by the U.S. Energy Information Agency (see https://www.eia.gov/tools/faqs/faq.php?id=86); emissions are for 2020 by the U.S. Environmental Protection Agency (see https://www.epa.gov/ghgemissions/inventory-us-greenhouse-gas-emissions-and-sinks-1990-2020).

70. New York City Mayor's Office of Sustainability, *One City Built to Last Technical Working Group Report: Transforming New York City Buildings for a Low-Carbon Future* (New York: New York City Mayor's Office of Sustainability, 2019).

71. Michael Waite and Vijay Modi, "Electricity Load Implications of Space Heating Decarbonization Pathways," *Joule* 4, no. 2 (2020): 376–94.

72. This history is summarized and excerpted from Avrami et al., "Energy and Historic Buildings."

73. Richard G. Stein, *Architecture and Energy* (Garden City, N.Y.: Anchor Books, 1978).

74. U.S. Department of Housing and Urban Development, *In the Bank, or up the Chimney? A Dollars and Cents Guide to Energy-Saving Home Improvements* (Washington, D.C.: HUD Office of Policy Development and Research, Division of Energy, Building Technology, and Standards, 1975); U.S. Energy Research and Development Administration, *Building Energy Handbook* (Washington, D.C.: Energy Research and Development Administration, Division of Building and Community Systems, 1976); U.S. Federal Energy Administration, *Guidelines for Saving Energy in Existing Buildings: Engineers, Architects, and Operators Manual (ECM 2)* (Washington, D.C.: Federal Energy Administration, Office of Energy Conservation and Environment, 1975); U.S. General Services Administration, *Energy Conservation Guidelines for Existing Office Buildings* (Washington, D.C.: General Services Administration, Public Buildings Service, 1977).

75. U.S. Department of Housing and Urban Development and U.S. Department of the Interior, *Guidelines for Rehabilitating Old Buildings: Principles to Consider When Planning Rehabilitation and New Construction Projects in Older Neighborhoods* (Washington, D.C.: National Park Service, 1977); U.S. Department of the Interior, National Park Service, *Secretary of the Interior's Standards*.

76. Advisory Council on Historic Preservation, *Preservation and Energy Conservation* (Washington, D.C.: Advisory Council on Historic Preservation, 1979), 14. See also Advisory Council on Historic Preservation, *Assessing the Energy Conservation Benefits of Historic Preservation: Methods and Examples* (Washington, D.C.: Advisory Council on Historic Preservation, 1979).

77. James G. Gross, James H. Pielert, and Patrick W. Cooke, *Impact of Building Regulations on Rehabilitation: Status and Technical Needs* (Washington, D.C.: U.S. Department of Commerce, National Bureau of Standards, 1979); Patrick W. Cooke, ed., *Selected Papers Dealing with Regulatory Concerns of Building Rehabilitation* (Washington, D.C.: U.S. Department of Commerce, National Bureau of Standards, 1979); Melvyn Green and Patrick W. Cooke, *Survey of Building Code Provisions for Historic Structures* (Washington, D.C.: U.S. Department of Commerce, National Bureau of Standards, 1976); Russell V. Keune, *Assessment of Current Building Regulatory Methods as Applied to the Needs of Historic Preservation Projects* (Washington, D.C.: Department of Commerce, National Bureau of Standards, 1978).

78. B. M. Smith, "Information Structure of Building Codes and Stan-

dards for the Needs of Existing Buildings," in Cooke, *Selected Papers Dealing with Regulatory Concerns*, 36.

79. Ann Webster Smith, introduction to *New Energy from Old Buildings*, by Diane Maddex (Washington, D.C.: National Trust for Historic Preservation, 1981), 47.

80. Washington, D.C., Preservation Review Board (2019); Ben Adler, "Old Meets New: The Debate over Photovoltaics in Historic Districts," *Architect*, May 9, 2013, https://www.architectmagazine.com/; Peter Jamison, "When Saving the Planet Spoils the Charm of Historic Houses," *Washington Post*, January 19, 2020, https://www.washingtonpost.com/.

81. Fredric L. Quivik, "Retrofitting with Passive Solar Energy," in Maddex, *New Energy from Old Buildings*, 147.

82. Manish K. Dixit, "Life Cycle Embodied Energy Analysis of Residential Buildings: A Review of Literature to Investigate Embodied Energy Parameters," *Renewable and Sustainable Energy Reviews* 79 (2017): 390–413.

83. Manish K. Dixit, "Life Cycle Recurrent Embodied Energy Calculation of Buildings: A Review," *Journal of Cleaner Production* 209 (2019): 731–54.

84. Lynnette Widder and Christoph Meinrenken, "Three Windows: Accounting for Embodied Resources and Cultural Value," in *The Routledge Handbook of Embodied Carbon in the Built Environment*, edited by Azari Rahman and Alice Moncaster, 359–76 (London: Routledge, 2023).

CONCLUSION

1. Peter M. Haas, "Introduction: Epistemic Communities and International Policy Coordination," *International Organization* 46, no. 1 (1992): 1–35, http://www.jstor.org/stable/2706951.

2. Erica Avrami, ed., *Preservation and the New Data Landscape* (New York: Columbia Books on Architecture and the City, 2019).

3. See https://www.huduser.gov/portal/home.html.

4. The author cochairs an expert advisory committee established by ACHP chair Sara C. Bronin to examine some of these policy challenges and opportunities.

5. For information about NPS grants, see https://www.nps.gov /subjects/historicpreservationfund/shpo-grants.htm.

6. Ned Kaufman, "Historic Places and the Diversity Deficit in Heritage Conservation," *CRM: The Journal of Heritage Stewardship* 1, no. 2 (2004), https://www.nps.gov/crps/CRMJournal/Summer2004/article3.html.

7. National Register of Historic Places, *How to Apply the National Register Criteria*.

8. Dublin, "Spatial Politics of Urban Character."

9. Sara Bronin, Paul S. Byard Memorial Lecture, Columbia University Graduate School of Architecture, Planning and Preservation, February 9, 2022.

10. Carstens and Varner, "Intersections in Public International Law."

11. Costonis, *Icons and Aliens.*

12. Robert Lake, "Bring Back Big Government," *International Journal of Urban and Regional Research* 26, no. 4 (2002): 815–22.

13. Lindblom, "Science of 'Muddling Through,'" 86.

Index

professionalization of, 90–93; property values in, 106–7; public engagement with, 20; relocation and, 132–33; restorative justice in, 117–22; revisions to, 173; site-based practices of, 7; social/ environmental aspects of, 3, 8, 156; social justice in, 11, 63–64, 155, 161–66; structural integrity of, 11; theoretical foundations of, 146; unjust outcomes, 117; urban policies and, 8, 136; victimization/valorization in, 32, 123. *See also* heritage enterprise
Preservation League of New York State, 184n33
preservation policy: advocacy-driven, 148; agency through, 174; analytical criteria for, 6; for community building, 89; cost/benefit range, 116; cultural differences in, 86; for decarbonization, 154; distributive effects of, 106; distributive justice through, 165; economic impact of, 106, 115–16; elements comprising, xi–xii; energy policy and, 53; future-oriented, 7–8, 170–74; health policy analogy for, 6, 8, 14, 158, 180n11; influence on neighborhood change, 111; integration into decision-making, 168; long-term implications of, 6–7; management of change, 13; origin stories of, 32; population densification and, 134; protection of freedom, 13, 63; reconciliatory intentions, 119–20; reform of, 32, 169, 173–74; restorative justice in, 119–20; serving diverse publics, 8, 90; social intentions of, 106; structural justice in, 122; sustainability goals of, 126; systemic

processes of, 79; tangible outcomes of, 148; target audiences, 105; transformative circumstances of, 4
preservation surveys: bias of, 191n32; of built environment, 77; funding for, 161; of Los Angeles, 69; of New York, 93–94, 96, 100; traditional, 79
preserved places: alterations to, 5; community impact of, 5; systemic change and, 5–6. *See also* heritage places; preservation, place-based
"Preserving the National Heritage: Policies, Partnership, and Actions" (Salzburg, 1995), 26
professionals, preservation: authority over review processes, 92; demographics of, 94; education for, 158, 163; energy concerns of, 148; engagement with social history, 167; first-order logic of, 93, 157–58; input into heritage governance, 90–93; navigation of system, 158; next generation of, 157; nonexpert agency and, 171; norms and languages of, 100; representation of diverse communities, 90; transcending of geopolitics, 92
property, cultural, 59; versus traditional property, 94–95
property, private: in *Berman v. Parker,* 109; community regulation of, 60; Constitutional protection of, 106; energy-centric renovation, 147–48; government-supported investment in, 147; in historic areas, 107; incentives for, 51; state claims to, 22–23
property rights: collective aesthetics in, 60; collective claims

Erica Avrami is the James Marston Fitch Associate Professor of Historic Preservation at Columbia University's Graduate School of Architecture, Planning, and Preservation and a research affiliate with the Columbia Climate School's Center for Sustainable Urban Development. She is editor of *Preservation, Sustainability, and Equity*; *Preservation and Social Inclusion*; and *Preservation and the New Data Landscape*; and coeditor of *Values in Heritage Management: Emerging Approaches and Research Directions*.